The Expense of Spirit

The Expense of Spirit

LOVE AND SEXUALITY IN ENGLISH RENAISSANCE DRAMA

MARY BETH ROSE

Cornell University Press

ITHACA AND LONDON

Cornell University Press gratefully acknowledges a grant from the Andrew W. Mellon Foundation that aided in bringing this book to publication.

First published 1988 by Cornell University
First printing, Cornell Paperbacks, 1991.

International Standard Book Number 0-8014-2189-6 (cloth)
International Standard Book Number 0-8014-9695-0 (paper)
Library of Congress Catalog Card Number 88-47742
Printed in the United States of America
*Librarians: Library of Congress cataloging information
appears on the last page of the book.*

⊗ The paper in this book meets the minimum requirements
of the American National Standard for Information Sciences—
Permanence of Paper for Printed Library Materials, ANSI Z39.48-1984.

For Larry, for my mother, Roberta Block Rose,
and in memory of my father, Lincoln Rose

Contents

Preface

In the sixteenth and seventeenth centuries profound changes in the conceptualization of private life began to crystallize into recognizably modern form; and scholars have connected these transformations with changes that took place in the economic, scientific, political, and religious spheres during the early modern period. This book combines an interest in the participation of literature in these processes of cultural change during the English Renaissance with an interest in the formation of modern sexual values. Specifically, it focuses on a public and popular literary form, the drama, comparing Elizabethan and Jacobean dramatic representations of love and sexuality with those in contemporary moral and religious writings on women, love, and marriage.

Renaissance drama provides a uniquely valuable register of cultural transformation. Given the broad appeal of the theater to many classes of English society, it is not surprising that recent studies analyzing the interaction between traditionally literary and nonliterary institutions and representations have found their impetus in the drama. Although most of these studies have focused at least in part on sexuality, they have been primarily concerned to examine the interlocking connections between literary expression and configurations of political power, placing their emphasis on the relation of sexuality to public life. The present book also makes connections between literary and nonliterary discourses; but representations of sexuality are examined more intensively from what I argue is the emerging, distinctive perspective of the private life.

Considering the tradition of Elizabethan and Jacobean drama as

ix

an ongoing historical process, this book attempts to trace a course of changing representations of sexuality over time. I have explored in detail the ways in which shifts can be identified and understood precisely by focusing on dramatic structure and form. Thus the altering prestige of marriage and eros and the shifting centrality and dignity attributed to private life in nonliterary discourse find their parallels in the transforming generic decorums of comedy and tragedy. Conversely, moral and religious writing often develops discussions of love and marriage from perspectives that are recognizably comic or tragic. A basic premise results that should have implications for connecting traditionally "literary" with traditionally "historical" discourses and events: namely, that these connections can best be demonstrated neither by comparing literary plots and characters to actual persons and behavior nor by dismissing fiction as evasive or unreal, but rather by tracing the changing location of conflict and the changing nature of subject matter throughout the course of a literary tradition. By including consideration of a number of playwrights working in a variety of dramatic forms, this book also contributes to the debate about the discursive status of comedy and tragedy as conservative and/or radical contributions to English Renaissance culture.

Every scholarly book is a communal endeavor, on a practical as well as an idealistic level. Most of the research for this book was conducted at the Newberry Library, under the auspices of the Monticello College Foundation. I owe a special debt of gratitude to the Foundation and to the staff of the Newberry, particularly to my colleagues Richard Brown and Paul Gehl, for supporting this study from a very early stage in my career. At that time Leonard Barkan, Ruth El Saffar, Michael Lieb, and M. L. Wine read drafts of the early chapters and offered invaluable encouragement and advice, as each of them has continued to do ever since.

The book was completed in Oxford, England, and I am indeed grateful to the National Endowment for the Humanities for the generous support that made this work possible. The British Academy also graciously provided crucial assistance. My seven-month stay in Oxford was enhanced by the hospitality of Pembroke College, and I particularly thank Paul Hyams, Eric Stanley, and John Woodhouse from Pembroke, as well as Julia Briggs of Hertford

College, for providing such a congenial collegial environment while I was in England.

Like others, I have debts too numerous to mention in the form of stimulating conversations that have influenced the writing of this book. Among those colleagues who have offered sensitive, thoughtful readings of all or part of the manuscript, I am especially grateful to David Bevington, Natalie Davis, Barbara Ewell, Shirley Garner, S. Clark Hulse, Arthur Kinney, Scott McMillin, Leah Marcus, Janel Mueller, Leo Salingar, and Teresa Toulouse.

Versions of the first two chapters of this book appeared in *Renaissance Drama*, N.S. 15 (1984), and in *English Literary Renaissance*, 14 (Autumn 1984), and I thank these publications for permission to use those materials. I am also very grateful to Bernhard Kendler of Cornell University Press for his responsiveness and courtesy, and for the encouragement he provided during the completion of the manuscript.

At every stage of writing I have profited from the intelligence, help, and friendship of Jean Pedersen and Frances Dolan. Catherine Gilhuly provided invaluable assistance in checking the text for accuracy. Jeff Auld has been continually interested, good-humored, and diligent throughout the preparation of the manuscript, and Marilyn DeBerry has finished the task with kindness and skill.

My greatest pleasure comes in dedicating this book to my parents and to my husband, Lawrence Rosen, whose exacting standards of scholarship, shrewd and compassionate insights into the formation of social relations, and generous interest in the social construction of dramatic forms have so enhanced my own. His companionship has made writing a book a happy adventure.

MARY BETH ROSE

Chicago, Illinois

The Expense of Spirit

Introduction

The vitality of Renaissance drama in England is deeply enmeshed in the struggles that characterized every aspect of English culture in the sixteenth and seventeenth centuries. As is well known, during the era that began with the Reformation and reached its crisis point with the Revolution, England experienced such shocks to its system as extraordinary demographic growth and price inflation, the opening of the land market that resulted from the dissolution of the monasteries, and significant increases in litigation, foreign trade, and other commercial activities, along with wide expansion in educational opportunities. The decades in which Renaissance drama proliferated strikingly (from c. 1580 to c. 1625 or, roughly, the late Elizabethan and Jacobean periods) were not only decades of intense cultural conflict, but also a time when, in a hierarchical society, economic potential and definitions of gender, social class, and status were perceived as provocatively fluid. It is the assumption of this study that drama is a form dependent on conflict for its realization and that, in the English Renaissance, cultural conflict can be seen as its raison d'être.

A public and popular form, the drama was accessible for most of this period to both sexes and to a mixture of social classes, with the probable exclusion of the very poor. Another major assumption in my analysis is that the drama not only articulates and represents cultural change, but also participates in it; seeks not only to define, but actively to generate, and in some cases to contain, cultural conflict. Far from acting as a fictional reflection of an imagined external reality that can somehow be grasped as true, the drama is a constituent of that reality and inseparable from it. In sum, I have conceived of the dramatic text as a symbolic form that creates, represents, and contains cultural change.

What follows focuses on the dynamics of this process as it concerns the representation of love and sexuality. The Elizabethan and Jacobean periods witnessed major transformations in the social construction of gender, the conceptualization of the position of women, and the ideology of the family, meaning the dominant set of accepted assumptions—often unexamined—that defines the family and provides the foundation on which it is built. Debate about altering sexual values was prolonged and intense in the English Renaissance, and all the important, controversial issues were dramatized in the plays of the period. This analysis attempts to show a parallel development between discussions of women, eros, and marriage in moral and religious writing and changing representations of love and sexuality in the drama, and to relate these changes to alterations in dramatic forms. The purposes are first, to illuminate the ways in which dramatic and moral languages combine to create, interpret, and transform a dominant sexual discourse; and, second, to trace a process of artistic change in the English dramatic tradition by focusing on the parallel relationship between changing sexual values and altering dramatic forms.

The grandest and most provocative study of English Renaissance sexuality to date is Lawrence Stone's *The Family, Sex and Marriage in England, 1500–1800* (1977). Though some of Stone's conclusions have been hotly debated, many of his arguments have withstood controversy, and I have relied on some of them in my account. For example, he demonstrates that in the conduct of marriage and the formation of the family during the sixteenth and seventeenth centuries there was a gradual shift from the predominant emphasis of the medieval aristocracy on arranged marriages as property-based alliances between kin groups to a contrasting emphasis on the conjugal couple and the isolated nuclear family; and, second, that these shifts accompanied changes in the official idealization of sexual behavior from the praise of celibacy and virginity in the Middle Ages to the Protestant glorification of "holy matrimony" as the eminently desirable sexual status in the post-Reformation English Renaissance.

Objections to these arguments tend to focus on the complex

nature of medieval sexuality and to question the originality of Protestant sexual discourse, two issues that affect the location of change. For example, as discussed in the first chapter of this book, Caroline Walker Bynum has demonstrated convincingly that the modern scholarly stress on asceticism disregards the wide and varied range of thought, feeling, and representation constituting the late medieval construction of eros. Others have argued that the valorization of celibacy had little to do with the actual behavior or feelings of medieval men and women: there were, for instance, commonsense counteridealizations of marriage to which ordinary people naturally responded. Second, scholars have alleged that Stone and other social historians have attributed far too much to Protestantism: the emphasis on an individual's consent to a marriage, to cite only one example, had always been encoded in Catholic canon law and was hardly an invention of the English Reformation; nor was the stress on a couple's affection for one another particularly new.

To state what perhaps will seem an obvious point, these objections carry different weight depending on the phenomena that one is attempting to discover and explain. What I am primarily interested in are dominant modes of conceptualization and the representation of belief. Most germane to my analysis are the facts that no matter how men and women in the Middle Ages may have felt or acted, and despite (perhaps along with) the complex construction of eros, dominant medieval homiletic and theological formulations officially idealized asceticism and celibacy as the most prestigious forms of sexual behavior; and Protestant sexual discourse explicitly and repeatedly abjured this idealization and replaced it with the glorification of marriage. Second, it is crucial to assert at the outset that the importance of English Protestant sexual discourse in the Renaissance lies not in its originality, but in its proliferation, elaboration, and wide accessibility to a variety of social groups, as well as in its attempt to construct marriage as a concretized relationship enacted in social life. As we will see throughout this book, the account of changing sexual discourses in the English Renaissance is not a story of origins, but an analysis of significant shifts in prestige, and in emphasis and degree.

One of the major arguments in this analysis is that there are two dominant forms of sexual discourse in the English Renaissance.

The first comprises a dualistic sensibility in which women and eros are perceived either as idealized beyond the realm of the physical (often they are viewed as leading to a consciousness of the divine, a transcendence of desire) or as degraded and sinful and, accompanying these assumptions, as frivolous, dangerous, and wasteful as well. I hope to show that these polarizations of women and sexuality inevitably coexist in the same discursive formation, one pole implying the other. The logic of this dualistic sensibility often construes marriage as at best a necessary evil, the means by which a fallen humanity reproduces itself and ensures the orderly succession of property. Second, and in contrast, there is the Protestant (largely Puritan) idealization of "holy matrimony," which constitutes a coherent, elaborate, and self-conscious effort to construct a new ideology of the private life. Although Protestant sexual discourse retains much of the erotic skepticism of the dualistic sensibility, it nevertheless unites love with marriage and conceives of marriage with great respect as the foundation of an ordered society. Protestant discourse is not dualistic, but complex and multifaceted, and one of its most significant and far-reaching changes is a shift in the prestige and centrality granted to the institution of marriage. Specifically, this discourse compares marriage to the church and the state, drawing out the equation among spiritual, public, and private realms by analogizing the husband to God and the king and the wife to the church and the kingdom. Once again (as is discussed in more detail in Chapter 3), the analogy connecting the family, the state, and the cosmos is an ancient invention, not a Protestant one. But the Protestants' elaborate deployment of this analogy, along with its wide dissemination in sermons and tracts in an age of printing, was a new development in sixteenth- and seventeenth-century English life. As Chapters 3 and 4 show, the attempt to grant new significance to private life by equating it with public and spiritual existence in pragmatic terms breaks down from the retention of domestic and political hierarchies that, issuing in a host of contradictions, subvert the attempted analogies and eventually result in the creation of separate spheres.

During the sixteenth and early seventeenth centuries, I argue, there is a gradual shift from the dualistic mentality to the predominance of the Protestant idealization of marriage. Naturally, such a shift in sensibility is not clear-cut; there is an inevitable overlapping of values and attitudes. Nor does one sexual consciousness ever supersede another entirely; clearly the dualistic sensibility is still an option in our culture. Nevertheless, a study of moral, religious, and dramatic writing in the English Renaissance reveals that the Protestant idealization of marriage gained a distinct ascendancy as the predominant, authoritative sexual discourse.

This book attempts to demonstrate these changes as their constituent and particular elements manifest themselves both in specific plays and in nondramatic writings. In locating a consideration of dramatic texts within a variety of forms of writing, and in viewing the drama as both creating and responding to cultural change, the analysis is allied to the efforts of much recent scholarship, including feminism and the new historicism. Yet along with other contrasts to which I will return, my own approach differs from that of some new historicists both in its emphasis upon changing values and in its focus upon dramatic form. New historicism is, of course, concerned with cultural conflict; but (and there are significant exceptions) in this scholarship the emphasis tends to fall less on the processes of change over time and more on the way the interrelations between literature and power reveal themselves in given texts at selected moments. Second, many new historicists eschew a focus on specifically aesthetic characteristics as static and falsely universalizing: in short, as empty formalism. Yet as scholars like Fredric Jameson have shown, literary forms and artistic conventions do not constitute static rhetorical paradigms that are transmitted without alteration through history; they are themselves social and ideological constructs, whose varying patterns, sudden appearances at distinct historical moments, and shifting dominance serve as significant registers of cultural transformation.

Attempting to illuminate the variety and complexity of sexual and dramatic change in the English Renaissance as well as their interconnections, I have focused and expanded upon traditional aesthetic configurations of dramatic structure and form. Dramatic forms are viewed as ways of categorizing experience and making it meaningful to people, as vehicles of interpretation that are altered and affected by nondramatic conceptualizations even while they themselves affect the course of cultural history. This book attempts to trace a dynamic process in which four dominant dramatic forms—romantic comedy, satire or city comedy, tragedy, and tragicomedy—may be seen from several perspectives. First, they can be viewed as contending simultaneously for adequacy of representation of changing sexual values within the particular structural demands of their distinctive genres. From this vantage point, certain formal conceptions of love and sexuality can be seen as more or less able to contain shifting views of women, eros, and marriage. Thus, developing in a cultural environment in which the prestige of marriage has increased significantly, Elizabethan romantic comedy attains formal coherence by idealizing marriage as a symbolic embodiment of social and spiritual harmony that reconciles sexual tensions. Yet as the conflicting implications of these tensions become more pressing, the contradictions that are generated themselves begin to contribute material for other forms. Jacobean satire severely scrutinizes traditional comic and social order by highlighting and exposing sexual tensions; and in Jacobean tragedy, the contradictions and paradoxes inscribed in the two dominant modes of Renaissance sexual discourse explode into destruction and protest. When these genres in turn confront conceptions to which their structural components cannot adapt (e.g., that illicit sexual desire need not result in fatal consequences), a less idealistic and demanding form, tragicomedy, becomes the vehicle for the articulation of newly shifting values.

Second, in the four chapters that follow, the four dramatic forms are viewed as variously capable of comprehending distinctive issues and problems in the changing representation of love and sexuality. How, precisely, do the conventional romantic comic preoccupations with eros and courtship, the satiric exposé of the collective delusions of social life, and the tragic focus on death and heroism interact with transforming sexual values in the Renaissance? Finally, given the options available in Elizabethan and Jacobean culture, should comic and tragic discourses be viewed as conservative, as radical, or as a complex mixture of both?

Chapter 1, "Moral Conceptions of Sexual Love in Elizabethan Comedy," examines the shift in predominance from a dualistic sensibility to the Protestant idealization of marriage by contrasting the relevant writings of eminent European humanists, including Castiglione, Vives, Erasmus, and Montaigne, whose works were widely translated in Renaissance England, to the effusion of sermons on holy matrimony written by Protestant preachers in the late sixteenth and early seventeenth centuries. By examining the growth of Elizabethan comedy from the early works of John Lyly through those of Robert Greene and Shakespeare, the chapter demonstrates a parallel development between this shift in sexual discourse and the changing representations of erotic love and marriage that characterize the development of the form. Lyly, whose comic structures embody the dualistic sensibility, rarely ended his plays with marriage and consequently was unable to experiment extensively with the genre; Greene developed romantic comedy to a limited extent; and Shakespeare realized its potential with *As You Like It* and *Twelfth Night* by creating more complex representations, in which sexual love and marriage have increased significantly in moral stature and prestige. This chapter also argues that despite its complexity, romantic comedy performed a predominantly conservative function in Elizabethan culture by evoking potentially disruptive sexual tensions only to represent them as harmoniously assimilated within the existing social structure.

Chapter 2 demonstrates the ways in which Jacobean satire constructs a more pointed critique of Renaissance sexual values than can penetrate the requisite wish-fulfillment structure of romantic comedy, precisely by transforming the conventions of that genre. Specifically, this chapter connects the phenomenon of social mobility with the struggle for sexual equality in Jacobean England by focusing on the figure of the disguised comic heroine as the symbolic composite of both. Ben Jonson's *Epicoene* and Thomas Middleton and Thomas Dekker's *The Roaring Girl*, both plays that center on a transvestite title figure, are examined in relation to the popular literature that constitutes the lively controversy over the nature and place of women in Renaissance England. The contrast between the two plays and the social commentary reveals the range of conceptual options that were available in Jacobean culture. By directly and self-consciously inverting romantic comic conventions, Jonson depicts sexual and social mobility with unmitigated ridicule, mocking them both, I argue, from a conservative and aristocratic point of view. In contrast, parallel treatments of women in men's clothing in *The Roaring Girl* and the satiric pamphlets *Hic Mulier* and *Haec-Vir* illuminate a deep, more comprehensive cultural ambivalence about social mobility, female independence, and equality between the sexes. Viewing the *Hic Mulier* debate in the context of contemporary moral and religious writing about women and fashion, the chapter demonstrates that a disjunction between content and form in the debate's structure depicts female freedom and equality as desirable and just, but also as impossible for a hierarchical society to absorb without unacceptable disruption. Similar aesthetic dislocation between content and form characterizes the representation of the man–clothed, virginal title figure in *The Roaring Girl*, who is simultaneously admired and excluded by the traditional comic society of married couples that forms on the stage at the end of the play.

Whereas Elizabethan romantic comedy evokes but contains sexual tensions within an idealization of marriage, Jacobean city comedy, in contrast, underscores these tensions, insisting on them. Yet even the more pointed scrutiny of satire contains (if barely and with noted ambivalence) the social and sexual paradoxes it highlights within a triumphant, festive present tense. However uncomfortable an audience may be with the resolution of a comic play, that discomfort centers on an imagination of the future, and the future remains outside the discursive terrain of comedy. In tragedy, on the other hand, the generic focus on individual heroism and death invites the consideration of the passage of time, forcing a confrontation between the future and the past: the social and sexual contradictions and inequities that are contained in comedy succeed in subverting the existing structures of society.

In considering the development of English Renaissance tragedy, what is remarkable for the purposes of this analysis are the transforming conceptions of heroism from Elizabethan to Jacobean interpretations of the form. Although there was no extensive, well-developed body of tragic theory in sixteenth- and seventeenth-century England, the theory that did exist viewed tragedy as intimately related to history, emphasizing the elevated stature of the characters and the importance of their individual destinies to the collective polity. Unlike comedy, which centered almost by definition on private, usually sexual, experience, tragedy focused on the concerns of public life. Elizabethan tragedy consequently represents a heroism of public action that highlights the protagonist's will to power, treating women and eros either as potentially destructive or as subliminally idealized, but always as peripheral to the represented action of a play. In short, Elizabethan tragedy constructs the representation of women and sexuality from the dualistic sexual sensibility described above, a process demonstrated in Chapter 3 in an analysis of Marlowe's *Tamburlaine*. In contrast, Jacobean tragedy constructs a heroism of endurance, rather than action, centering on private life, exploring sexual experience in detail, and presenting a surprising number of women as the heroes of tragic plays. In Chapter 3, I relate this transforming conception of tragic heroism—the idea of what constitutes tragic experience—to the rising prestige of marriage in the English Renaissance. Specifically, examination of Protestant sermons and conduct books about holy matrimony reveals that marriage is constructed in explicitly heroic terms, as the most critical endeavor of one's whole life, as a quest, or "a voyage on a dangerous sea," as the arena in which one pursues salvation or damnation, as inevitable destiny. Furthermore, the heroism being constructed is one of patient suffering, rather than willful action; as such, I argue, it is a heroism particularly suited to women. Within the terms of the discourse that I have called the heroics of marriage, women begin to be represented in English Renaissance tragedy as powerful agents of cultural change.

In tracing the connections between altering sexual values and changing concepts of tragic heroism, I focus on *Othello* and *The Duchess of Malfi* as particularly illuminating examples of this process. *Othello* can be seen to depict the decline of the heroism of action that is associated with the disappearing past, whereas in *The Duchess* that decline has already taken place, and the need to construct a future is imperative. In both plays the heroics of marriage is embodied in the female protagonists and associated with the future. Yet the heroics of marriage breaks down from external opposition and from internal contradictions that center on conflicting imperatives of gender, power, and social class. By examining the deaths of Desdemona and the Duchess of Malfi as symbolic foci of tragic experience, I argue that tragedy functions paradoxically as both a radical and a conservative discourse in the representation of sexual and cultural change.

Jacobean tragicomedy continues to dismantle traditional conceptions of heroism in the representation of love and sexuality. A transitional and unstable form, tragicomedy, despite its surface evasions and fantasy, is entirely dependent upon an awareness of Jacobean social processes and artistic traditions if it is to be understood. As a hybrid genre, tragicomedy combines old sexual discourses in new ways, never quite transforming them but, at the same time, creating the conditions in which they can be transformed and thus constituting the critical link between Renaissance and Restoration drama. To explore this process, I have focused on chivalry as a metaphor and vehicle for cultural change, examining in particular the relation between heroism and sexuality in three plays: Shakespeare's *Troilus and Cressida*, *The Two Noble Kinsmen* (probably a collaboration between Shakespeare and John Fletcher), and *The Knight of Malta* (probably a joint effort between Fletcher and a frequent collaborator, Philip Massinger), all ironic renditions of knightly heroes in love. Analyzing the ways in which issues that, treated bitterly by Shakespeare, are represented with increasing levity and parody in the Fletcher plays, I argue that Jacobean tragicomedy represents a final relinquishing of a treasured Renaissance vision of the past.

Although my method throughout this book involves detailed analyses of individual plays and documents, often isolating moments in time for purposes of comparison, broad patterns of change focusing on conceptions of public and private life are also suggested. As we have seen, the rising prestige of marriage in Renaissance England helps to account for the development of both comedy and tragedy. Elizabethan comedy attains formal coherence by idealizing marriage, whereas in tragedy the private life, after being treated as subordinate, destructive, and peripheral, is elevated in stature to the center of tragic significance. The heroics of marriage is, of course, constructed precisely by equating private experience with the political and spiritual realms: these are the analogies that give love and sexuality an added prestige. Yet when these analogies break down from the contradictory retention of hierarchies of age, rank, class, and, particularly, gender, private experience does not retreat to its former marginal status. As I have tried to show in the last chapter of this study, in tragicomedy private life begins to be represented as a once again separate, but newly equivalent, sphere. The continued representation of private experience as a serious center of significance in its own right constitutes the ongoing legacy of the heroics of marriage.

Recent historical studies of Renaissance literature have recognized the importance of understanding representations of love and sexuality. Yet these representations are considered significant primarily insofar as they illuminate the manipulations of Elizabethan and Jacobean political power and mechanisms of economic exchange. "Love is not love," asserts a recent critic, wittily playing on the famous Shakespearean line in a perceptive account of the political ploys embedded in Elizabethan sonnets. The dignity of eros and marriage was indeed enhanced when they were analogized to political and spiritual power. Yet to assume that political power is more real—more worthy of analysis—than sexual love and marriage is to ignore the equivalence given to the terms of an analogy and to overlook the mixed, complex, and overlapping nature of public and private experience. Ultimately, this emphasis distorts by depriving the private life of historical content. For whatever else it may be, love, definitely, is love. Giving each realm of experience its due can help to make visible new aspects of Renaissance drama and to create a new perspective on the course of cultural change.

Tracing the transforming dramatic representations of love and sexuality in Elizabethan and Jacobean England provides insight into the ways in which people conceived of their emotional experience and represented it not only to the world but to themselves. When the most intimate emotions are given popular, public expression in dramatic forms, we can perceive the paradoxes and contradictions that constituted the mental formulations of sexual love as England moved into the modern age. The drama not only illuminates the inner life of the surrounding culture but plays a significant part in creating it. An awareness of this reciprocal relation between sexual values and their symbolic representation in dramatic forms should become increasingly germane as scholars move more deeply into unearthing the history of the private life.

I

Moral Conceptions of Sexual Love in Elizabethan Comedy

i

Elizabethan romantic comedy is traditionally regarded as a dramatic form that can be distinguished as a generic celebration of marriage. Contrasting the erotic teleology of romantic comedy (which she calls "pure comedy") with the moral corrective of satire and the tragicomic emphasis on plot, Helen Gardner has written that "the great symbol of pure comedy is marriage, by which the world is renewed, and its endings are always instinct with a sense of fresh beginnings. Its rhythm is the rhythm of the life of mankind, which goes on and renews itself as the life of nature does. . . . The young wed, so that they may become in turn the older generation, whose children will wed, and so on, as long as the world lasts. . . . The end of comedy declares that life goes on."[1]

In romantic comedy, then, the sexual love that leads to marriage symbolizes the ongoing life of society, which in Elizabethan terms suggests a spiritually integrated cosmos. Although recent scholarship has been carefully dissecting the ideological program that sustains this comic syndrome, pointing to the devious subversions of its unity and the complex qualifications of its ideals, no analysis has disputed that the multileveled idealization of marriage is a powerful informing presence in Elizabethan comedy.[2] Yet this celebra-

1. Helen Gardner, "*As You Like It*," in *Modern Shakespearean Criticism: Essays on Style, Dramaturgy, and the Major Plays*, ed. Alvin B. Kernan (New York: Harcourt, Brace & World, 1970), pp. 193–94.
2. See, e.g., Louis Adrian Montrose, "'Shaping Fantasies': Figurations of Gender and Power in Elizabethan Culture," *Representations*, 1 (Spring 1983),

tory sexual and social configuration, which Shakespeare discerned and exploited until it had been thoroughly imagined and expressed, was by no means always developed or even implicit in earlier Elizabethan comedies. John Lyly was the first Elizabethan playwright to clarify the aesthetic realization that the theme of erotic love could be used to organize the disparate materials of early romantic comedy into a coherent design; but unlike the comedies of Shakespeare, Lyly's plays never acclaim sexual love and rarely end in a festive celebration of marriage. This chapter seeks to trace the ways in which Elizabethan comic form developed in plays by Lyly, Robert Greene, and Shakespeare in accordance with the precise erotic teleology Gardner describes by relating changes in the dramatic representation of love and marriage to similar patterns of change in conceptualizations of love and marriage in the nondramatic literature, particularly in Elizabethan moral and religious writing, including sermons and courtesy and conduct books.

Two salient modes of conceptualizing eros and marriage emerge from the complex controversy over changing sexual values articulated in Elizabethan conduct literature: a dualistic sensibility, in which sexual love is idealized beyond physical existence on the one hand or derided as lust on the other, and which views marriage as a necessary evil; and a more realistic, multifaceted sensibility, which, while retaining much of the skepticism about erotic love contained in the first view, nevertheless begins to conceive of affectionate marriage with great respect as the basis of an ordered society. Taking into account the inevitable overlapping and intermingling of shifting values and attitudes, historians have shown that in late sixteenth- and early seventeenth-century England, the second sensibility was gaining ground over the first.[3] What I suggest is a parallel development between this shift in *mentalité* and the changing representations of sexual love and marriage that characterize the growth of Elizabethan comedy: Lyly, whose comic structures

61–94; and Phyllis Rackin, "Androgyny, Mimesis, and the Marriage of the Boy Heroine on the English Renaissance Stage," *PMLA*, 102 (January 1987), 29–41.

3. This change in sensibility is particularly apparent in the upper and middle classes, to whom my remarks are limited. The most comprehensive treatment of this subject is Lawrence Stone, *The Family, Sex and Marriage in England, 1500–1800* (New York: Harper & Row, 1977).

embody the dualistic sensibility, was unable to develop romantic comedy beyond a certain point; Greene developed the form to a limited extent; and Shakespeare brought it to fruition with *As You Like It* and *Twelfth Night*, dramatizing more complex representations, in which sexual love and marriage have acquired greater centrality and prestige.

My purpose in comparing the changing attitudes articulated in Renaissance sexual discourse to the altering dramatic representations of sexual love is not, therefore, to demonstrate causal connections between them, but to show that the concepts and values that inform the one can be seen as informing the other, and that the shifts discernible in one form are similarly discernible in the other. As a result my method involves suggesting reciprocal influences among kinds of evidence often thought to have a different value: the imagination of the individual artist, the aesthetic requirements of the comic form, and contemporary moral and religious writings about love and marriage. What emerges is a picture of alterations in the sexual conditions of possibility in the English Renaissance that suggests a new perspective on the cultural context and development of Elizabethan comedy.

ii

Lawrence Stone and other historians of the relations between the sexes have demonstrated convincingly that the institution of marriage enjoyed a considerable rise in prestige in post-Reformation England.[4] The precise origins and chronology of this change in sensibility are as difficult to determine as is the actual sexual conduct of medieval and Renaissance men and women. In terms not of actual behavior, but of the moral prestige granted to heterosexual love and marriage, however, it is clear that those medieval conceptualizations of heterosexual relations which were officially articu-

4. See, e.g., Stone, pp. 135–38. Also see Christopher Hill, "The Spiritualization of the Household," in his *Society and Puritanism in Pre-Revolutionary England* (New York: Schocken Books, 1964), pp. 443–81; and C. L. Powell, *English Domestic Relations, 1487–1653* (New York: Columbia University Press, 1917).

lated by homilists, theologians, and poets often stressed and valorized asceticism.

Once made, such a generalization about centuries of thought, feeling, and representation must of course be qualified. Caroline Walker Bynum has definitively demonstrated that the modern scholarly emphasis on medieval asceticism is based on a radical privileging of genital sexuality and an accompanying disregard of the wide range and detailed exploration of erotic feeling and representation that characterize medieval spirituality. It is also true that a commonsensical, concrete counterideal of married love existed among ordinary people throughout the Middle Ages.[5] Yet for purposes of this discussion, which centers on the rising prestige of the secular institution of marriage in sixteenth- and seventeenth-century England, it remains appropriate to stress the striking contrast with the late medieval idealization of celibacy. Sexual love was considered out of the question as a basis for marriage, which the upper classes regarded as an alliance for the enhancement of family property and as an outlet for the avoidance of fornication. It is true that Saint Jerome, who felt that love between men and women was at best "to be endured, not enjoyed," and preferably "to be avoided if at all possible," represents the extreme of medieval opinion; nevertheless, carnal love, even for purposes of procreation, was usually conceptualized as tainted with some odor of sin and was at best regarded as morally neutral. Celibacy was upheld as the ideal behavior to be emulated, not only by priests and nuns, but by the whole community.[6] Even Saint Paul, cited so often by sixteenth- and seventeenth-century Protestant preachers

5. Caroline Walker Bynum, *Jesus as Mother: Studies in the Spirituality of the High Middle Ages* (Berkeley: University of California Press, 1982), esp. pp. 110–69, and "The Body of Christ in the Later Middle Ages: A Reply to Leo Steinberg," *Renaissance Quarterly*, 3 (Autumn 1986), 399–439. See also Henry Ansgar Kelly, *Love and Marriage in the Age of Chaucer* (Ithaca, N.Y.: Cornell University Press, 1975), pp. 247, 284–85, 300, 315; Jane Tibbetts Schulenburg, "The Heroics of Virginity: Brides of Christ and Sacrificial Mutilation," in *Women in the Middle Ages and the Renaissance: Literary and Historical Perspectives*, ed. Mary Beth Rose (Syracuse, N.Y.: Syracuse University Press, 1986), pp. 29–72; and *Western Sexuality: Practice and Precept in Past and Present Times*, ed. Philippe Ariès and André Béjin, trans. Anthony Forster (Oxford: Basil Blackwell, 1985).

6. Kelly, p. 315; Stone, p. 135.

as the main scriptural authority in their vehement defenses of marriage, could be seen to consider marriage as merely a necessary evil: "For I would that all men were even as I myself am . . . [i.e., celibate]," he writes in 1 Corinthians. "It is good for them if they abide even as I doe. But if they cannot absteine, let them marrie: for it is better to marrie then to burne" (7.7–9).

During the English Renaissance, conjugal loyalty and affection replaced celibacy as the officially idealized pattern of heterosexual conduct.[7] Like other forms of medieval thought, however, much of the consciousness of love, marriage, and sexuality persisted into the Renaissance.[8] Stone reports that "marriage among the property-owning classes in sixteenth-century England was . . . a collective decision of family and kin, not an individual one. . . . Property and power were the predominant issues which governed negotiations for marriage."[9] Individual, rather than parental choice of a spouse, let alone prior affection between potential mates, seemed foolish, undesirable. The eminent sixteenth-century humanist Vives, whose works were accessible in English, observes, for example, that "they that mary for loue shall leade theyr lyfe in sorowe."[10] Montaigne, whose translated essays were also available after 1603, is less hostile to erotic love than Vives; nevertheless, he affirms what he construes to be the essential incompatibility of erotic love and marriage:

> *Loue disdaineth a man should holde of other then himselfe*, and dealeth but faintly with acquaintances begun and entertained under another title; as marriage is. Alliances, respects and meanes, by all

7. Stone, pp. 135–38; Hill, pp. 443–81. Also see Louis B. Wright, *Middle-Class Culture in Elizabethan England* (Chapel Hill: University of North Carolina Press, 1935), pp. 201–27; Ian Maclean, *The Renaissance Notion of Woman* (Cambridge: Cambridge University Press, 1980), p. 59; and Carroll Camden, *The Elizabethan Woman* (New York: Elsevier, 1952), pp. 109–49.

8. Linda T. Fitz, "What Says the Married Woman: Marriage Theory and Feminism in the English Renaissance," *Mosaic*, 13 (Winter 1980), 1–22; Peter Laslett, *The World We Have Lost: England before the Industrial Age* (New York: Scribner's, 1965), pp. 130–31.

9. Stone, p. 87.

10. John Louis Vives, *Instruction of a christen woman*, trans. Rycharde Hyrde (1529; rpt. London, 1557), bk. 1, chap. 16, "Howe the mayde shall seeke an husbande."

reason, waighe as much or more, as the graces and beawtie. A man doth not marrie for himselfe, whatsoever he alledgeth; but as much or more for his posteritie and familie. The use and interest of mariage concerneth our off-spring, a great way beyond us. Therefore doth this fashion please me, to guide it rather by a third hand, and by anothers sence, then our owne: All which, how much doth it dissent from amorous conventions? . . . *I see no mariages faile sooner, or more troubled, then such as are concluded for beauties sake, and hudled up for amorous desires.* There are required more solide foundations, and more constant grounds . . . this earnest youthly heate serveth to no purpose.[11]

Furthermore, while celibacy no longer flourished as an idealized mode of behavior after the Reformation, the distrust of sexual desire and the ideals of maidenly virtue—virginity—and wifely chastity continued to preoccupy the Renaissance imagination of the moral and spiritual life well into the seventeenth century.

It is worth dwelling briefly on the tremendous spiritual weight put on sexuality in the Renaissance. A good example is the emphasis placed on premarital female virginity. Many have argued that the perceived necessity for premarital female chastity, as well as the double standard of sexual morality, arose originally from the economic need to legitimize property for the purposes of inheritance;[12] however this may be, the ideal of virginity accrued moral and theological overtones and became for poets a useful means of dramatizing female social and spiritual life. One need only think of Britomart, Spenser's embattled knight of chastity, dueling her way through a world full of erotic peril. In the courtesy book *Instruction of a christen woman* (1529), dedicated to Catherine of Aragon, Vives elaborates powerfully the consequences that loss of virginity entails for a young woman:

> Turn hir whiche way she will, she shall fynde all thynges sorowfull and heauy, walyng and mourning, and angry and displeaserfull. What sorowe will hir kynneffolkes make, when euery one shall thynke them selfe dysshonested by one shame of that maide?

11. Michaell de Montaigne, *The Essayes*, trans. John Florio (London, 1603), p. 510, italics his.

12. Stone, p. 637; Keith Thomas, "The Double Standard," *Journal of the History of Ideas*, 20 (1959), 195–216.

What mourninge, what teares, what wepyng of the father and mother and bryngers up? Doest thou quiete theim with this pleasure for soo muche care and labour? Is this the rewarde of the bringyng up? What cursyng will there bee of hir acquaintance? . . . What mockinge and bablynge of those maides, that enuied hir before? What a loathynge and abhorrynge of those that loued hir. What flyinge of hir company . . . when euery mother wyll keepe not onely their daughters but also their sonnes from the infection of such an unthryftie mayde. And wooars also, if she had any, all flee away from hir. . . . I reherce the hate and angre of folkes for I knowe that many fathers have cut the throtes of their daughters, bretherne of their sisters, and kinnesmen of their kynneswomen.[13]

Could any young woman possibly have endured such an onslaught of threatened damnation, social ostracism, personal guilt and despair, open ridicule, and family catastrophe? In a chapter discussing when a maid should leave the house (to which his answer is never, unless absolutely necessary, and in that case certainly never alone), Vives evokes a world of sexual desire that, like the world of Spenser's Britomart, is fraught with spiritual dangers. "Howe so euer she turneth hirselfe from god unto men, whether shee like them or be liked of them, shee forsaketh Christe, and of Christes spouse sodeynly becometh an adulterer."[14] This statement, striking in its lucidity, starkly conveys the perils of sexuality, the evils of it, and the human responsibility for it; Vives has here clarified the association of sexuality with sin. Female entrance into the sexual world, whether through body or mind, by choice or unwittingly, whether by reciprocating male affections or merely remaining the passive object of them, is equivalent to sin, *is* sin. Even when sexual love is viewed with a less foreboding gloom, it is often regarded as bitterly degrading, bestial, and absurd. Once again we can turn to Montaigne for the liveliest and most direct articulation of this attitude:

When all is done, I finde that *loue is nothing els but an insatiate thirst*

13. Vives, bk. 1, chap. 7, "Of the kepying of virginitee and chastitee."
14. Vives, bk. 1, chap. 12, "How the mayde shall behaue hyr selfe forth abrode."

of enioying a greedily desired subiect . . . which becometh faulty by immoderation & defectiue by indiscretion. . . . Now considering oftentimes the ridiculous tickling, or titilation of this pleasure, the absurd, giddie and harebraind motions wherewith it . . . agitates . . . that unaduised rage, that furious and with cruelty enflamed visage in loues lustfull and sweetest effects: and then a grave, sterne, severe surly countenance in so fond-fond an action . . . I beleeue that which *Plato* sayes to be true, that *man was made by the Gods for them to toy and play withall.* . . . And that nature in mockery leaft us the most troublesome of our actions the most common: thereby to equal us, & without distinction to set the foolish and the wise, us and the beasts. . . . In all other things you may observe decorum, and maintaine some decencie: . . . this cannot onely be imagined, but vicious or ridiculous.[15]

Moral bankruptcy and degeneracy, fear, humiliation, and a kind of ridiculous madness: what fools these mortals be! Such negative associations are made over and over again in Renaissance discussions of the place of sexuality in social and moral life. But were there not more positive conceptions of erotic love—beyond, that is, such occasional, begrudging tributes as Robert Burton's parenthetical concession that love "by a perpetual generation makes and preserves mankind, propagates the Church"?[16] One answer, of course, is that just as classical writers had treated love both philosophically and sensually, so Christian writers recognized both a sacred and a profane love.[17] This dualistic, idealizing cast of thought granted love the highest respect and prestige when it was conceived of either as separate from, or as having transcended, sexual desire. I cannot do justice here to the profound and complex legacy that the Renaissance inherited from this mode of conceptualizing love, which had been articulated systematically in Christian orthodoxy.[18] But of the many literary variations on the theme

15. Montaigne, p. 527, italics his.
16. Robert Burton, *The Anatomy of Melancholy*, in *Seventeenth Century Prose and Poetry*, ed. Alexander M. Witherspoon and Frank J. Warnke (New York: Harcourt, Brace & World, 1963), p. 192.
17. John Charles Nelson, *The Renaissance Theory of Love* (New York: Columbia University Press, 1958), p. 67.
18. See, for example, Irving Singer, *The Nature of Love* (Chicago: University of Chicago Press, 1984); Maurice Valency, *In Praise of Love* (New York:

of this tradition that are of immediate relevance to English Renaissance drama, Neoplatonism and the related phenomenon of Petrarchism are salient.

The ideas of the Florentine Neoplatonist Marsilio Ficino are expanded and popularized in Castiglione's *The Courtier*, which was translated by Thomas Hoby in 1561. In the fourth book of *The Courtier* the favored figure of the ladder of love, inherited from Plato's *Symposium*, is set forth in eloquent detail. In this image the beauty of the female beloved inspires the male lover to ascend by stages a metaphorical ladder, leading him to the beauty that "shall make a universal conceite, and bring the multitude of them to the unitie of one alone, that is generally spred over all the nature of man." Now able to ascend by contemplating its own beauty, the soul of the lover then transcends this stage, along with all earthly things, to gaze on "the maine sea of the pure heauenly beautie." Castiglione allows for the appropriateness of sensual love in the young, but the mature, civilized society has transcended sexuality. Whereas the female beloved serves the crucial but limited function of original inspiration, the true Neoplatonic lover will keep "alwaies fast in minde, that the bodie is a most diverse thing from beautie, and not onely not encreaseth, but diminisheth the perfection of it." The speech in which the ladder of love is described includes many of the characteristically idealistic love themes: sacrifice (in this case of the soul to God through burning or consuming of the body), liberation from the self, transcendence, transformation, the ideals of contemplation and union with God.[19]

Sears Jayne points out that Platonism became permanently associated in the English Renaissance with Petrarchism.[20] The Neoplatonic ideas of love both as "a cosmic phenomenon informing the universe and apparent in nature" and as an independent force transcending nature and creating its own world directly influenced

---

Octagon, 1975); and Denis de Rougemont, *Love in the Western World*, trans. Montgomery Belgion (New York: Harcourt Brace, 1940).

19. Baldesar Castiglione, *The Courtier*, trans. Thomas Hobby (London, 1588). See bk. 4, which Hobby describes as telling "of honest loue."

20. Cited in Neal L. Goldstein, "*Love's Labor's Lost* and the Renaissance Vision of Love," *Shakespeare Quarterly*, 25 (Summer 1974), 339.

the Petrarchan tradition through Castiglione and Pietro Bembo.[21] As in Castiglione, the beloved in Petrarch's poetry remains an idealized, unattainable icon. Although in Petrarch the lover oscillates "between restrained wooing and distant adoration," actual union is envisaged only in dreams. Leonard Forster stresses the central importance of the lover's experience of love as dual, as "interpenetration of pleasure and pain. . . . The elaboration and exploitation of antitheses is the essence of Petrarchism."[22] The Petrarchan style and diction, which reached England via Wyatt and Surrey in the first half of the sixteenth century, was most notably exploited in the latter half by Sidney, Spenser, and Shakespeare and their followers in the numerous, fashionable sonnet sequences of that period, sequences that created an image of a courtly, melancholy, obsessive lover, doomed to frustration and rejection, a little foolish for putting so much hope and faith in the desire for a woman.

According to the mentality being described, sexual desire, even when conceived as leading to a consciousness of the divine, was never considered beneficial or good in itself. Loved women were better left exalted, remote, and untouched. It is therefore not surprising to discover that where idealization of women occurred, misogyny was rarely far behind. With significant exceptions, English Petrarchism and its corollary, anti-Petrarchism, tend to articulate that consciousness which exalts and idealizes the image of Woman while simultaneously regarding actual women with neglect or contempt.[23] Notwithstanding the persistence of this mode of thought in our culture, what is both new and significant in the English Renaissance is that this dualizing, polarizing consciousness begins to break down, to lose its authority as the predominant, or at least as the only, articulated view of women and sexuality. A burgeoning awareness of a more complex, problematic moral and emotional reality ensues; and it is in this changing moral atmo-

21. Leonard Forster, *The Icy Fire: Five Studies in European Petrarchism* (Cambridge: Cambridge University Press, 1969), p. 21.

22. Forster, pp. 1–60.

23. Regarding exceptions, see, e.g., C. S. Lewis's discussion of Spenser as the poet of married love in *The Allegory of Love: A Study in Medieval Tradition* (London: Oxford University Press, 1977), pp. 297–360.

sphere that romantic comedy, with its celebration of married love, comes into its own as a dramatic form.

In the development under discussion, the work of John Lyly represents an encounter between the dualistic, idealizing Petrarchan sensibility to which he was heir and the more realistic, multifaceted view of married love that was beginning to announce its presence both in the drama and in the moral and religious outpourings of the surrounding society.[24] Lyly was the first major Elizabethan playwright to recognize the importance of the erotic love theme to the coherence and design of his plays; consequently, he was the first to organize romantic comedy by subordinating the disruptive medley of spectacle, song, ritual, pageant, magic, folklore, slapstick, and farce that constituted it to a central love story. Lyly emerged from the tradition of aristocratic early sixteenth-century humanism in which literature existed in service to the prince and the state, not as an independent profession. As G. K. Hunter has demonstrated, Lyly's values and beliefs, his apparent disdain of writing for the increasingly powerful, popular, public theater, doomed him to outlive his early success and to die in disappointed poverty, having hopelessly depended on favors from Queen Elizabeth that never were forthcoming.[25] But the anachronistic humanist idealism that tied Lyly to an outmoded literary tradition caused him to conceive of his plays as select entertainments, dramatizations of the elegant, refined manners of a stately court; as a result, though Lyly retained many of the native traditions that gave Elizabethan comedies their vitality, he also imposed on them a new sense of integration, balance, and grace. Neverthe-

24. Cf. Robert Weimann, *Shakespeare and the Popular Tradition in the Theater*, ed. Robert Schwartz (Baltimore, Md.: Johns Hopkins University Press, 1978), p. 197: "It is a new sense of the interdependence of character and society, and a fully responsive interplay between dramatic speech and dramatic action in the process of reproducing the cause and effect of human behavior that defines 'realism' in the Renaissance theater." Weimann also makes the point (p. 173) that Lyly stood "at the very threshold" of such a complex apprehension, remaining "too bewildered to realize that the contradictions (which he points out) are about to yield a new and superior kind of unity."

25. G. K. Hunter, *John Lyly: The Humanist as Courtier* (London: Routledge & Kegan Paul, 1962).

less, the lack of flexibility in his conception of sexual love prevented Lyly from developing romantic comedy in accordance with the changing sensibility around him.

In his early success, *Euphues* (1578), and its successor, *Euphues and His England* (1580), Lyly creates an image of love and sexuality that he develops throughout his plays, and that is recognizable as emanating from that polarizing consciousness which posits idealization of women or misogyny, chaste worship or lust, as the only possibilities for love. In these two tracts, Lyly establishes a prose style that, with its witty similitudes, puns, antitheses, and parallelisms, mirrors his ideal of a learned, courtly, graceful, and sophisticated society. As a means of recommending manners and morals to their readers, both of these courtesy books relate the adventures of two elegant young men, Euphues and Philautus, whose coming of age Lyly depicts as an ongoing encounter with temptation in the form of love and desire. In the indiscriminate, capricious fickleness of most of the female characters and the continually wrongheaded, hopelessly infatuated state of Philautus, Lyly depicts sexual desire as a compulsive, impersonal, and ridiculous passion, which can be understood only as a direct contrast to reason and wisdom. "What new skirmishes dost thou now feele betweene reason and appetite, loue and wisdom, daunger and desire" Philautus asks, rhetorically echoing conventional Petrarchan sentiments and antitheses. All in all we are expected to perceive that "the desease of loue . . . is impatient, the desire extreame, whose assaultes neyther the wise can resist by pollicie nor the valiaunt by strength." One wants to protest that the sensible could ignore this self-indulgence by intelligence, so utterly self-centered, obsessive, and infantile an experience does love become when Lyly presents it. As might be expected, Euphues' heroism consists in his transcending sexual desire, his realization that "the effect of loue is faith, not lust, delightfull conference, not detestable concupiscence, which beginneth with folly and endeth with repentaunce."[26] At the end of *Euphues and His England* we find this polarized perspective figured forth concretely. In a concluding diatribe, Euphues, having returned to Italy from a visit to England determined to devote the

26. John Lyly, *Euphues and His England*, in *The Complete Works of John Lyly*, vol. 2, ed. R. Warwick Bond (Oxford: Clarendon, 1902), pp. 89–112, 158.

remainder of his life to solitary idealization of the Virgin Queen, exhorts the Italian women, whom he misogynistically maligns, to be like the English women, whom he sentimentally idealizes. Philautus ends up in a second-best, rebound marriage that pointedly does not ensue from any of his perpetual courtships.

This configuration, in which love remains a marginal experience, finding fulfillment either in the dream life or in an unsatisfactory lowering of expectations, becomes a structural principle in Lyly's plays. *Sapho and Phao* (1584) concludes with the image of an idolized female monarch, victorious over desire and remaining an object of the chaste, constant adoration of a solitary admirer and subject. Although *Endymion* (1588) ends with several happy couplings, the hero of the play conceives an impossible, idealizing love for the Moon, who, descending to the action in the form of a chaste and benevolent queen, rewards the hero for his solitary devotion by restoring his youth and granting him permission to worship her from afar for the rest of his life with celibate, contemplative, Neoplatonic joy.

Lyly's preference, clearly, is for sublimation; and his habitual tendency is to dissociate sexual love, which he distrusts, from social order, which he idealizes. In Lyly's earliest play, *Campaspe* (1584), a distracted Alexander the Great at last magnanimously transcends his love for a lower-class woman who does not return it. The potential threat to the orderly, efficient running of society implicit in Alexander's sexual desire is domesticated to a harmless, frivolous interlude, a digression in the career of his greatness. Lyly replicates this situation in *Sapho and Phao*: the virtuous monarch, Sapho, overcomes her unseemly attraction to a lower-class boatman, Phao, and usurps the capricious authority of Venus by capturing Cupid, in an elegant victory over desire.

In Lyly, then, sexual desire, though powerful and unavoidable, cannot be incorporated in a civil, humane society. Instead it must be conquered, overcome. Lyly accounts mythically for the inevitable association of chaos and sexuality in one of his most absurd, charming, and misogynistic plays, *The Woman in the Moon* (1593). Here his conception of female weakness and duplicity is allegorized in Pandora, a drastic parody of the remote, idealized Petrarchan lady. Pandora, a sort of ur-woman, is created by Nature and then abandoned to the whimsical mercy of the envious planets. In a mad, obsessive, and uncivil chase, several shepherds pursue the helplessly victimized, indiscriminate, perpetually inconstant and deceptive Pandora through a series of comically futile attempts to possess her. In one of Lyly's repeated images of sexual desire, Pandora, like the heroine of *Euphues*, ends by being attracted to a clown.

In spite of Pandora's outrageous behavior, the real cause of these ridiculous effects is actually male desire. The play begins with an image of the longing shepherds kneeling to Nature, begging and praying for the creation of a female. The three reasons the shepherds give for desiring a woman turn out to be the very reasons cited in the Elizabethan *Book of Common Prayer* as the justifications for marriage: the procreation of children, the avoidance of fornication; and the need for companionship.[27] Nevertheless, marriage, if and when it enters the scene at all, has little prestige in a Lyly play. The shepherds in *The Woman in the Moon* end by praising a single life, while Pandora is assigned to permanent residence in the moon—remote and heavenly, but also wayward, fickle, and false.

It should be emphasized that although erotic love, which, with one exception, is always Lyly's subject, is continually presented in his work as a threat to the brilliant, graceful society patterned in Euphuistic prose, the tone of his comedies is invariably delicate, witty, and light. This refinement of mood is partially achieved by the ordered introduction of the mixture of musical, magical, folkloric, allegorical, and mythological material which Elizabethan comic playwrights loved: singing and dancing; magic fountains and wells; Ovidian transformations; gods and goddesses; fairies and monsters; ugly, wise old hags who speak with the cynical clairvoyance of desire. All of these characters and motifs, woven together with witty repartee, constitute not a narrative of rising intensity with which we are asked to identify, but a series of static tableaux, balanced against one another, that we are asked to admire.[28]

Lyly's allegorical characters and static, balanced scenes serve as emotional distancing devices. M. C. Bradbrook has noted aptly

---

27. *The First and Second Prayer Books of Edward VI* (1549; rpt. London: J. H. Dent, 1949), pp. 252–58.

28. Cf. Hunter, p. 103.

that in Lyly's comedies passion is merely a postulate;[29] the evocation of felt emotion is not part of the playwright's courtly representation of love as a wooing game, a witty lark that provides an amusing, if occasionally dangerous, diversion from the serious activities of society. When erotic love is first appropriated from the Petrarchan lyric and begins to be dramatized, it is seen as abstract, magical, playful.

Along with the fact that erotic love is dramatized abstractly as a frivolous game, I believe there is another reason why Lyly's basically negative and skeptical portrayal of love and sexuality never violates the brittle whimsy of his comedies. Although sexual desire, whether or not it leads to marriage, is viewed by Lyly and many others as dangerous, humiliating, anarchic, and absurd, still the consequences of indulging it appear determined beforehand. There is no need to take a complicated, certainly not a suspenseful, view of the matter; the moral position of sexuality is fixed and predictable: "All this the world knows . . . well." What I am suggesting is that the consciousness that polarizes love is inherently undramatic.[30] This dichotomizing perspective, in which love becomes either degrading lust or spiritual idealization, traditionally took poetic form in the lyric, a genre designed to explore individual emotion, not to represent situational conflicts that drive toward resolution among various characters. Lyly's sense of dramatic conflict is epitomized in *Campaspe*, in which, in a story of unrequited love, he never once dramatizes a scene alone between the frustrated, powerful lover Alexander the Great and his unresponsive, captive beloved, Campaspe. As a result, love is depicted as an isolating, self-absorbed experience; the meaningful conflict is clarified not as an emotional struggle between Alexander and Campaspe, but as an abstract debate taking place in Alexander's

29. M. C. Bradbrook, *The Growth and Structure of Elizabethan Comedy* (Cambridge: Cambridge University Press, 1979), p. 65.

30. Cf. Robert J. Meyer, "'Pleasure Reconciled to Virtue': The Mystery of Love in Lyly's *Gallathea*," *Studies in English Literature*, 21 (1981), 193–208, in which the author correctly warns us not to assess Lyly's "masque-like" and "non-developing" drama in terms other than its own. My purpose is not to judge Lyly's dramaturgy as inferior, but to point out why, given his moral perspective on sexual love and his structural techniques, Lyly could develop romantic comedy only to a limited extent.

mind, an intellectual exercise. Furthermore, in an imaginative vision that, like Lyly's, idealizes the superiority of the elegant, contemplative soul, which has managed to remove itself from the muddy contingencies of physical existence, we must recognize a level of perception that is profoundly anticomic, particularly insofar as comedy is associated morally, emotionally, psychologically, and symbolically with birth, rebirth, the cycle of the seasons, with ongoing, natural life.[31]

Northrop Frye has clarified the necessary structural relationship between fulfilled sexual love and the form of romantic comedy as Shakespeare discerned and perfected it. Frye shows that the sense of vitality underlying comedy often takes the form of a drive toward identity that, in romantic comedy, is always erotic. The harsh and irrational laws impeding the fulfillment of the sexual drive of the hero and heroine must be overcome in order to bring about the freedom and self-knowledge that will form the basis of the new society symbolized in the festive conclusion. Romantic comedy, then, dramatizes that longing for a happy ending which is a wish-fulfillment fantasy of attaining all of one's desires without social, emotional, or moral cost: "Jack shall have Jill / Nought shall go ill." It should be mentioned that by wish-fulfillment Frye does not mean escapism, although romantic comedy can serve that purpose. Frye stresses instead what he calls "an imaginative model of desire." In his comedies Shakespeare pits the world of individual imagination and sexual desire against the more tangible world of social and historical fact, causing the spectator to question the reality of both worlds and then reconciling the claims of both in a final, inclusive vision of the social and spiritual harmony symbolized in marriage.[32]

31. See Susanne K. Langer, *Feeling and Form* (London: Routledge & Kegan Paul, 1953), pp. 326–50.

32. Northrop Frye, *A Natural Perspective* (New York: Columbia University Press, 1965), p. 117. See also his "The Argument of Comedy," in Kernan, pp. 165–73, and *Anatomy of Criticism* (Princeton, N.J.: Princeton University Press, 1957), p. 184. Cf. Montrose, who points out (p. 69) that "Frye's account of Shakespearean comic action emphasizes intergenerational tension at the expense of those other forms of social and familial tension from which it is only artificially separable; in particular, he radically undervalues the centrality of sexual politics to these plays by unquestioningly identifying the

Interestingly, in a later play, *Mother Bombie* (1589), Lyly moves toward a comic plot in which wit and vitality are joined to sexual desire. But the emphasis in this play remains with the servants' intriguing, not with the inherent drama of erotic love that gives shape to romantic comedy. Love still is not represented as a felt emotion. Lyly consequently fails to unite love with marriage. G. K. Hunter believes, not without justice, that what Lyly gains in narrative and integrative power in this play, he sacrifices in delicacy and grace.[33]

The fact that Lyly moves in *Mother Bombie* toward an uncharacteristically festive conclusion celebrating marriage, no matter how unsuccessful the attempt, indicates that he is beginning to detect a more profound pattern at the heart of the comic form. Although Lyly can discern this possibility, his polarized conception of love and sexuality prevents him from either fully imagining its ramifications or realizing them artistically. These achievements instead can be found to coexist in the drama with a different set of articulated beliefs which, while retaining much of the Renaissance sense of the wicked bestiality and folly of sexual desire, nevertheless includes these skeptical elements in a larger configuration that unites love with marriage and conceives of the combination as the foundation of an ordered society. I am not, of course, arguing that polarized conceptions of love and sexuality, expressed in Neoplatonic and Petrarchan patterns and images, disappeared from post-Lylyan Elizabethan comedy, but that these conceptions became part of an expanded vision that incorporates the dualistic

---

heroines' interests with those of the heroes." Although Frye needs a corrective, it remains true that in Shakespearean romantic comedy, much of the point is that the heroine herself comes to identify her interests with those of the hero; this syndrome, in fact, may be seen as the location of the comic wish-fulfillment generated by the male perspective, including both Frye's and Shakespeare's. The conservatism of Shakespearean comedy in terms of sexual politics can best be perceived in contrast to the satiric comedies and tragedies written by his contemporaries, where the inequities of the Jacobean sexual hierarchy are not suppressed, but themselves constitute the subject of various plays. See Chapters 2 and 3 of this book. The best critique of Frye appears in Fredric Jameson, *The Political Unconscious: Narrative as a Socially Symbolic Act* (Ithaca, N.Y.: Cornell University Press, 1981), esp. pp. 68–74.

33. Hunter, pp. 227–28, 243.

sensibility but is not limited to it. The fact that romantic comedy, a dramatic form celebrating erotic love and marriage, flourished in the environment of a new sensibility which embraced marriage both as the spiritual foundation of society and as the repository of hope for personal happiness strongly suggests a parallel develop- ment between the increasingly complex, optimistic comic repre- sentations of eros that followed Lyly's plays and the more positive, complex, moral conceptions of sexual love and marriage that were beginning to be articulated in Protestant conduct literature.

iii

Although it did not originate with the Protestant (largely Pu- ritan) theologians of the sixteenth and early seventeenth centuries, this optimistic vision of marriage was articulated explicitly, fully, and repeatedly by them. As Lawrence Stone points out, "Sancti- fication of marriage—'holy matrimony'—was a constant theme of Protestant sermons . . . which were directed to all classes in British society."[34] More than forty-five years ago, in a seminal article entitled "The Puritan Art of Love," William and Malleville Haller showed that "it was the Puritan preachers who set forth an ideal pattern of love and marriage based upon traditional Christian mo- rality, vitalized for popular imagination in terms of the English Bible, and adapted to the new conditions in which men were hav- ing to live."[35]

Reiterating the holiness of the married state, the Puritan preach- ers went about idealizing marriage and the family with all the fervid determination that their Catholic forefathers had lavished upon celibacy and virginity. The Puritans no longer felt the need to attack the prestige of celibacy: "There is no man now so dull as to think it is a sin to marry," Heinrich Bullinger announces confi- dently in the important *Golden boke of christen matrimonye*, trans- lated by Miles Coverdale in 1543.[36] In the Puritan outpourings of

34. Stone, pp. 135–36.

35. William Haller and Malleville Haller, "The Puritan Art of Love," *Hunt- ington Library Quarterly*, 5 (1941–42), 242.

36. Heinrich Bullinger, *The golden boke of christen matrimonye*, trans. Miles Coverdale, with a preface by Thomas Becon (London, 1543). Cf. William

sermons, conduct books, and spiritual autobiographies, marriage becomes "the type and source of all human relations, the seminary and model of all polities, the church and the state in little, the image and reflection of Christ's union with his elect."[37] John Dod and Robert Cleaver's influential courtesy book, *A Godlie forme of householde Government* (1598), makes it plain that the proper running of one's household had become, like the preservation of virginity, a matter of the greatest spiritual importance, of salvation and damnation.[38]

Several salient themes mark those Puritan tracts which idealize marriage as the basis of an ordered society. First, rather than stressing the avoidance of fornication or even the procreation of children, these documents emphasize a third motive for marriage, which was added by Archbishop Thomas Cranmer to the *Book of Common Prayer* in 1549:[39] companionship, or the relief of what Milton was later to call "that . . . God forbidden loneliness."[40] This new emphasis on the spiritual, rather than the physical quality of the marriage relation, along with the Puritan stress on the unique relationship between each individual and God, accompanied a recognition of the value of individual, rather than parental, choice of a marriage partner, the importance of the woman as helpmate and companion, the need for love in marriage, and finally, the desire for personal happiness.[41]

Perkins, *Christian Oeconomie or Houshold Government* (London, 1631), in *Workes,* 3:683. Perkins sees celibacy as a kind of punishment for those isolated and marginal figures who are unable to participate in normal social life.

37. Haller and Haller, p. 270.

38. John Dod and Robert Cleaver, *A Godlie forme of householde Government* (London, 1598). See, e.g., "Epistle Dedicatorie."

39. See Stone, p. 136.

40. John Milton, *The Doctrine and Discipline of Divorce,* in *John Milton: Complete Poems and Prose,* ed. Merritt Y. Hughes (Indianapolis, Ind.: Odyssey, 1957), p. 707.

41. See Jack Goody, *The Development of the Family and Marriage in Europe* (Cambridge: Cambridge University Press, 1983), esp. pp. 24–26, where Goody argues that an emphasis on consent in marriage, or on the mutual affection of the conjugal couple, "was in no way peculiar to the English." Though Goody maintains that these emphases were inventions neither of English Protestantism nor of bourgeois capitalism, he does acknowledge "a general move away from the solidarity of kin groups to the independence of

The Puritans linked happiness inseparably by hope to their ideal of love and marriage. In remarking drily that "it was a nice and subtle happiness these men conceived for themselves when they abandoned celibacy and embraced matrimony," the Hallers are referring to the latent contradictions in Puritan thought on this subject.[42] While insisting on the obedience and subordination of women, for example, the Puritans simultaneously stressed woman's importance, both as a companion to her husband and as supervisor of the newly exalted household.[43] Furthermore, the fact that Puritan doctrine gives woman's soul full equality with man's in the sight of God grants woman an undeniable dignity. Similarly, the Puritans continue to express a wholehearted distrust of sexual desire, dwelling—often with obsessive relish—on "abhominable adulterers, stinking whoremongers, uncleane fornicatours, and detestable Sodomites";[44] yet their perception that sex in the context of marriage—when practiced with moderation, of course, and as a solemn religious duty—is a "holy and undefiled action"[45] does grant consummated erotic love a distinct prestige. Further, although the Puritans strongly emphasize the importance of individual choice of a mate, deriding "the buying & selling of children among parents . . . [and] the forced marriages,"[46] they nevertheless insist on parental consent to a match. Finally, though the preachers reiterate that adultery, which should be punished with death, is the only reason to dissolve a marriage, the logical extension of their arguments about the absolute necessity of companionship results eventually in Milton's divorce tracts, where, in arguments that surely would have horrified the preachers, Milton declares that incompatibility alone is sufficient cause to declare a marriage void.

---

the conjugal couple, and even of its constituent members as individuals." The main relevance of Protestant sexual discourse to this study, however, is not its originality, but the wide extent to which it repeated and disseminated these ideals and the problem of embodying them in social relations. See Introduction and Chapter 3.

42. Haller and Haller, p. 250.

43. Hill, pp. 443–81.

44. Becon, "Preface," in Bullinger.

45. Perkins, p. 689.

46. Samuell Hieron, "The Marriage Blessing," in *The Sermons of Master Samuell Hieron* (London, 1635), p. 405.

The Puritan tracts therefore constitute a complex expression of double-mindedness: women must be totally subordinate while also being fully capable and equal; freedom of choice in marriage must be pursued while absolute obedience to parents is maintained; individual personality and desire must be asserted and fulfilled, but spiritual authority and social stability must never be violated. The preachers did not acknowledge these potential contradictions, however much their unforeseen consequences may have revealed the strains inherent in them. It is one of the striking features of post-Lylyan romantic comedy that a similarly complex, apparently inconsistent or paradoxical awareness of the moral ambivalence of sexual desire, freedom of choice in marriage, and the social and spiritual position of women is both evoked and resolved; and that the reconciliation of these erotic tensions itself becomes the subject of the drama.

Robert Greene's popular comedy, *Friar Bacon and Friar Bungay*, written in 1589–90 for the public theater, provides an excellent example of the reciprocal relation between this complex moral and sexual awareness and the development of romantic comedy. *Friar Bacon* is a characteristically chaotic medley, but as in a Lyly comedy, a dominant love story gives the play its shape. Unlike Lyly, however, Greene develops the love story as a conflict that arises from the diverse social, emotional, and sexual needs of three individuals and then moves through a suspenseful confrontation to a resolution in which all protagonists are married and happy.[47] A brief review of the plot will recall how this works.

Edward, the Prince of Wales, amusing himself by hunting in the country, becomes infatuated with Margaret, a farmer's daughter, whom he attempts to seduce while disguised as a farmer. But Margaret is not interested, and, his ploy failing, Edward sends his friend Lord Lacy to plead his case for him. Lacy and Margaret fall in love. The germane point about this material is that Greene works through the ensuing erotic complications to a wish-fulfill-

47. See Norman Sanders, "The Comedy of Greene and Shakespeare," in *Early Shakespeare*, Stratford-upon-Avon Studies, no. 3, ed. J. R. Brown and B. Harris (London: Edward Arnold, 1961), p. 40. Sanders observes that Greene realized the dramatic possibilities of love—"the surprises, psychological quirks and inconsistencies of human love which constitute its logic in art as in life."

ment conclusion in which "nought shall go ill" by dramatizing love and sexuality as variable, complex components in the moral and social lives of his characters. Edward, the future king of England, cannot possibly marry a commoner and is merely trifling with Margaret; unlike Lyly's Alexander, who overcomes his inappropriate infatuation in isolation and goes off alone to heroic martial exploits, Edward relents in a fully dramatized confrontation with Margaret and Lacy, from which he exits happily and honorably to marry the princess of his father's choice. Lacy, an earl, in turn proves *his* worthiness by ignoring conventional class barriers and marrying the farmer's daughter, Margaret of Fressingfield, the woman of his own personal choice. Interestingly, all of Edward's wooing is rhetorical, allegorical, and cast in the conventional antitheses of the Petrarchan lover. "Her bashful white mixed with the morning's red / Luna doth boast upon her love cheeks" (1.56–57), he recites, recalling the Renaissance sense of the abstract impersonality of sexual desire.[48] In contrast, Lacy speaks of his love with a straightforward passion full of concrete references to his immediate, individual situation: addressing Edward he says, "Love taught me that your honor did but jest / That princes were in fancy but as men, / How that the lovely maid of Fressingfield / Was fitter to be Lacy's wedded wife / Than concubine unto the Prince of Wales" (8.19–23).

Finally, it is Margaret's character—her wit, vitality, gratitude, and chastity—that gives love its felicity and dignity, making possible the harmonious and stable society of the conclusion, in which the two marriages simultaneously take place. At one juncture, Margaret, wrongly thinking Lacy has betrayed her, decides to become a nun. "And now I hate myself for that I loved / And doted more on him than on my God . . . / All is but lust, but love of heavens" (14.13–14, 18), she says, despairingly polarizing the position of love in the moral life. But the point is that Margaret is in despair when she makes this speech. The scene in which Lacy confronts her in her nun's habit and persuades her to marry him

---

48. All quotations, identified in the text by scene and line numbers, are from Robert Greene, *Friar Bacon and Friar Bungay,* in *Drama of the English Renaissance,* vol. 1: *The Tudor Period,* ed. Russell A. Fraser and Norman Rabkin (New York: Macmillan, 1976), pp. 359–82.

reads like a final farewell to medieval ideals of love and sexuality: "Either a solemn nunnery or the court; / God or Lord Lacy. Which contents you best, / To be a nun, or else Lord Lacy's wife?" (14.82–84). She replies, "The flesh is frail . . . / Off goes the habit of a maiden's heart; / And, seeing Fortune will . . . / All the shroud of holy nuns, farewell. / Lacy for me, if he will be my Lord" (14.86, 89–92).

Thus does *Friar Bacon* provide a fledgling example of the way in which Elizabethan comedy, like the Puritan marriage tracts, manages to have things both ways. In the courtship of Lacy and Margaret, individual choice and sexual desire leading to marriage are conjoined and affirmed. But Greene also suggests the anarchy and folly of sexual desire by having two of Margaret's suitors destroy each other, as well as by having Edward change costumes for a time with the Fool. Similarly, the Margaret-Lacy union recommends the harmonious breakdown of traditional class and rank barriers. But Edward's happy acceptance of an arranged marriage assures the audience that the courtly, aristocratic hierarchy, despite the welcome intrusion of the pastoral world, has remained intact. And although it is the heroine's sexual powers—both of resistance and of surrender—that have brought about these congenial conditions, she nevertheless acknowledges her subordination at the end of the play in a speech of joyfully grateful obedience. The private claims of individual personality and desire have been asserted, recognized, and assimilated into a public vision of social harmony.

Northrop Frye has remarked that "the presiding genius of comedy is Eros, and Eros has to adapt himself to the moral facts of society."[49] As we have seen, Lyly's polarized attitude toward eros as either deviant or ideal makes such an adjustment impossible. Greene takes romantic comedy a step further by working both with Lyly's perspective and with a different set of moral terms, one in which sexual love gains legitimacy as the true source of a coherent society. Although many elements in *Friar Bacon* remain chaotic and virtually unassimilable, the love story does give the play a distinct shape; therefore it moves significantly toward the vision of inclusiveness symbolized in marriage that is the crowning achievement of Elizabethan comedy. The movement from Lyly to

49. Frye, *Anatomy of Criticism*, p. 181.

Greene thus constitutes a development from a view of sexual love as abstract and impersonal, polarized, static, emotionally simple, and morally predictable to another vision that, while retaining much of the skepticism of the first perspective, incorporates it into a view of eros as more concrete, individualized, dynamic and suspenseful, essentially creative, and morally and emotionally complex.

It was by his unique ability both to discern and to express this movement that Shakespeare brought romantic comedy to fruition. The early comedy *Love's Labor's Lost* (1594–95) can be read in this light as a self-conscious comment on what Shakespeare perceived to be the structurally inevitable relationship between sexual values and the comic form. *Love's Labor's Lost* begins with the youthful King of Navarre and three lords swearing to retire from social life for three years, declaring war against their "own affections / And the huge army of the world's desires" (1.1.9–10).[50] The absurdity of this oath, which is broken immediately when four eligible young ladies appear, is in part a revelation of the absurdity of sexual desire itself, with its imperious, mechanical urgency. But more important than the silliness of the vow of celibacy is its unnaturalness and futility. "The sea will ebb and flow, heaven show his face: / Young blood doth not obey an old decree" (4.3.211–12), states Berowne, the wittiest of the young lords, at the moment of the play when self-knowledge begins. The rejection of celibacy, however, is not enough; the King, Berowne, and company also must learn the meaning of eros as both a civilizing force and a force that must be civilized. Shakespeare conveys their sophomoric callowness as an infatuation with verbal wit, an enchantment with their own cleverness. Upon deciding to pursue his heart's desire, Berowne immediately begins to posture and attitudinize in the conventional courtly manner of a Petrarchan lover, the manner that Edward assumes in *Friar Bacon*. The wit and charm engendered by this pose recall Lyly; as in Lyly, these qualities make up the substance of the play. But *Love's Labor's Lost* eventually rejects the courtly love syndrome as sterile, shallow,

50. All quotations, identified in the text by act, scene, and line numbers, are from William Shakespeare, *Love's Labor's Lost*, ed. Alfred Harbage (Baltimore, Md.: Penguin, 1973).

and static. Love conceived as a frivolous game is simply inadequate: when the men approach the women in ridiculous disguises,
the women see through them at once. Sensing that the men are not
quite ready for grown-up reality, which in Elizabethan comedy
means married love, the women, true to romance tradition, demand a year of separation complete with appointed tasks for their
lovers before marriage can take place. The play therefore ends with
the promise of marriage and not the actuality; the exchange of
overblown rhetoric and narcissistic posturing for a plain style and
shared experience has not yet come to pass. Consequently, the
profound emotional and psychological demands of the comic form
have not been completely met, a fact acknowledged directly in a
brief conversation between Berowne and the King. Berowne
grumbles:

> Our wooing doth not end like an old play;
> Jack hath not Jill. These ladies' courtesy
> Might well have made our sport a comedy.
> *King.* Come, sir, it wants a twelvemonth and a day
> And then 'twill end.
> *Ber.* That's too long for a play.
> [5.2.864–68]

Shakespeare is announcing clearly here the structural secret of
romantic comedy. This clarification of the relationship between
fulfilled sexual desire and the comic form releases his ability to
represent love as the complex spiritual, emotional, and psychic
force that guarantees the perpetuation of society. What is stated so
boldly in *Love's Labor's Lost* is fully dramatized in the comedies
that follow: for example, *Love's Labor's Lost* concludes with a song
celebrating summer and winter and suggesting the alliance among
fruitful sexual love, the predictably recurring cycle of the seasons,
and the ongoing life of society; in ensuing comedies, like *A Midsummer Night's Dream* (1595) and *As You Like It* (1599), this seasonal imagery becomes fully integrated into the action and poetry,
clarifying the inevitable association between human sexuality and
great creating nature.

The King of Castile, a character in *Friar Bacon*, remarks at one
point that "men must have wives and women will be wed"

(12.20). "The world must be / peopled" (2.3.233–34), says Benedick in *Much Ado about Nothing* (1598),[51] and there are no possibilities of life to which romantic comedy assigns greater value
than these. This dramatic celebration of generative sexuality would
not have been possible without the significant increase in the prestige of marriage that, as historians have shown, took place in the
Renaissance. The movement out of the forest and back into court
that dramatizes the harmonious alliance between sexual and social
life characterizes Shakespeare's pastoral comedies and is also evident in *Friar Bacon*, but it is never completed in a Lyly play. Shakespeare manages to develop Greene's optimism about sexual love
and social life while eliminating his crude awkwardness, just as he
refines Lyly's skepticism while retaining his grace and sense of
design.

When viewed in terms of chronological development, Shakespeare's romantic comedies, like the Puritan marriage tracts, reveal
an increasing sense of confidence that sexuality as individual assertion can be organized for society's good. At the same time—and
the difference from modern conceptions of romantic love is crucial—sexual desire is never idealized for its own sake, never seen as
by itself leading to personal happiness, never conceived as a positive value—as love—apart from marriage or procreation. The
anxiety that haunts and humiliates writers of Renaissance sexual
discourse is always present in Shakespearean comedy, mocking the
hope of unique or ideal love with its distrustful sense of the mechanical impersonality of sex. It is the imperative, arbitrary quality
of sexual desire that makes it seem bestial and foolish to the Elizabethans, but in Shakespearean comedy submission to this imperative also joins humanity to nature in fruitful union. Sexuality
therefore presents itself as a paradox: the human need for sexual
relationships could lead to the mindless disruption of society, but
without fulfillment of this need, there would be no ordered society
at all.

Shakespeare's rendering of Berowne in *Love's Labor's Lost* as

51. All quotations, identified in the text by act, scene, and line numbers, are
from William Shakespeare, *Much Ado about Nothing*, ed. A. R. Humphreys
(New York: Methuen, 1981).

commenting with freely conscious knowingness on the absurdity of his own desires reveals an early effort to encompass the paradoxes of sex; but the abstract choreography of the play makes full dramatization of this issue impossible. The dramatic conflict of *A Midsummer Night's Dream* is, of course, set in motion by the issue of individual choice of a mate versus forced marriage. Although the young lovers triumph over irrational parental opposition to their desires, their victory is suffused with irony. The lovers imagine that they are defiantly asserting their individuality; but the lack of differentiation among them and the mix-up in the forest clarify both their lack of uniqueness and the arbitrary quality of their choices. Demetrius never does know what hit him when he returns to Helena, any more than he ever did when he loved and rejected her in the first place. The arrogance and complacence of both Theseus and the young lovers are further qualified by the final assertion of the irrational, imaginative authority of the fairies; and the absurd, arbitrary, and mysterious nature of sexual desire is distilled in the joyful parody of Bottom's dream. Though the tensions inherent in achieving erotic identity are never resolved, the suggestion in *A Midsummer Night's Dream* is that harmony is attained by the intervention of a benevolent, reconciliatory Providence, which manifests itself on the social level in the final wedding feast.

As Arthur Kirsch has shown in his analysis of *Much Ado About Nothing*, the tensions between freedom of choice and submission to authority are not entirely imposed from without, but are rooted psychologically in sexuality itself.[52] Claudio and Hero never acknowledge these internal tensions between the immediate demands of their desires and their deeper fears of surrender and rejection in love. They become engaged thoughtlessly, following the conventional clichés of society while never imagining the complex, mixed nature of sexual love; as a result of their psychological and emotional oblivion, they remain completely vulnerable to doubt and fear. Claudio and Hero are contrasted to the witty Beatrice and Benedick, who, more thoughtful and consequently more wary of love's complications and paradoxes, pride themselves on their independence. But this brilliant couple needs the manipula-

52. Arthur Kirsch, *Shakespeare and the Experience of Love* (Cambridge: Cambridge University Press, 1981), pp. 40–70.

tive, busybody society of *Much Ado* to liberate them from the lonely trap of their uniqueness. Released from their fears, they are free to join society by loving one another. Benedick and Beatrice are one of the first outstanding pairs of lovers in Shakespeare, the first to command complete sympathy because of their personalities. "Man is a giddy thing and this is my conclusion" (5.4.107), Benedick announces at the end of *Much Ado*, revealing that the paradoxical awareness of sexual desire, enjoyed by the audience of *A Midsummer Night's Dream* with a kind of superior irony, is appropriated in *Much Ado* by Benedick and Beatrice themselves, who are humbly aware that in seeming to lose their identities, they have in fact gained self-knowledge. In the sense of gratitude for life that is consequently released in them, Shakespeare exhibits the same awareness of the joyful mysteries of sexual love that he always portrays. But I believe that in individualizing Benedick and Beatrice to the extent that he has, and in allowing them to achieve self-knowledge, he reveals an enhanced respect for the human dignity of sexual life as well.[53]

As I have tried to show in discussing the Puritan marriage tracts, the increasing moral prestige of love and marriage in the Renaissance was accompanied by a wider acknowledgment of the social, emotional, and spiritual dignity of women, whose freedoms of action and influence were nevertheless explicitly and severely limited. Developing an insight latent in Greene, Shakespeare seems to have assimilated these paradoxical facts imaginatively by giving women the heroic roles in many of his major comedies; their heroism consists, however, in choosing to preserve the status quo by wisely and lovingly assimilating themselves to it. Rosalind in *As You Like It* is the supreme romantic comic heroine.[54] With her realism, openness, and depth, she seems blessed with self-knowl-

---

53. Cf. R. A. Foakes, "The Owl and the Cuckoo: Voices of Maturity in Shakespeare's Comedies," in *Shakespearean Comedy,* Stratford-upon-Avon Studies, no. 14, ed. J. R. Brown and B. Harris (London: Edward Arnold, 1972), p. 132; and B. K. Lewalski, "Love, Appearance and Reality: Much Ado about Something," *Studies in English Literature,* 8 (1968), 243. For an opposite view of Beatrice and Benedick, see A. P. Rossiter, "*Much Ado about Nothing,*" in *Shakespeare: The Comedies,* ed. Kenneth Muir (Englewood Cliffs, N.J.: Prentice-Hall, 1965), p. 51.

54. Cf. Clara Claiborne Park, "As We Like It: How a Girl Can Be Smart

edge from the beginning, superbly adapted to exploit successfully the ironies of experience and desire. The mastery of her erotic quest is epitomized in her education of Orlando, in whom she instills a knowledge of the demands of love for a real woman in actual life that allows him to grow beyond the shallow, remote conventionalities of the Petrarchan lover.[55] The extent to which Rosalind's individuality remains in complete spiritual harmony with nature becomes apparent in the way she controls the timely release of erotic energy embodied in the array of marriages at the end of the play. Just as the negative components of sexual desire are largely displaced onto Claudio and Hero in *Much Ado*, so the other couples in the procession at the end of *As You Like It* suggest the less attractive aspects of sexuality, leaving the Rosalind-Orlando union relatively free of ironic qualification. The fact that Rosalind finds the freedom to accomplish all that she does while disguised as a boy and then sheds this disguise at the end of the play again brings to mind the insoluble contradictions of the female condition, much as these contradictions present themselves in the Puritan marriage tracts. But Shakespeare emphasizes reconciliation, not contradiction; nothing like the sentimental, didactic surrender of Margaret in *Friar Bacon* mars the predominant (and intended) feeling of harmony at the end of *As You Like It*. If the audience is meant to be reminded of any paradox about the loving surrender of individual identity to society, it is the Christian one of losing in order to gain, dying in order to live.

That the potentially contradictory functions of Rosalind's disguise should be reconciled symbolically in marriage clarifies the idea that the erotic teleology of Elizabethan comedy demands an "imaginative model of desire" based on the harmonious resolution of sexual conflict. Given his skeptical, polarized view of sexual love, Lyly could not make the desired reconciliation demanded by the wish-fulfillment pattern at the heart of the comic form. Greene discerned the need to harmonize both the anarchic and the civiliz-

---

and Still Popular," in *The Woman's Part*, ed. Carolyn Ruth Swift Lenz, Gayle Greene, and Carol Thomas Neely (Urbana: University of Illinois Press, 1980), pp. 100–116.

55. Cf. Kent Talbot Van Berg, "Theatrical Fiction and the Reality of Love in *As You Like It*," *PMLA*, 90 (October 1975), 885–93.

ing components of sexual desire into a vision of social and spiritual harmony. But it was Shakespeare who perfected this vision, drawing out all its implications with neither awkwardness nor sentimentality. The witty vitality with which Shakespeare endows the lovers in *Much Ado* and *As You Like It* contributes to an enhanced sense of their individuality and self-knowledge; since the imperative, urgent impersonality of sexual desire was what made it seem both dangerous and ridiculous to the Elizabethans, these more distinctive characterizations consequently suggest a greater respect for the human dignity of sexual experience. But comedy cannot accommodate too much individuality, any more than it can lose its sense of the ridiculous. As is well known, comedy focuses not on the destiny of the individual, which ends in death, but on the destiny of human society as a whole, which is perpetual.[56] Interestingly, in his last romantic comedy, *Twelfth Night* (1600), the play in which Shakespeare completely masters and exhausts the possibilities of this form of drama, he focuses less on the self-knowledge of the characters and more on the intervention of a benevolent Providence in sorting out human affairs satisfactorily.[57] On the one hand, the idea of a benevolent Providence assisting human destiny illuminates all of his romantic comedies; on the other, the lovers in *Twelfth Night* are distinctly more individualized than those in *Love's Labor's Lost* or *A Midsummer Night's Dream*. But it is a question of emphasis and degree.

Elizabethan romantic comedy was able to achieve its aim—the representation of a harmonious, spiritually integrated society symbolized in marriage—in a cultural environment in which love and

56. See Gardner, pp. 193–94.

57. Cf. Leo Salingar, *Shakespeare and the Traditions of Comedy* (Cambridge: Cambridge University Press, 1974), pp. 240–42. Salingar believes that "*Twelfth Night* is the summing-up of a major phase in Shakespeare's writing, the last romantic play at the end of a decade, because it deals with the psychological value of revelry and its limits as well; it is a comedy about comedy. . . . As the play advances, psychological mistakes dissolve into 'errors' of identity; Time and Nature, assuming the guise of Fortune, are stronger than characters' 'reason,' their conscious will. Although the actors have been given some of the depth and self-awareness of individuals in real life, they are caught up in a situation that evidently belongs less and less to real life and increasingly to the stage."

marriage were gaining moral prestige and, as a corollary, personal happiness and freedom began to be considered goals worth pursuing. Currently a debate has arisen about whether Puritan marriage ideology, which, like Rosalind's disguise in *As You Like It*, enhanced female dignity and autonomy while at the same time explicitly reinforcing the double standard, has positive or negative effects for women.[58] The important point here is the clear correspondence between the potentially contradictory view of sexual values presented in the Puritan tracts and the representation of sexual tensions in Elizabethan comedy. In both forms we can see certain conceptual antitheses beginning to take shape: personal freedom and social convention, happiness and stability, civilization and its discontents. But neither the theologians nor the comic playwrights drew final attention to the conflicts implicit in their conceptions of erotic love and marriage. As we will see in the discussion of tragedy (Chapter 3), the Puritan preachers simply did not perceive the inherent contradictions in their sexual values. Although the playwrights discerned the outlines of comic structure in the drama of sexual desire seeking and finding satisfaction, they represented potentially conflicting social and erotic forces mainly in order to reconcile them. In Shakespearean comedy happiness and stability are the same.

Keith Thomas has linked the preponderance of sexual humor in Tudor and Stuart England to a pervasive anxiety about changing sexual relationships. Thomas recognizes that among its many functions, comedy can perform the conservative one of introducing potentially disruptive elements only to represent them as harmoniously assimilated within the existing social structure.[59] As the implications of the idealization of marriage and the claims of the individual self became more pressing, conflicts that were evoked but contained in one form of drama became grist for the mill of other forms. In Jacobean England love and sexuality began to be subjected to the savage scrutiny of satire and tragedy.

58. See Fitz; and Juliet Dusinberre, *Shakespeare and the Nature of Women* (London: Macmillan, 1975).

59. Keith Thomas, "The Place of Laughter in Tudor and Stuart England," *Times Literary Supplement,* 21 January 1977, pp. 77–81. Also see Mary Douglas, "The Social Control of Cognition: Some Factors in Joke Perception," *Man*, 3 (September 1968), 361–76.

2

Sexual Disguise and Social Mobility
in Jacobean City Comedy

i

In its representation of love and sexuality, Elizabethan romantic comedy is not concerned with the problematic enactment of social and sexual roles in the institution of marriage. Rather, it concentrates on the complexities of eros, dramatized as sexual desire seeking and finding fulfillment in the heroes' successful resolution of the process of courtship. In contrast, Jacobean city comedy brings into the light of representation precisely those dissociations and contradictions in English Renaissance sexual ideology which romantic comedy evokes but seeks to reconcile and contain.[1] Jacobean satire, or city comedy, is a genre designed to dramatize the complex process of conducting economic and social relations in a newly forming urban environment. As is well known, city comedy as such began in the late 1590s with Ben Jonson's humor plays, achieved recognizable generic conventions by about 1605, and thrived during, roughly, the first decade of the seventeenth century, when dramatists perceived the city of London as the setting in which those conflicts caused by the political, religious, and economic upheavals that transformed Renaissance England were being enacted most intensely.[2]

1. See Louis Adrian Montrose, "'Shaping Fantasies': Figurations of Gender and Power in Elizabethan Culture," *Representations*, 1 (Spring 1983), 61–94; and Jonathan Dollimore, "Subjectivity, Sexuality, and Transgression: The Jacobean Connection," *Renaissance Drama*, N.S. 17 (1986), 53–81.
2. Brian Gibbon, *Jacobean City Comedy: A Study of Satiric Plays by Jonson,*

43

Historians have demonstrated that from the mid-sixteenth to the mid-seventeenth centuries, extraordinary demographic growth and price inflation, the opening of the land market that resulted from the dissolution of the monasteries at the Reformation, the increase in litigation, foreign trade, and other commercial activities, and the expansion of education combined to create new problems of severe poverty and uprootedness for the lower orders and, at the same time, unheard-of opportunities for social mobility among the middle and upper classes. By 1600 both the victims of change and the protagonists of opportunity were drawn to the metropolis. Developing during this peak period of social upheaval, city comedy explores the struggle for survival and preeminence among the inhabitants of a society in which economic potential and definitions of social class and status are suddenly perceived as provocatively fluid.[3]

Although the population of London increased more rapidly than that of the country at large during the sixteenth century, the overwhelming majority of English people remained living in the rural sections of the country. According to historians, Tudor and Stuart perceptions of the rapidly changing social order reveal an ideologi-

---

Marston, and Middleton (London: Methuen, 1980), p. 2; Alexander Leggatt, *Citizen Comedy in the Age of Shakespeare* (Toronto: University of Toronto Press, 1973); Margot Heinemann, *Puritanism and Theatre: Thomas Middleton and Opposition Drama under the Early Stuarts* (Cambridge: Cambridge University Press, 1980), pp. 3–24.

3. See Lawrence Stone, *The Crisis of the Aristocracy, 1558–1641* (Oxford: Clarendon, 1965), as well as his "Social Mobility in England, 1500–1700," *Past and Present*, 33 (1966), 16–55, in which he explores both the upward and downward mobility of the middle and upper classes. David Cressy, in "Describing the Social Order of Elizabethan and Stuart England," *Literature and History*, 3 (March 1976), 29–44, revises some of Stone's breakdown of the status hierarchy, including his separation of the peerage from the rest of the upper gentry. Cressy believes (p. 36) that subdivisions in the category of "gentleman" are not helpful: "Even contemporaries confessed difficulty distinguishing the status grades in practice." The evidence from Jonson's *Epicoene*, however, supports Stone's emphasis on the importance of status gradations among the upper classes, precisely because boundaries within their ranks were conceived of as fluid. Also see Keith Wrightson, *English Society, 1580–1680* (New Brunswick, N.J.: Rutgers University Press, 1982), pp. 17–38; Leggatt, pp. 3–4; Gibbon; and Peter Laslett, *The World We Have Lost: England before the Industrial Age* (New York: Scribner's, 1965), pp. 22–52.

cal disjunction within "a society whose legal system and status system were based on possession of land at a time when non-landed skills, wealth and power were increasingly significant."[4] Though city comedy has been treated exclusively as a searing satiric indictment of emerging urban economic values and social struggles, recent scholarship has perceived a greater flexibility in the genre's depiction of social change.[5] Establishing an eloquent, pro-

4. Cressy, p. 29. See also Stone, "Social Mobility in England," pp. 20, 34, and passim; and Wrightson, pp. 24–28. On pp. 127–28, Wrightson describes the "shifting balance between the urban and rural populations of England" that ensued as the drift of the rural population toward the towns contributed to rapid urbanization.

5. The classic treatment of the genre as an indictment of acquisitiveness is L. C. Knights's *Drama and Society in the Age of Jonson* (London: Chatto & Windus, 1937). Leggatt argues (pp. 150–51) that city comedy moves between poles of subversion and assertions of traditional morality. City comedy is "concerned with social relations in their most material form—sex and marriage, money and property." Whereas characters in later comedies "show a concern for more delicate social adjustments," the characters in city comedy reveal "an urgent concern for the material side of life and little else. . . . [City comedy's] social morality is finally a morality of property and possession. Each man should keep and use what is rightfully his, whether his land or his wife: the moralizing comedies rebuke the neglect of wives and the squandering of wealth in roughly similar terms." Leggatt adds interestingly that "the characters of citizen comedy are too close to the sources of their security, and too anxious about them, to have any time for . . . niceties." For another traditional view of English Renaissance satire as an attack on emerging capitalism and "an indirect assertion of the innate fineness of the ideals of the old landed aristocrats," see Oscar James Campbell, *Comicall Satyre and Shakespeare's "Troilus and Cressida"* (San Marino, Calif.: 1938), pp. 15–20, 43.

For more recent and revisionary views of the purposes and concerns of Jacobean satiric comedy, see Walter Cohen, *Drama of a Nation: Public Theater in Renaissance England and Spain* (Ithaca, N.Y.: Cornell University Press, 1985), pp. 282–301. Cohen views the attacks on bourgeois morality in Jacobean satire as a defensive strategy of the aristocracy, or a sign of "aristocratic failure." See also Heinemann; and Don E. Wayne, "Drama and Society in the Age of Jonson: An Alternative View," *Renaissance Drama*, N.S. 13 (1982), 103–29. As his title suggests, Wayne revises Knights's views by exploring Ben Jonson's ambivalence toward the emerging bourgeois culture that nourished and empowered, as well as disgusted, him. Susan Wells, in "Jacobean City Comedy and the Ideology of the City," *ELH*, 48 (1981), 37–60, makes interesting and provocative suggestions about the origins and purposes of city comedy; see the discussion that follows in the text.

vocative connection between economics and aesthetics, Susan Wells argues that the major achievement of city comedy is to conjoin the traditional rural and festive values of the carnival (and of romantic comedy) with the emerging urban values of trade and commerce. This process allows the genre to examine and profoundly criticize social processes at the same time that it avoids tragedy: "The relations of exchange and accumulation [are immersed] . . . in the norms and customs of the feast, so that these relations could be either celebrated in traditional terms or called into question by their confrontation with them. . . . When accumulation is successful . . . we experience it as cleverness rather than greed." Varying its emphases from play to play, city comedy thus accommodates both satiric critique and festive celebration, severely scrutinizing commercial urban society while retaining a comic tone.[6]

Scholarship continually has emphasized that the sexual discourse in city comedy, with its obligatory prostitutes and notorious adulteries, inhabits the critical rather than the celebratory end of this spectrum. Arguments focus on the satiric exposure of the corrupt connections between money and sex, marriage and property, lust and greed, which are viewed as a trenchant indictment of the commercialization of feeling and human relationships.[7] However, marriage as a property-based arrangement had long been a traditional value; it is the transformation and distortion of this aristocratic and rural ideal to the increasingly bourgeois urban environment of London that Jacobean satire subjects to harsh and vicious scrutiny.[8]

The plays frequently rely on the equation of sexuality with sin to examine the economics of marriage and the commercial exploitation of eros. Yet though this focus is lively and well developed throughout the genre, it does not constitute the truly original con-

6. Wells, pp. 54, 56, and passim.

7. See, e.g., Knights, pp. 125–26; Gibbon; Leggatt, p. 151; and Richard Horwich, "Wives, Courtesans, and the Economics of Love in Jacobean City Comedy," *Comparative Drama*, 7, no. 4 (Winter 1973–74), 291–309.

8. See Jack Goody, *The Development of the Family and Marriage in Europe* (Cambridge: Cambridge University Press, 1983), p. 119: "The change to feudal order led to marriage policies designed to protect what one had, and specifically to an emerging principle of devolution based on primogeniture."

tribution that city comedy makes to the dramatic representation of sexuality. That contribution stems less from a generic preoccupation with economics per se than from an equally pressing concern with the unprecedented social mobility of Elizabethan and Jacobean society. When connected with the idea of social mobility—a perceived fluidity among social ranks and classes and instability in the determination of social status[9]—the satiric view of sexuality takes dramatic form as the struggle for female independence and equality between the sexes. This chapter attempts to demonstrate that city comedy's probing and original exploration of the link between sexual equality and social mobility can best be perceived in the playwrights' exploitation of the multiple dramatic possibilities inherent in the metaphor of sexual disguise, or cross-dressing. Although they represent very different treatments of the subject, Ben Jonson's *Epicoene* (1609) and Thomas Middleton and Thomas Dekker's *The Roaring Girl* (c. 1608–11) both contain a transvestite title figure; by refining the conventions of romantic comedy, each text ensures that society's effort to manipulate and identify that figure constitutes the central symbolic and dramatic issue of the play. In what follows I will examine the plays, along with related nonfictional texts concerned with Jacobean transvestism, in order to demonstrate the range of positions about female independence and equality between the sexes that English Renaissance culture was capable of exploring.

In pursuit of the analysis and exposure of urban corruption, city comedy generally participates with gusto in the polarizing discourse that either views sexual love as leading to a plane of existence beyond the physical or degrades it as lust, and in which idealization of women and misogyny become the only possibilities for construing the female sex.[10] A brief glance at Thomas Middleton's *A Chaste Maid in Cheapside* (1613) and John Marston's *The Dutch Courtesan* (c. 1603–5), two plays in which sexuality and its consequences carry the major symbolic burden of the action, can help to underscore this point. Middleton's *Chaste Maid* is the starkest example of city comedy's general view of eros-as-lust and

9. Stone, "Social Mobility in England," Wrightson, and Cressy all stress the threat to stability that fluidity among ranks and classes posed to a society that valued and believed in hierarchy and defined itself in hierarchical terms.
10. Cf. Leggatt, pp. 99–124.

lust-as-commodity. The play is full of children—all of them il-legitimate—and much of the action consists of efforts to align biology with sentiment, traditional social structure, and the law. These attempts only partially succeed. Upper and middle classes exploit each other in the former's drive to preserve and perpetuate itself and the latter's endeavor both to profit financially from the aristocratic desire to retain ascendancy and to join in that ascendancy as much as possible. Thus Sir Walter Whorehound, the decadent knight, fathers a family on the middle-class Mrs. Allwit, whose husband gladly accepts the effortless money he makes from the situation; while the snobbish, greedy Yellowhammers, goldsmiths, eagerly seek to marry their daughter to the knight, Sir Walter, although he is clearly corrupt and she loves someone else. The most important upper-class couple in the play, Sir Oliver and Lady Kix, are sterile, unable to produce an heir and consequently threatened with losing their property.

At the center of all the intrigue stands the odd and original figure of Touchwood Sr., an embodiment of comic eros, whose copious and perpetual fertility, combined with poverty, forces him to separate temporarily from his wife. Middleton views Touchwood Sr.'s sexual desire (and Touchwood Sr. *as* desire) as complex and amoral, the unyielding, paradoxical human necessity that both creates chaos and ensures the perpetuation of society. The action is filled out by Touchwood's illegitimate children, including the child that (unknown to her husband, who joyfully thinks it is his), he fathers on Lady Kix, as well as several offspring who remain socially unaccounted for and yet seem to possess a benevolent, transforming power.[11] The greedy, social-climbing society of *A Chaste Maid* is partially redeemed by the exposure of many of the characters' lying, malevolent tricks and by the achievement of the romantic, desired, and financially solvent marriage of the Yellowhammers' daughter that Touchwood Sr. brings about. Yet the identity of Lady Kix's child, who will, presumably, save the upper classes from extinction, remains a deception; and the conclusion makes comically clear that although Touchwood Sr. is returned to his wife, his adultery with Lady Kix will continue. The malicious wit

11. See William W. E. Slights, "The Incarnations of Comedy," *University of Toronto Quarterly*, 51 (Fall 1981), 13–27.

of the play therefore resides in the final dissociation between the arbitrary predominance of sexual need and the inadequate way in which social institutions like marriage contain and embody it.

In Marston's *The Dutch Courtesan* the anarchic sexual desire that suffuses the entire society of Middleton's play is focused and writ large in the female hero-villain, Franchesina the prostitute, who seeks to murder her former lover when he leaves her in order to marry. Marston perceives no possibility of happiness in eros , only the probability of danger. "There is no God in blood, no reason in desire" (4.2.13), announces Malheureux, one of the males whom Franchesina seduces.[12] With its title character a murderous whore, *The Dutch Courtesan* clearly reveals the links city comedy establishes between female sexuality and spiritual and social evil: "When woman's in the heart, in the soul hell" (4.2.30).[13] Though *The Dutch Courtesan* also satirizes upward mobility and commercialism, which it interprets as snobbery and greed, the main comic action constitutes revealing and purging the whore at the center of the play, who becomes a composite of the antisocial, a projected embodiment of the passions that must be expelled in order for society to continue. In contrast, the petty cheaters, thieves, and social climbers who populate the action are allowed to forgive each other and remain onstage at the end of the play. *The Dutch Courtesan* therefore clarifies the way in which misogyny becomes a structural principle in city comedy. Marston overlooks the fact that Franchesina's whoredom depends upon the sexual desire of her male clientele; his view of women and sexuality is remarkably simple and clear. Not surprisingly, the whore Franchesina is complemented by the saint, Beatrice, the idealized Griselda figure whose chastity, unswerving loyalty, and patient goodness convert the hero from profligacy and command his love.

12. Quotations, identified in the text by act, scene, and line numbers, are from John Marston, *The Dutch Courtesan*, in *Drama of the English Renaissance*, vol. 2: *The Stuart Period*, ed. Russell A. Fraser and Norman Rabkin (New York: Macmillan, 1976), pp. 241–68.

13. Cf. Campbell, p. 44: "In spite of all . . . literary precedents, the preoccupation of all the members of this English school [i.e., of satirists] with the sins and perversions of sex is so marked that a critic must assume either that the satirists, in particular Marston, were pathologically attracted to the unsavory subject or that lustful practices constituted in their time the most

With their varying emphases and differences in tone, *A Chaste Maid* and *The Dutch Courtesan* illustrate the variety of connections city comedy establishes between sexuality and the complexities of social corruption in an urban environment. It is true that the genre frequently relies on the romantic comic convention of the desired marriage to conclude the action in obedience to its comic purpose and, in however qualified, deflected, and obligatory a fashion, to establish a festive tone; this is an important point to which I will return. Here I wish to emphasize that, whether represented with Marston's appalled indignation as the generation of social and moral evil that finds its source in women, or viewed with Middleton's detached and cynical wit as the anarchic power that defies containment by law and tradition, sexuality in city comedy is equated primarily with social disjunction and with sin.

ii

This sexual logic receives its most refined, startling treatment in Ben Jonson's harsh and brilliant *Epicoene* (c. 1609). Unlike Middleton and Marston, Jonson is not interested in the unruliness of sexual desire; indeed, *Epicoene, or The Silent Woman,* is particularly devoid of erotic love. Instead Jonson focuses his satire on social mobility, the scramble for position, power, status, and prestige. His concern with sexuality therefore centers on the challenge posed to the traditional Renaissance social hierarchy, in which females are dependent and subordinate, by women's attempt at independence and equality with men.

In further contrast to other city comedies, the social range of *Epicoene* is relatively narrow, comprising a virtually exclusive focus on the struggle for money and gradations of status among

---

dangerous enemy to social decency." Despite Campbell's anachronistic Victorian distaste for the "unsavory subject" of sexuality, his remarks do point to the frequency as well as the intensity of the exclusive equation of sexuality with evil and sin in English Renaissance satire. In *The Cankered Muse: Satire of the English Renaissance* (New Haven, Conn.: Yale University Press, 1959), pp. 21–28, Alvin Kernan discusses the problem of the satirist's twisted and pathological preoccupations implicating him in the depravity he is meant to expose.

the upper classes and excluding an examination of middle-class commercialism.[14] Lawrence Stone has demonstrated that one of the salient features of social change in Renaissance England was "a remarkable increase in the number of the upper classes, which trebled at a period when the total population barely doubled." While the upper classes became more numerous, equality expanded among their ranks. With the opening of the land market, "the wealth and power of the greater gentry increased relative to those of the aristocracy; and secondly members of the trades and professions rose in wealth, numbers and social status relative to the landed classes."[15] This latter development, coinciding with expanded educational opportunities, greatly increased occupational options for figures like younger sons of the propertied classes, who, owing to primogeniture, frequently found themselves with elite status but without inherited land, and who were left to their own devices.[16] With opportunity, therefore, came risk. Traditionally marginal figures like younger sons now also were forced to compete in an environment where "movement across the gap between ruling and subject classes was becoming increasingly possible, and elite identity had begun to be a function of actions rather than of birth—to be achieved rather than ascribed,"[17]—and consequently they faced the danger of losing their elite status altogether.

Written at the peak of this "phase of unprecedented individual mobility, upwards and downwards," *Epicoene* presents an anatomy of these processes of social change among the upper classes in Jacobean London.[18] All of the characters are in social positions marginal to the elite: that is, they are all struggling to achieve,

14. As Cressy shows (p. 30), in traditional English Renaissance descriptions of the social order, such as Sir Thomas Smith's, William Harrison's, or William Camden's, the poor are excluded entirely.

15. Stone, "Social Mobility in England," pp. 23–24, 29.

16. Stone, "Social Mobility in England," pp. 37–38. For a good treatment of this issue in Shakespeare, see Louis Adrian Montrose, "'The Place of a Brother' in *As You Like It*: Social Process and Comic Form," *Shakespeare Quarterly*, 32 (Spring 1981), 28–54.

17. Frank Whigham, *Ambition and Privilege: The Social Tropes of Elizabethan Courtesy Theory* (Berkeley: University of California Press, 1984), p. 5.

18. Stone, "Social Mobility in England," p. 33. According to Stone, mobility peaked in the 1610s, when it was "250% higher than in the 1560s." Also see Wrightson, pp. 140–42.

exploit, or retain elite identity, which none of them can take for granted as a stable birthright.[19] Recent studies have emphasized the intensity of the ambition inspired by social instability and the competition for patronage and power centered on the English court.[20] In *Epicoene* the court becomes the symbolic focus of social ambition. Several of the characters make clear that they have been or feel they belong there; even the misanthropic Morose takes pride in his "breeding" at court (2.3.34–36; 3.2.265–68).[21] Nevertheless, the action takes place entirely in private residences, at one remove from the still unattained source of value and aspiration represented by the court. It is the nature of social aspiration and the techniques enacted to achieve its goals that Jonson scrutinizes and satirizes in the play.

The characters' attempts to escape marginality range from ludicrous self-inflation to shrewd strategies for survival. The three witty protagonists, Clerimont, Truewit, and Dauphine, have been well described as "men like Donne and others in Jonson's circle of friends, enjoying a sophisticated idleness somewhere between the court and the City while they wait for the property that will establish them or the patronage that will direct their abilities or scholarship into a purposeful career."[22] Among these "wits, and braveries o' the time" (1.1.83–84), Dauphine is distinguished by his rank (he is a knight, whereas Truewit and Clerimont are merely gentlemen) and by the fact that the plot centers on his successful attempt to secure an inheritance by tricking his reluctant uncle Morose (he gains a third of Morose's income by enticing Morose into a sham marriage and then helping him to escape). Morose is also only a

19. Cf. Wallace MacCaffrey, quoted in Whigham, p. 11: "The greediest and most restless were those with the least in hand and the most to wish for—the great army of younger brothers, or the jostling crowd of lesser gentry, men with little patrimony or none at all, either threatened with the loss of status or desperately anxious to attain it."

20. See Louis Adrian Montrose, "Celebration and Insinuation: Sir Philip Sidney and the Motives of Elizabethan Courtship," *Renaissance Drama*, N.S. 8 (1977), 3–35; Arthur Marotti, "'Love Is Not Love': Elizabethan Sonnet Sequences and the Social Order," *ELH*, 49 (1982), 396–428; and especially Whigham.

21. All citations and quotations, identified in the text by act, scene, and line numbers, are from Ben Jonson, *Epicoene*, in Fraser and Rabkin, pp. 102–41.

22. L. G. Salingar, "Farce and Fashion in 'The Silent Woman,'" *Essays and Studies*, N.S. 20 (1967), 38.

gentleman, and it is clear that his dislike of his nephew is rooted in jealousy of Dauphine's higher rank.[23] With malicious glee he plots to bankrupt Dauphine, depriving him of all available opportunities to elevate himself through commercial ventures and rendering his title worthless. "It [Dauphine's title] shall not have money to discharge one tavern-reckoning, to invite the old creditors to forbear it knighthood, or the new, that should be, to trust it knighthood. . . . it shall want clothes, and by reason of that, wit, to fool to lawyers. It shall not have hope to repair itself by Constantinople, Ireland, or Virginia" (2.3.124–37). When the play opens, therefore, Dauphine is a candidate for downward mobility. Among the wits, he alone shows concern to graduate from social limbo: only Dauphine makes an active effort to establish himself securely. The exchange between Truewit and Clerimont in the first scene, where Truewit reproaches himself and Clerimont for frivolous idleness, makes this distinction clear:

> *Tru.* See but our common disease! with what justice can we complain, that great men will not look upon us, nor be at leisure to give our affairs such dispatch as we expect, when we will never do it to ourselves? Nor hear, nor regard ourselves?
>
> *Cler.* Foh! thou hast read Plutarch's *Morals*, now, or some such tedious fellow; and it shows so vilely with thee, 'fore God, 'twill spoil thy wit utterly. . . . leave this stoicity alone till thou makest sermons.
>
> *Tru.* Well, sir; if it will not take. . . . I'll do good to no man against his will, certainly.
>
> [1.1.61–74]

Thus Jonson raises the issue of idle frivolity in order to dismiss it. But Truewit's reflectiveness in this exchange, however disingenuous and brief, serves to separate him and Clerimont from the fools, who share the protagonists' social ambitions without possessing their wit. The remaining *dramatis personae* in *Epicoene* are absurd and pretentious upstarts, whose aspirations Jonson locates very precisely within Jacobean social processes. Like the wits, the

23. Cf. Salingar, who describes Morose (p. 38) as "an ex-courtier, who considers himself a man of the old school and keenly resents his nephew's title."

fools are "near the court, but not of it."[24] Sir Amorous La Foole is a younger son whose knighthood is an accident rather than a birthright. "I . . . have spent some crowns since I was a page in court, to my Lord Lofty, and after, my lady's gentleman-usher, who got me knighted in Ireland, since it pleased my elder brother to die," he boasts (1.1.409–13).[25] Not only has La Foole sold his land to spend his money "upon ladies" and ostentatious courtly pleasures (1.1.416–20); his intense anxiety to gain approval reveals a complete lack of decorum, gentility, and urban know-how: "He will salute a judge upon the bench, and a bishop in the pulpit, a lawyer when he is pleading at the bar, and a lady when she is dancing in a masque" (1.1.324–27). Furthermore, Jonson implies that there are (perhaps always have been) more such indecorous characters at loose: "They all come out of our house, the La Fooles o' the north, the La Fooles of the west, the La Fooles of the east and south—we are as ancient a family as any is in Europe" (1.1.388–91). Jonson elaborates this attack on the newly forming knighthood—which was, of course, one of the most controversial phenomena of James's reign[26]—in his creation of Sir John (Jack) Daw, whose boasts of sexual conquest combine with poetic and intellectual pretensions ("There's Aristotle, a mere commonplace fellow; Plato, a discourse; Thucydides and Livy, tedious and dry; Tacitus, an entire knot" [2.2.58–60]) to reach a zenith of folly in his expectation of becoming a councilor of state (1.1.312–14; 2.2.120–21; 5.1.39). Indeed, Jonson's representation of expanding educational opportunities in the Renaissance is entirely negative in *Epicoene*. A shallow pretense to humanistic learning is the one vice that infects the fools of all social classes and ranks. Captain Otter, for example, whose infantile ambitions to impress his social superiors border on the pathetic, "does Latin it as much as your barber" (2.4.53–54).

24. See Salingar, pp. 39–46, where he discusses all the topical references in *Epicoene*, describing the marginality of the Londoners in the play in terms of the "post-Elizabethan London of 'the Wits and Braveries o' the time, as they call 'hem,' who are near the court but not of it, who lodge in the city but do not belong to it, who are beginning to form a separate, gossip-filled milieu of their own, the future 'town.'"

25. Stone, in "Social Mobility in England," p. 33, interestingly clarifies why Jonson could use Ireland to ridicule the *arriviste*: "Those who entered the Irish scene in the 1590s . . . found themselves endowed with great wealth which was easily converted into status by the purchase of an Irish title."

26. Stone, *Crisis of the Aristocracy*, pp. 71–82; Cressy, p. 34.

That a barber should attempt to speak Latin—what could be more hilarious? Disguised later in the play (5.1) as a lawyer and a priest, both captain and barber make many grammatical errors.

The shallowness, futility, mediocrity, snobbery, boasting, duplicity, infantile obsession, and intellectual pretension that are diffused among the male fools of the play combine with a vengeance in the females. It has been noted that there are no women characters in *Epicoene* who can match the three male wits in cleverness, charm, and verbal agility.[27] In fact, no unmarried, attractive, witty, or even young women exist in the play. Indeed, for Jonson in *Epicoene* the only dramatically interesting women are disloyal wives, who, past their prime, "live from their husbands; and give entertainment to all the wits, and braveries o' the time" (1.1.82–84). Like all their male counterparts, they inhabit a social limbo, "an order between courtiers and country-madams" (1.1.81–82); and like the male fools, they are superficial, fashion-conscious pedants and snobs. Their pretensions to taste and culture outdo those of the male fools. Absurdly, they have formed their own exclusive society and "call themselves the collegiates" (1.1.81). Jack Daw's fantasy of erudition and political skill and La Foole's giddy, inappropriately lavish hospitality are fatuous and misguided. But where the men's delusions are culturally grandiose, the women's preoccupations with status and power remain hopelessly trivial, centering on arcane distinctions in pedigree and disputes about who will enter a room first:

> *Mrs. Ot.*　'Tis my place.
> *Mav.*　You shall pardon me, Mistress Otter.
> *Mrs. Ot.*　Why, I am a collegiate.
> *Mav.*　But not in ordinary.
> *Mrs. Ot.*　But I am.
> *Mav.*　We'll dispute that within. [*Exeunt* Ladies]
> *Cler.*　Would this had lasted a little longer.
> *Tru.*　And that they had sent for the heralds.
> [3.2.337–44]

Like the opinions and preferences of the foolish knights, those of the ladies derive entirely from the opinions of others. Indeed none

27. See Barbara Baines and Mary C. Williams, "The Contemporary and Classical Antifeminist Tradition in Jonson's *Epicoene*," *Renaissance Papers*

of the fools can properly be said to *desire* anything at all; their only real passion is for conformity: "They have nothing, not the use of their senses, but by tradition" (3.1.262–63).[28] The ladies, however, are even more vulnerable and empty than the men. Like the collegiates, Daw and La Foole profess undying friendship for one another, which their actions disprove. But where the wits easily exploit the knights' cowardice to lead each to mistrust the other, both Daw and La Foole prove reluctant enemies and are pleased to make amends. In contrast, the ladies rush to betray and slander one another with eager, purposeful malice (cf. 4.2 and 5.1). Thus it is not enough to point out that the women in *Epicoene* share the vices of the male fools: they are, pointedly, worse than the men. The male fools are contemptible, but the women are beneath contempt.

As is by now well known, with the exception of some single women and widows, women of all classes in English Renaissance society, like other dependent persons, servants, and apprentices, were considered "in some sense outside the social order" and were "categorically rejected . . . as subjects and citizens in the commonwealth."[29] Considerable evidence has arisen to suggest that women in the early seventeenth century were beginning to contest their dependent and unequal status to some extent, a development that is examined later in this chapter. Here it suffices to note that from the text of *Epicoene* it is clear that Jonson was aware of the struggle and regarded any such female challenge to traditional social and sexual order as offensively ludicrous. Though the collegiates' lewdness is frequently discussed, no actual evidence of it ever surfaces among the thick layers of things, names, and objects, the myriad data and detail of the play. Their pursuit of Dauphine, for example, emerges from competitive conformity rather than eros. Although sexual boasting abounds in *Epicoene* (e.g., 5.1.76–101; 4.1.77–160; 4.1.1–62), no adulteries ever take place. Instead,

---

(1977), 43–58; and Anne Barton, *Ben Jonson, Dramatist* (Cambridge: Cambridge University Press, 1984), pp. 120–35.

28. Cf. Stephen J. Greenblatt, "The False Ending in *Volpone*," *Journal of English and Germanic Philology*, 75 (1976), 90–104, in which Greenblatt stresses the characters' emptiness, paralysis, and impotence, in light of which Volpone's and Mosca's acquisitiveness can be understood as both a substitute for desire and potency and a mask to hide their absence.

29. Cressy, pp. 30, 34.

among the array of the collegiates' lusts and vanities, other offenses are targeted for peculiarly prominent ridicule: that they have banded together as a group, forming, in a sense, an alternative commonwealth (1.1.80–87); that they are living "from their husbands" (1.1.82); that they are using birth control (4.2.58–62); that they assume knowledge of intellectual subjects and claim prowess in matters of culture and taste (2.1.146–81). With the possible and only partial exception of using birth control, all of these actions suggest not the dangerous temptations of eros, but the drive toward female equality and independence, which Jonson depicts as an aggressive attempt to usurp male authority.

Jonson sums up and caricatures his view of women's desire for independence in his portrait of the ridiculous marriage of Captain and Mrs. Otter, the satiric force of which derives from its complete inversion of traditional sexual hierarchies. The uxorious Captain, who hates his wife, is financially dependent on her, forced to call her his "princess" and to obey her irrational whims. She in turn commands and maligns him, perpetually reestablishing her dominion. The only marriage actually represented in the play, the Otters' union is middle class; interestingly, Jacobean moral and religious writing indicates that the movement toward female freedom was seen as originating in middle-class values.[30] But the grossness of Mrs. Otter's assumption of preeminence merely exaggerates and parodies the "Amazonian impudence" of the "great" ladies' exercise of power over men. They are continually outrageous, unspeakably grotesque. In all of Jacobean drama, no misogyny is so detailed and unmitigated, so utterly triumphant, as Ben Jonson's is in *Epicoene*.[31]

In his representation of the collegiates' assumption of "most

---

30. See, e.g., John Earle, *Micro-cosmographie* (London, 1633), no. 36. In his "character" of "A meere Gull Citizen," Earle expresses his greatest ridicule and contempt for what he perceives as the shopkeeper-citizen's relations of relative equality with his wife. The citizen is "one that do's nothing without his chuck, that is, his Wife, with whom he is billing still in conspiracy, and the wantoner she is, the more power shee ha's over him: and shee never stoopes so low after him, but is the onely woman goes better of a Widdow then a Maide."

31. Baines and Williams trace some of the classical and Renaissance sources of the misogyny in *Epicoene*.

masculine, or rather hermaphroditical authority" (1.1.85–86), Jonson associates social mobility with sexual monstrosity and sexual monstrosity with women's attempt at equality. The androgynous Epicoene's instantaneous conversion from obedient silence to domestic tyranny following "her" marriage to Morose of course epitomizes this process. Thus it would seem that traditional Renaissance sexual values—polarization of sexual roles, the subordination of women, and marriage based on a balance of affection and property—constitute the norm against which the play's biting satire operates. Yet the representation of sexuality in *Epicoene* is more complicated than this formulation would indicate. Jonson's purposes—indeed, his *coup*—can be illuminated further by examining his transformation of the conventions of romantic comedy.

As noted above, no matter how vicious the satire, sketchy the portrait, or deflected the treatment, city comedy frequently relies on the romantic comic convention of desired marriage to conclude the action within festive traditions and retain a comic tone.[32] Jonson, however, does not merely deflect or deemphasize marriage in *Epicoene*; he calls attention to this romantic convention by inverting it. *Epicoene* ostentatiously depicts not the construction but the undoing of a marriage, ending not in a promise of consummation, but in a declaration of impotence.[33] Similarly, Jonson transforms the traditional use of sexual disguise in romantic comedy. Though there is some precedent for male characters disguising themselves as women,[34] male actors portraying female characters who are in turn disguised as male characters are a much more frequent dramatic event. Romantic comedy exploits both the metatheatrical and the symbolic ambiguities of this situation. In romantic comedy the female hero's androgyny represents an ambiguous identifica-

32. Cf. Cohen, p. 283.

33. Cf. R. V. Holdsworth, ed., *Epicoene*, New Mermaids edition (London: Ernest Benn, 1979), pp. xxviii–xxix; and Ian Donaldson, "'A Martyrs Resolution': Jonson's *Epicoene*," *Review of English Studies*, N.S. 18 (1967), 13.

34. See Holdsworth, p. xxv; L. A. Beaurline, ed. *Epicoene*, Regents Renaissance Drama (Lincoln: University of Nebraska Press, 1966), pp. xiii–xiv; and Salingar, p. 30. All three point to Aretino's *Il Marescalco* (1533) as a source for a male character disguised as a female. Beaurline also notes that John Day's *The Isle of Gulls* (1606) had used a man disguised as a woman to satirize the Jacobean court. Another famous example would, of course, be Pyrocles disguised as an Amazon in Sidney's *Arcadia*.

tion with and experience of male sexuality that is eventually contained. But the androgyny of the title character in *Epicoene* (a term defined in the *OED* as "one who partakes of the characteristics of both sexes") is merely a sham. Since the audience is not included in the joke of his true sexual identity, Epicoene's female disguise dramatizes no ambiguity, contains no complexity: as it turns out, the only possible silent woman—the best woman—is, simply, a man.[35]

What is the effect of these twists, jokes, and generic inversions? The play's representation of eros offers an intriguing answer. Although it is dramatized with ambivalence, heterosexual desire becomes the propelling force in romantic comedy. In contrast, heterosexual love is never actually experienced in *Epicoene*; instead, it is regarded by all the characters, particularly the males, with subtle but distinct aversion. Truewit's numerous misogynistic tirades are notorious (1.1.109–144; 2.1.70–208; 4.1.37–160; 4.2.687–94), and Jonas Barish has demonstrated convincingly how Jonson adapts both Ovid and Juvenal in these speeches, rendering the courtly polish of the former and the moral indignation of the latter in turn less appealing and more devastating.[36] In his ironic, cynical speeches praising cosmetics, for example, Truewit does not merely fragment women into teeth, eyebrows, and nails; he articulates a vivid disgust with the female body, a conviction that women should "practice any art to mend breath, cleanse teeth, repair eyebrows; paint and profess it" (1.1.115–16)—in other words, to repair what is by nature vicious and ugly: "They have a natural inclination sways 'hem generally to the worst, when they are left to themselves" (4.2.692–93). There is no allusion to female beauty in *Epicoene*, only a nauseated reaction to an "oiled face," "ill foot," "fat hand," "scald nails," "sour breath," "black and rugged teeth" (1.1.15–16, 4.1.40–49).[37] The point of Truewit's discourse about

35. For an interesting account of a nonsatiric treatment of a similar idea in Shakespeare's sonnets, see Judith Kegan Gardiner, "The Marriage of Male Minds in Shakespeare's Sonnets," *Journal of English and Germanic Philology*, (1985), 328–47.

36. Jonas Barish, "Ovid, Juvenal, and *The Silent Woman*," *PMLA*, 71 (1956), 213–24. See also Annette Drew-Bear, "Face-Painting Scenes in Ben Jonson's Plays," *Studies in Philology*, 77 (1980), 388–401.

37. See Nancy J. Vickers, "Diana Described: Scattered Woman and Scat-

seeking women out in order to discover "whom to love, whom to play with, whom to touch once, whom to hold ever" is drastically subverted by his conviction, expressed in the same speech, that loving women is conceivable only when "variety arrests . . . judgment" (4.1.66–68). His recommendation of physical force as a method of courtship ("it is to them an acceptable violence, and has oft-times the place of the greatest courtesy" [4.1.90–91])[38] has winning and one-upsmanship as its major goal, rather than sexual intercourse, which Truewit regards as an occasional necessity and equates with sin: "Nor will it be out of your gain to make love to her too. . . . All blabbing is taken away when she comes to be a part of the crime" (4.1.133–36). Truewit's physical aversion to women is epitomized when Mrs. Otter, overhearing her husband ridicule her for having bad breath, seeks revenge by asking Truewit for a kiss:

> *Mrs. Ot.* O treacherous liar! Kiss me, sweet Master Truewit,
> and prove him a slandering knave.
> *Tru.* I'll rather believe you, lady.
> [4.1.249–51]

Similarly, Morose's professions of erotic feeling for his alleged bride-to-be, Epicoene, are clearly pedantic, Petrarchan nonsense ("Out of the first fire of meeting eyes, they say, love is stricken: do you feel any such motion suddenly shot into you, from any part you see in me? Ha, lady?" [2.3.29–32]). As noted, his desire to marry stems from jealousy of Dauphine's title, not from sexual need.

Besides, his bride, Epicoene, is a man. Perhaps in response to King James's sexual preferences, Jonson's treatment of homosexuality is slightly less hostile than the unquestionable revulsion toward heterosexual love expressed in the play. It is true that Daw and La Foole are ridiculed for confessing unwittingly that they

---

tered Rhyme," in *Writing and Sexual Difference*, ed. Elizabeth Abel (Chicago: University of Chicago Press, 1980), pp. 95–109, for a discussion of the fragmentation of the female in male-authored poetry.

38. For a different view of the relations between the sexes in the play, see Barbara Millard, "'An Acceptable Violence': Sexual Contest in Jonson's *Epicoene*," *Medieval and Renaissance Drama in England*, 1 (1984), 143–58.

have been "in the great bed at Ware together in our time" (5.1.65–66); and it is implied with equally piercing mockery that the collegiates prefer boy pages wearing female wigs and gowns to adult male lovers.[39] It is also possible that the play was banned after its first performance for an overtly political, ironic reference to transvestism that Jonson was apparently unable to resist including, although the allusion obviously satirizes the Jacobean court.[40] Yet it is Clerimont, one of the three hero-wits, who is said to have "a mistress abroad" and "an ingle at home" (1.1.27–28), with a clear and acceptable preference for the latter. Most important, by excluding Truewit, Clerimont, and the audience from the secret of Epicoene's true sexual identity, Jonson slyly implies that it is impossible to tell the difference between the sexes. That the play's bride and best woman turns out to be a man also constitutes a witty twist with multiple sexual implications.

The heroic solution to reconciling eros with city life, however, lies neither in homosexuality nor in heterosexuality, but rather in the absence of sexual desire. It is his complete lack of eroticism (along with his knightly rank) that makes Dauphine the hero of the play. When the collegiates are persuaded to pursue him, he, unlike Truewit and Clerimont, is never tempted by their offers of sexual favors and never seeks their approval (4.1.34–36; 4.2.510–13); he wishes only to be rid of them (5.1.150–60). And his immunity to

---

39. For women's aversion to men, see 4.2.2–4, 1.1.14–20, and 2.1.170–72.

40. The allusion in question is in 5.1.24–25, when La Foole refers to "the Prince of Moldavia, and . . . his mistress, Mistress Epicoene"; it refers to Stephano Janiculo, who escaped a Turkish prison disguised as a woman and pretended to be engaged to Lady Arabella Stuart, the king's cousin. According to Beaurline, p. xix, when Lady Stuart complained the play was banned. In contrast, Barton speculates (pp. 131–32) that *Epicoene* stopped being performed because it was simply unpopular. She cites Drummond, who in his *Conversations* remarked of Jonson's *Epicoene*, "When his Play of a Silent woman was first acted, ther was found verses after on the stage against him, concluding that, that play was well named the Silent Woman. ther was never one man to say plaudite to it." Whatever the reasons, there is no recorded performance of *Epicoene* after the first at the Whitefriars Theater by the Children of Her Majesty's Revels in 1609, until it was revived at court in 1636. The play was entered for publication in 1610 and again in 1612, but no edition exists before the one Jonson prepared for the 1616 edition of his *Works* (see Barton, pp. 131–32).

eros is accompanied by a lack of sociability. Only Dauphine is actually capable of the secretive behavior, the avoidance of intimacy, most valued by the wits (1.1.292–304).[41] No matter how cynically, both Truewit and Clerimont are fully engaged in sexual and sociopolitical pursuits; but Dauphine stays in his room, reading. At one point Truewit reprimands him as an antisocial dreamer: "You must leave to live i' your chamber, then, a month together upon *Amadis de Gaul*, or *Don Quixote*, as you are wont; and come abroad where the matter is frequent, to court, to tiltings, public shows and feasts, to plays, and church sometimes" (4.1.60–64).

Dauphine is therefore related to the misanthropic Morose not only by blood but by a shared tendency toward isolation. Scholars have noted often that Jonson portrays Morose with distinct ambivalence. Morose's hatred of noise—his hatred, that is, of social life—can best be viewed as an extreme distortion of his father's worthy advice: to "collect and contain my mind, not suffering it to flow loosely; that I should look to what things were necessary to the carriage of my life, and what not; embracing the one and eschewing the other" (5.1.243–47). This speech comes as near to expressing a Jonsonian norm of rational behavior as any statement in *Epicoene*.[42] It is typical of Jonson to complicate his comedy by giving the most sympathetic speech to the most ludicrous character in the play.

Dauphine, of course, is less grotesque than Morose; but Jonson treats him with an ambivalence that, although it is more subtle, is nevertheless distinct. Dauphine has the last laugh in the play, but it is clear that he is something of a sadist. During the ruse played on Daw and La Foole, the latter, thinking his life is in danger, offers his left arm. "Take it by all means," Dauphine advises eagerly, and Truewit, shocked, replies, "How! Maim a man for ever, for a jest? What a conscience hast thou!" (4.2.398–400). When the foolish knights do receive a milder form of corporal punishment, it is Dauphine who administers the kicks. After he has tricked Morose

41. Cf. Barton, pp. 128–29.

42. Cf. Barton, p. 131; and Thomas M. Greene, "Ben Jonson and the Centered Self," *Studies in English Literature*, 10 (1970), 325–48. See also Greenblatt; and Jonas Barish, *The Antitheatrical Prejudice* (Berkeley: University of California Press, 1981), pp. 132–54.

out of one-third of his income, humiliated him into declaring impotence publicly, and reduced him to silence, Dauphine concludes his part in the play by wishing death on his uncle: "I'll not trouble you till you trouble me with your funeral, which I care not how soon it come" (5.1.672). This, indeed, is maiming a man for a jest.

Dauphine, then, has travestied and undone marriage and desire, brought death and impotence into the concluding scene. Yet although Truewit has the final speech, it is Dauphine who orchestrates the comedy and becomes the "master-wit" of the play. His crowning achievement is getting the money and securing the title without, as it were, getting the girl. Therefore, in *Epicoene* it is not eros that will guarantee the perpetuation of society, but acquisition, secrecy, and wit, all exercised in service of preserving traditional rank and hierarchy. As will be demonstrated in the next chapter, such harsh repression of sexual desire is usually associated with tragedy. But Jonson's triumph in *Epicoene* is to avoid the complexities of the tragic representation of sexuality by dispensing with eros altogether. Indeed, it is precisely because the inversion of romantic comic conventions is so absolute, deliberate, and direct in *Epicoene* that the play remains within comedy's discursive terrain. By developing to its logical extreme the satiric discourse that equates sexuality with corruption, disjunction, and sin, Jonson "lurched . . . the better half of the garland" from his fellow playwrights and managed to celebrate the continuation of society not by including and containing sexual desire, but by banishing it altogether.

Dauphine's defeat of eros, combined with his social isolation, reveals a profound misanthropy at the heart of *Epicoene*. Equating social and sexual aspiration, Jonson mercilessly ridicules them both. Much more than Jonson's other comedies, *Epicoene*, with its narrow range of social reference directed toward a private theater audience, can be said to be written from the point of view of the aristocracy. Recently Walter Cohen has argued that the emergence of satiric drama in the Renaissance indicates "the failure of the aristocracy to adapt to social and political change." The vigor of satiric plays, Cohen continues, is rooted in "a simultaneous aristocratic desire to exclude the citizen classes from the national polity and fear that the opposite might actually be occurring. . . . If one could not read the citizen classes out of the nation, one could at least write them out of the plays. Something of this strategy may be detected as early as Jonson's *Epicene.*"[43]

As Cohen's remarks imply, chronologically speaking, the social and sexual conservatism of *Epicoene* is extreme. On the one hand, the play's very extremity, its lack of mitigation, lays bare the logic of the polarizing satiric discourse that equates sexuality with sin; on the other hand, the narrowness of social reference precludes representation of the variety of points of view toward social and sexual mobility that were in fact available. Thomas Middleton and Thomas Dekker's city comedy *The Roaring Girl* (c. 1608–11), another play with a transvestite title figure written at roughly the same time as *Epicoene*, provides a contrast. Composed for a relatively heterogeneous, public theater audience, *The Roaring Girl* offers a more comprehensive picture of the variety and range of attitudes toward sexual and social mobility that were prevalent in Renaissance England.

iii

The central figure in *The Roaring Girl* is a woman named Moll Frith, whose distinguishing feature is that she walks around Jacobean London dressed in male clothing. It should be stressed that Moll is not in disguise: she is neither a disguised player, a man pretending to be a woman, nor is she a disguised character, whose

---

43. Cohen, pp. 282, 290. The alternative spelling of the play's title is Cohen's. See also Michael Shapiro, "Audience vs. Dramatist in Jonson's *Epicoene* and Other Plays of the Children's Troupes," *English Literary Renaissance*, 3 (1973), 400–417. In this interesting and imaginative essay, Shapiro argues (p. 401) that playwrights who composed for children's companies performing in private theaters faced the special task of containing the intrusive, condescending response of a self-dramatizing aristocratic audience seeking to assert its superiority: "Although it is impossible to analyze the private theater audiences sociologically, or even to know how typical they were of upper-class Englishmen, opportunities for self-dramatization probably attracted members of the upper classes who felt their social status to be precarious: either old-line aristocrats struggling to maintain their standing; or gentry, *nouveaux riches*, and young inns-of-court men striving for higher status." Shapiro's analysis of the probable audience of *Epicoene* resembles my own of the society Jonson is interested in representing in the play.

role requires a woman pretending to be a man. Unlike Epicoene or the disguised heroines of romantic comedy, Moll seeks not to conceal her sexual identity, but rather to display it. Although certain of the *dramatis personae* in *The Roaring Girl* occasionally fail to recognize her immediately, the fact that Moll is a woman is well known to every character in the play. She simply presents herself in society as a woman wearing men's clothes. Demanding merely by her presence that people reconcile her apparent sexual contradictions, she arouses unspeakable social and sexual anxieties in the established society of the play. Indeed, Middleton and Dekker create Moll as the fulcrum of *The Roaring Girl*, and the other characters' reactions to her tend to define them as social and moral beings. As a result, society's effort to assess the identity of this female figure in male attire becomes the central dramatic and symbolic issue of the play.

Recognizing the title figure's assumption of male attire as the symbolic focus of social and moral concern in *The Roaring Girl* allows us to connect the play with the intense, often bitterly funny debate about women wearing men's clothes that was taking place in contemporary moral and religious writing, and that came to a head in 1620 with a pair of pamphlets entitled, respectively, *Hic Mulier: Or, The Man-Woman*, and *Haec-Vir: Or The Womanish-Man*.[44] Indeed, the figure of the female in male apparel emerges from the documents of this controversy much as Moll Frith does from the text of *The Roaring Girl*: as an embodiment of female independence boldly challenging established social and sexual values and, by the fact of her existence, requiring evaluation and response. Although historians of Renaissance conduct literature as well as literary critics have discussed the *Hic Mulier/Haec-Vir* controversy, scholars only recently have begun to view *The Roaring Girl*, with its "man-woman" heroine, in the context of this debate.[45] Both because the controversial issue involved has an

44. The full names of these colorful pamphlets are as follows: *Hic Mulier: Or, The Man-Woman: Being a Medicine to cure the Coltish Disease of the Staggers in the Masculine-Feminines of our Times*, and *Haec-Vir: Or The Womanish Man: Being an Answer to a late Booke intituled Hic-Mulier*. All quotations from the pamphlets are from the edition published by *The Rota* at the University of Exeter, the Scolar Press, 1973.

45. See Louis B. Wright, Middle-Class Culture in Elizabethan England

ongoing importance in Renaissance England and because I am not seeking to establish a direct influence between documents and play, the small chronological discrepancy between the performance and publication of *The Roaring Girl* (c. 1608–11) and the high point of the debate (1620) is not relevant to my purposes here; rather, I am interested in exploring the fact that the figure of the female in male attire is portrayed in both dramatic and social contexts with simultaneous admiration, desire, abhorrence, and fear. The following discussion attempts to demonstrate the ways in which parallel treatments of women in men's clothing in the drama and the debate illuminate this phenomenon of fashion as the focus of considerable moral and social anxiety aroused by changing sexual values in Jacobean England. Taken together, artistic representation and social commentary suggest not the unmitigated conservatism of *Epicoene*, but a deep cultural ambivalence in the British Renaissance about female independence and equality between the sexes.

iv

Elizabethan and Jacobean sermons and conduct books continually castigate the fickleness of fashion and the vanity of sumptuous apparel. To cite one very typical example, the writer of the sermon "Against Excess of Apparel" in *Certain Sermons or Homilies Appointed to Be Read in the Time of Queen Elizabeth* sees the English preoccupation with the novelties of fashion as a futile expenditure of energy, indicating an endlessly detrimental spiritual restlessness: "We are never contented, and therefore we prosper not."[46] Fur-

---

(Chapel Hill: University of North Carolina Press, 1935), pp. 494–97; Carroll Camden, *The Elizabethan Woman* (New York: Elsevier, 1952), pp. 263–67; Juliet Dusinberre, *Shakespeare and the Nature of Women* (London: Macmillan, 1975), pp. 231–71; Linda T. Fitz, "What Says the Married Woman: Marriage Theory and Feminism in the English Renaissance," *Mosaic*, 13 (Winter 1980), 1–22; and Linda [Fitz] Woodbridge, *Women and the English Renaissance: Literature and the Nature of Womankind, 1540–1620* (Urbana: University of Illinois Press, 1984), pp. 139–51. See also my essay "Women in Men's Clothing: Apparel and Social Stability in *The Roaring Girl*," *English Literary Renaissance*, 14 (1984), 367–91; and Dollimore, pp. 65–72.

46. "Against Excess of Apparel," in *Certain Sermons or Homilies Appointed to Be Read in Churches in the Time of Queen Elizabeth* (London: Society for Promoting Christian Knowledge, 1908), p. 327.

thermore, like Ben Jonson in *Epicoene,* the conservative spirit frequently links propriety of dress with the coherence of society and views as a threat to social stability the tendency of the pretentious or the newly prosperous to dress so elegantly that it has become increasingly difficult to distinguish among social classes by the varied attire of their members.[47] Along with the upwardly mobile and the fop, women (like the collegiates) are singled out in this criticism as creators of chaos, seeking to seduce men other than their husbands by wearing enticing clothes and being generally disobedient, disrespectful, shallow, demonic, and extravagant in their preoccupation with fashion.[48]

From these characteristic themes the phenomenon of women dressing in male clothing begins gradually to assume a distinct identity as a separate issue; or, more accurately, as an issue that, in its symbolic significance, articulates a variety of social and moral concerns. The few available references to the phenomenon in the 1500s are largely parenthetical. In the early part of the sixteenth century, the idea of women wearing men's clothes apparently seemed too appalling even to be feared. Ever zealous of female virtue, Vives, for example, issues an ultimatum on the subject in *Instruction of a christen woman* (c. 1529) only as a last line in his chapter on feminine dress, a mere afterthought to the more important prohibitions against brazenness and extravagance in female attire. Citing Deuteronomy 22.5, he writes, "A woman shall use no mannes raymente, elles lette hir thinke she hath the mans stomacke, but take hede to the woordes of our Lorde: sayinge, A woman shall not put on mans apparell: for so to doo is abhominable afore God. But I truste no woman will doo it, excepte she be paste both honestee and shame."[49] Vives's confidence in womanly docility was, however, misplaced. In George Gascoigne's satire *The Steel Glas* (1576), complaints about women in male attire, although

---

47. See, e.g., "Against Excess of Apparel"; Thomas Nashe, *Christs Teares over Jerusalem* (1593), in John Dover Wilson, *Life in Shakespeare's England* (Cambridge: Cambridge University Press, 1920), p. 125; and Phillip Stubbes, *Anatomy of Abuses* (1583), ed. Frederick J. Furnivall, The New Shakespeare Society (London, 1877–79), pp. 33–34.

48. See, for example, William Harrison, *Description of England, 1587,* in Wilson, pp. 124–25. Cf. Wright, p. 493; Camden, pp. 257–67; and Fitz.

49. John Louis Vives, *Instruction of a christen woman,* trans. Richard Hyrde (1529; rpt. London, 1557), bk. 1, chap. 9, "Of raymentes." Deuteronomy

still relegated to epilogue status, are nevertheless becoming decidedly more pointed and vociferous:

> What be they? women? masking in mens weedes?
> With dutchkin dublets, and with Ierkins iaggde?
> With high copt hattes, and fethers flaunt a flaunt?
> They be so sure even *Wo* to *Men* in dede.[50]

The astonished despair of female modesty expressed in Gascoigne's mournful pun takes the form of accusations of sexual and, by clear inference, social, moral, and cosmic perversion in the rhetoric of Phillip Stubbes. Writing in 1583, in the midst of a general denunciation of the apparel of both sexes, Stubbes mentions women with "dublets and Jerkins as men have heer, buttoned up the brest, and made with wings, welts, and pinions on the shoulder points, as mans apparel is." Stubbes lucidly states his indignant alarm at the possibility of not being able to distinguish between the sexes: "Our Apparell was given us as a signe distinctive to discern betwixt sex and sex, and therefore one to weare the Apparel of another sex is to . . . adulterate the veritie of his owne kinde. Wherefore these Women may not improperly be called *Hermaphroditi*, that is, Monsters of bothe kindes, half women, half men."[51]

Though Stubbes's rhetoric is always colorfully extravagant, the topic of women in male attire continued to elicit highly emotional reactions at a growing rate, particularly in the second decade of the seventeenth century, when, amidst a marked increase in satiric attacks upon women in general, references to the "monstrous . . . *Woman* of the *Masculine Gender*" multiplied notably.[52] As Louis B.

22:5 reads: "The Woman shall not wear that which pertaineth unto a man, neither shall a man put on a woman's garment: for all that do so *are* abomination unto the Lord thy God."

50. George Gascoigne, *The Steele Glas* (1576), in *English Reprints*, ed. Edward Arber, vol. 5 (London, 1869), pp. 82–83.

51. Stubbes, p. 73. Cf. Harrison, pp. 124–25.

52. Henry Fitzgeffrey, *Notes from Black-fryers* (1617), cited by Wright, p. 492. See Wright, pp. 483–94, for other references to the "man-woman," including Barnabe Rich, in *The Honestie of this Age* (1614); Alexander Niccholes, in *A Discourse of Marriage And Wiving* (1615 ed.); and Thomas Adams, in *Mystical Bedlam* (1615).

Wright has demonstrated, this growth in both the volume and the hostility of satire against women represented the misogynistic, ultraconservative voice in the lively debate about woman's nature, behavior, and role that was taking place in the moral and religious writing of the early decades of the century.[53] It is in this camp that *Epicoene* belongs. According to Wright and other critics, the content of the conduct literature can be distinguished roughly along class lines: where "learned and courtly" works tend to discuss women in the abstract and spiritualized terms of Neoplatonic philosophy, middle-class tracts dispute more practical and social issues, such as the appropriateness of female apparel.[54] Although the documents in the controversy surrounding women in male attire indicate that both upper- and middle-class females followed the fashion, they are much too partisan and factually imprecise to convey the actual extent to which the style was adopted.[55]

Nevertheless, by 1620 the phenomenon of women in men's clothing had become prominent enough to evoke an outraged protest from King James, recorded in a letter of J. Chamberlain to Sir D. Carleton, dated 25 January 1620: "Yesterday the bishop of London called together all his clergie about this towne, and told them he had expresse commandment from the King to will them to inveigh vehemently against the insolencie of our women, and theyre wearing of brode brimed hats, pointed dublets, theyre haire cut short or shorne, and some of them stilettoes or poniards, and such other trinckets of like moment; adding withall that if pulpit admonitions will not reforme them he would proceed by another

53. Wright, p. 490. Anger against women reached its zenith in Joseph Swetnam's misogynistic tract *The Araignment of Lewd, Idle, Froward, and unconstant Women* (1615), which had ten printings by 1634 and inspired several responses (see Wright, pp. 486–93), including a stage play, *Swetnam, the Woman-hater, Arraigned by Women* (1620).

54. Wright, p. 507; Fitz, pp. 2–3.

55. Along with the numerous isolated references to the *Hic Mulier* phenomenon cited in Wright, these documents include the *Hic Mulier* and *Haec-Vir* pamphlets noted above and another pamphlet, *Mulde Sacke: Or The Apologie of Hic Mulier: To the late Declamation against her* (1620). By referring to the *Hic Mulier* phenomenon as a "transvestite movement," or even as a "rough-and-ready unisex movement," Fitz implies (p. 15) more coherence and range to the fashion than these pamphlets can document. Cf. Woodbridge [Fitz], pp. 139–51.

course; the truth is the world is very much out of order." On 12 February Chamberlain added: "Our pulpits ring continually of the insolence and impudence of women, and to helpe the matter forward the players have likewise taken them to taske, and so to the ballades and ballad-singers, so that they can come nowhere but theyre eares tingle; and if all this will not serve, the King threatens to fall upon theyre husbands, parents or frends that have or shold have power over them, and make them pay for it."[56] The king's protest amounted to a declaration of war. Though undoubtedly resulting in part from James's considerable misogyny, the actions following his protest also revealed that, among all the satiric targets on the subject of female fashion, women in men's clothing had assumed threatening enough proportions in the conservative mind to be singled out in a conscientious and thorough attempt to eliminate the style from social life. In February 1620 the pamphlets *Hic Mulier*, which represented the conservative viewpoint, and *Haec-Vir*, which defended the practice of women wearing male attire, appeared. Because the pamphlets are anonymous, it is impossible to link their opinions to the gender of their author or authors.[57] More important, the subject of the unconventional man-woman had evolved into a full-fledged debate, in which conservative and liberal positions were clearly and elaborately defined.

Wright believes that the hostile, conservative response to women in men's clothing was a defensive reaction against an increasingly successful demand both for moral and spiritual equality between the sexes and for greater social freedom for women: freedom, for example, from confinement to the home, from the double standard of sexual morality, from wife beating and forced marriage. "The average [i.e., middle-class] woman," Wright concludes,

56. Quoted in Edward Phillips Statham, *A Jacobean Letter-Writer: The Life and Times of John Chamberlain* (London: Kegan Paul, Trench, Trubner, 1920), pp. 182–83.

57. We should not, I think, take for granted that misogynistic and feminist attitudes can be aligned neatly with gender in the Renaissance. The relative paucity of literature of the early 1600s in which women are clearly speaking for themselves makes specifically female attitudes very difficult to distinguish and assess. Resolving the problem of the correlation between gender and attitude is not, however, a prerequisite to the present analysis, which seeks to compare the sexual values clearly articulated in the *Hic Mulier/Haec-Vir* debate with the artistic conception of a *Hic Mulier* figure in *The Roaring Girl*.

"was becoming articulate in her own defense and . . . was demanding social independence unknown in previous generations." According to Wright, the female adoption of male apparel aggressively and visibly dramatized a bid for social independence, which constituted a largely successful and coherent challenge to existing sexual values that is reflected in *Haec-Vir*, a pamphlet Wright believes to be "the *Areopagitica* of the London woman, a woman who had attained greater freedom than any of her predecessors or than any of her European contemporaries."[58] We can discern the challenge that women in male attire presented to the existing imbalance of power between the sexes in the vindictive bitterness of the opposition to the androgynous style. Yet Linda Woodbridge has provided a useful and fascinating corrective to the hopeful interpretation of the extent and coherence of Jacobean feminism advanced by Wright and critics like Juliet Dusinberre by stressing the restrictiveness, rather than the liberating potential, of middle-class conduct literature. In her discussion of the controversy surrounding women in men's clothing, Woodbridge points out some serious oversights in Wright's optimistic view of the *Hic Mulier/Haec-Vir* debate; nevertheless, she ends by conceding that "Wright is quite justified in his . . . assessment" of a resounding victory for female freedom articulated in this controversy.[59] My own analysis of the debate suggests an attitude toward the *Hic Mulier* phenomenon and the sexual freedom it represented that is more complex either than Wright perceives or Woodbridge explores, an attitude that both acknowledges injustice and fears

58. Wright, pp. 490, 497. Although I disagree with Wright about the extent to which Renaissance women's challenge was successful or even coherent, his idea that the hostile conservative response to female attempts at sexual independence was a reaction to a demand corresponds with the interpretation I have given to Ben Jonson's misogyny in *Epicoene*.

59. Writing as Fitz, pp. 16–17. For example, Woodbridge [Fitz] sees as unfortunate the argument in *Haec-Vir* (sig. C2v) that it is a law of nature that differences between the sexes be preserved by designated dress and behavior. She also remarks that "Renaissance women so far accepted the masculine rules of the game that they felt they had to adopt the clothing and external attributes of the male sex in order to be 'free.' This was true in drama as in life: witness the transvestite heroines of Shakespeare's romantic comedies." Cf. Woodbridge [Fitz], who perceives (pp. 148–49) the "eventual collapse of *Haec-Vir* into orthodoxy" but again concludes that the pamphlet is a significant statement of female freedom.

change, that wants sexual freedom yet perceives its attainment as conflicting with an equally desirable social stability.

V

After an introductory lament that "since the daies of *Adam* women were never so Masculine" (sig. A3), the pamphlet *Hic Mulier* or *The Man-Woman* begins by propounding a familiar Renaissance ideal of woman as chaste, maternal, compassionate, discreet, and obedient, a model of behavior and sentiment from which the notorious man-woman is believed to depart "with a deformitie neuer before dream'd of" (sig. A4ᵛ).[60] In contrast to this modestly attired paragon, the *Hic Mulier* figure, sporting a "cloudy Ruffianly broad-brim'd Hatte, and wanton Feather . . . the loose, lasciuious ciuill embracement of a French doublet . . . most ruffianly short lockes . . . for Needles, Swords . . . for Prayer bookes, bawdy Iigs," is "not halfe man, halfe woman . . . but all Odyous, all Divell" (sig. A4ʳ–B1ᵛ). In elaborating the polemical intention of this pamphlet—to eliminate the heinous fashion by demonizing its proponents—the author builds a case around two major arguments.

As might be expected, the first group of arguments centers on the dangerous sexual chaos that the author assumes will result from the breakdown of rigid gender distinctions, symbolized by the man-woman's attire. Like Jonson portraying female attempts at independence in *Epicoene*, the writer perceives in Hic Mulier's choice of male clothes unconventional sexual behavior; therefore, this figure automatically becomes a whore, promiscuous in her own conduct and inspiring by her lewd example a pernicious illicit sexuality in others. As is implied in the description of her "loose, lasciuious ciuill embracement of a French doublet, being all unbutton'd to entice" (sig. B1ᵛ), she will allow, even invite, "a shameless libertie to every loose passion" (sig. C2). Despite—indeed, because of—her mannishness, then, Hic Mulier displays and encourages a free-floating sexuality, a possibility that the author

60. See Suzanne W. Hull, *Chaste Silent & Obedient: English Books for Women, 1475–1640* (San Marino, Calif.: Huntington Library, 1982). Hull provides an ample bibliography of documents that articulate the Renaissance ideal of womanhood.

views as socially destabilizing and therefore disastrous, "most pernicious to the Common-wealth" (sig. C2). This interesting association between socially threatening female sexiness and the breakdown of polarized gender identities and sexual roles becomes very important in *The Roaring Girl*. The fear seems to be that without rigidly assigned, gender-linked roles and behavior, legitimate, faithful erotic relations between the sexes will become impossible, and the integrity of the family will consequently disintegrate: "they [i.e., the men-women] are neither men, nor women, but iust good for nothing . . . they care not into what dangers they plunge either their Fortunes or Reputations, the disgrace of the whole Sexe, or the blot and obloquy of their private Families" (sig. B2–C2).

However ominous eros and the breakdown of sexual polarization may be, their unleashing does not preoccupy the author as much as do questions of social status and hierarchy.[61] As in *Epicoene*, the implied norm behind the satire in the pamphlet is a stable society that derives its coherence from the strict preservation of such essential distinctions as class, fortune, and rank. Not only do women in men's clothing come from various classes in society; they also have the unfortunate habit of dressing alike, obscuring both the clarity of their gender and the badge of their social status, and thereby endangering critically both unquestioned aristocratic ascendancy and the predictable orderliness of social relations. To convey the seriousness of this offense, the author employs the

61. In "Attitudes of Members of the House of Commons to the Regulation of 'Personal Conduct' in Late Elizabethan and Early Stuart England," *Bulletin of the Institute of Historical Research*, 46 (1973), 41–71, Joan Kent substantiates from a legal point of view the argument made in this chapter. Kent argues (pp. 50, 57) that legislation attempting to regulate conduct was designed to reinforce the social structure in a time when defining and consolidating that structure were becoming increasingly difficult. Referring specifically to sumptuary legislation, she shows that the early seventeenth-century bills against excess of apparel seem to have been regarded by some members of the House of Commons "as a threat to the very social distinctions which earlier bills had been designed to mirror and reinforce." Specifically, regulations in Jacobean England reflected a new disjunction between economics and status distinctions. The only provision on apparel to become law between 1576 and 1604 was a clause for the repeal of statutes, "which withdrew all previous regulations on dress without replacing them." Also see Whigham, pp. 155–69.

rhetorical device of associating the hated style by turns with decaying aristocrats and gentry ("the adulterate branches of rich stocks" [sig. B1]), with women of base birth ("stinking vapours drawne from dunghils" [sig. B1]), with females of the upper classes "knowne great" ("no more shall their greatness or wealth save them from one particle of disgrace" [sig. B1ᵛ,B2ᵛ]), and with middle-class wives (tailors have "metamorphosed more modest old garments . . . for the use of Freemens wives than hath been worne in Court, Suburbs, or Countrey" [sig. C1ᵛ]). All of these complaints lead to the indignant outburst: "It is an infection that emulates the plague, and throwes itselfe amongst women of all degrees. . . . Shall we be all co-heires of one honor, one estate, and one habit?" (sig. B1ᵛ-B4ᵛ). Like death and disease, then, the female in male attire served as a leveler; and just as such issues as the inflated sale of honors by the crown seemed to the conservative mind to be undermining social coherence by threatening the traditional prestige of inherited nobility, so the phenomenon of women of different social positions dressing in similar male clothing appeared intolerably chaotic. As Woodbridge has shown, English Renaissance women, particularly in the middle classes, used their apparel as a showpiece to advertise the prosperity of their fathers and husbands.[62] That women should perversely refuse, by donning look-alike male clothes, to serve their crucial function as bearers of social status and class distinction is the issue that arouses the author's most vindictive antipathy: "Let . . . the powerfull Statute of apparell but lift up his Battle-Axe . . . so as every one may bee knowne by the true badge of their bloud, or Fortune: and then these *Chymera's* of deformitie will bee sent backe to hell, and there burne to Cynders in the flames of their owne malice" (sig. C1ᵛ).

Hic Mulier ends with an invective against all social change (sig. C3). Given the hectic violence of this author's conservatism, it is not surprising that the rebuttal in the pamphlet *Haec-Vir: Or The Womanish Man,* which appeared seven days later, would dwell on the folly of thoughtlessly adhering to social custom. Interestingly, *Haec-Vir* ignores the issue of whether women of different social categories dressing alike as men disrupt the alignment of social

---

62. Writing as Fitz, pp. 9–10. Also see Wright, pp. 490–91; and Dusinberre, pp. 234–35.

classes; instead, the second pamphlet argues solely in terms of gender and sexual roles. Rather than appearing as the product of a single mind, *Haec-Vir* is presented as a dialogue between two characters, the *Hic Mulier* and the *Haec-Vir* figures, suggesting by its very form and by the introduction of a new figure, the womanish man, a greater openness to discussion and to cooperation between the sexes. The irrationality of the author of the first pamphlet is also clarified and undercut at the beginning of the second when the two figures conduct a witty exchange about their mutual inability to identify one another's gender. Thus a tolerant and urbane tone is set in which Hic Mulier (now a sympathetic figure) can defend her behavior.

Hic Mulier's defense elaborates in positive terms the fact that her attire symbolizes a demand for recognition of spiritual and moral equality between the sexes, a recognition that she regards as her birthright: "We are free-borne as Men, have as free election, and as free spirits, we are compounded of like parts, and may with like liberty make benefit of our Creations" (sig. B3). Consequently, she counters Haec-Vir's charge that assuming male apparel makes her a mere slave to the novelties of fashion both by defining her outfit as a symbol of her freedom of choice and by redefining slavery as Haec-Vir's mindless submission to the tyranny of pointless custom, "for then custome, nothing is more absurd, nothing more foolish" (sig. B2). The customs she resents as most false and destructive to female freedom and equality are those gender-linked stereotypes which constrain female behavior to compliance, subordination, pathos, and passivity: "But you say wee are barbarous and shameles and cast off all softnes, to runne wilde through a wildernesse of opinions. In this you express more cruelty then in all the rest, because I stand not with my hands on my belly like a baby at *Bartholomew Fayre* . . . that am not dumbe when wantons court mee, as if Asse-like I were ready for all burthens, or because I weep not when iniury gripes me, like a woorried Deere in the fangs of many Curres: am I therefore barbarous or shamelesse?" (sig. B3). "*I stand not with my hands on my belly like a baby* at Bartholomew Fayre . . . *as if Asse-like I were ready for all burthens.*" Hic Mulier argues that to reduce woman to the position of static icon, allegedly "so much better in that she is something purer" (sig. B1ᵛ) than man, is actually to infantilize and dehumanize her by denying her full participation in adult reality, which she optimistically defines as a world of creative movement and change, in which man can "alter, frame and fashion, according as his will and delight shall rule him" (sig. B1ᵛ). This conception, which locates adult reality in the creative opportunities provided by public life, recognizes that women are unjustly confined by tradition to perpetual fantasy and immaturity. It therefore forms the most strikingly modern of Hic Mulier's arguments.

The eloquence and clarity with which these convictions are expressed make the retrenchment that occurs in the pamphlet's conclusion all the more startling. Having established herself as the rational contender in the debate, the man-woman suddenly withdraws before the irrational onslaught of Haec-Vir, the womanish man who ignores her arguments, rather than systematically rebutting them. Suddenly the focus shifts to the way that Haec-Vir (who, it has been suggested, represents the homosexuality of the Jacobean court)[63] has relinquished his manhood and become a fop—aberrant male behavior that is now viewed as the sole reason for the existence of the notorious man-woman. In an astonishing abandonment of her considerable powers of logic, Hic Mulier nostalgically evokes chivalric gallantry, recalling the bygone days when men were men: "Hence we have preserved (though to our owne shames) those manly things which you have forsaken, which would you againe accept, and restore to us the Blushes we lay'd by, when first wee put on your Masculine garments; doubt not but chaste thoughts and bashfulnesse will againe dwell in us . . . then will we love and serve you; then will wee heare and obey you; then will wee like rich Iewels hang at your eares to take our Instructions" (sig. C2ᵛ, C3ᵛ). It is a bargain, an offer he can't refuse. The dialogue concludes with Haec-Vir having the last word, just as he had had the first, and the entire phenomenon of women in men's clothing is rationalized as an attempt not to achieve unrealized social freedom for women, but rather to return society to the idealized sexual norm of gender polarization and male dominance. As in King James's protest and the end of *Hic Mulier*, responsibility for the unconventional style of female dress, now recognized by all as deformed, is seen to rest with men because power does.[64]

---

63. Dusinberre, pp. 234–35, 239.
64. See *Hic Mulier* (sig. C2v): "To you . . . that are Fathers, Husbands, or

Although the concluding section of *Haec-Vir* articulates this drastic shift in perspective, it is nevertheless short, and it fails to cancel or even to qualify the dominant logic of Hic Mulier's stirring defense of her freedom, a speech that remains the focus of the second pamphlet. We are therefore left with a disjunction between the stubbornly rebellious, salient content of the second pamphlet and the conservative structure of the debate as a whole. On the one hand, the dominant content of *Haec-Vir* convincingly challenges the justice and reality of the existing sexual power structure by enumerating the illusory, sentimental, and destructive premises on which it is based. On the other, the form of the debate as a whole perpetuates the status quo by attempting to absorb this cogent demand for change into a larger movement of realigning the established society into conformity with an old ideal, a rhetorical endeavor that does not, however, entirely succeed in quelling the vigor of the opposition. As a result of this disjunction between content and form, the debate shows female independence and equality between the sexes as desirable and just, but also as impossible for a hierarchical society to absorb without unacceptable disruption.

vi

A pronounced ambivalence toward sexual equality as represented by the *Hic Mulier* figure is discernible in the *Hic Mulier/Haec-Vir* debate, then, and this attitude can be viewed in aesthetic terms as a disjunction between content and form. In *The*

Sustainers of these new *Hermaphrodites*, belongs the cure of this Impostume; it is you that give fuell to the flames of their wilde indiscretion." Cf. J. Chamberlain, in Statham, pp. 182–83: "A tax upon unruly female relatives! . . . the King threatens to fall upon theyre husbands, parents or frends that have or shold have power over them, and make them pay for it." Kent discusses (pp. 55–56) the legislative attempts in the early seventeenth century to make heads of households responsible for the conduct of wives, servants, and children, particularly for behavior in such areas as church attendance. For more on the issue of female responsibility see Marie B. Rowlands, "Recusant Women, 1560–1640," in *Women in English Society, 1500–1800*, ed. Mary Prior (London: Methuen, 1985), pp. 149–80.

Roaring Girl a similar dislocation between thematic content and dramatic form can be perceived in the representation of the title character, Moll Frith, a point to which I will return. Middleton and Dekker modeled their unusual central figure after a real-life "roaring girl," popularly known in Jacobean London as "Moll Cutpurse." As this name implies, the real Moll was an underworld figure, notorious as a thief, whore, brawler, and bawd. Much of the reliable evidence we have about her exists in the court records made after her several arrests, for offenses that included a scandalous appearance at the Fortune Theater, where *The Roaring Girl* was performed, and where she "sat . . . uppon the stage in the publique viewe of all the people there p[rese]nte in mans apparrell & playd uppon her lute & sange a songe."[65] Most of the existing criticism of *The Roaring Girl* attempts to date the play with reference to this incident.[66]

Whatever the precise connections between the events in the life of the actual Mary Frith and the performance and publication of *The Roaring Girl*, the court records show that the playwrights drew heavily on the habits and physical appearance of the real-life Moll, with her brawling, singing, and smoking, her lute, her boots, her sword, and above all, her breeches; as has been suggested, it is also probable that Middleton and Dekker were attempting to benefit from the *au courant* notoriety of the actual Moll in the timing of their play.[67] Nevertheless, in his address to the

65. Quoted in P. A. Mulholland, "The Date of *The Roaring Girl*," *Review of English Studies*, 28 (1977), 22, 30–31. See also Andor Gomme, Introduction to Thomas Middleton and Thomas Dekker, *The Roaring Girl* (London: Ernest Benn, 1976), pp. xiii–xix; and Margaret Dowling, "A Note on Moll Cutpurse—'The Roaring Girl,'" *Review of English Studies*, 10 (1934), 67–71. There is a pamphlet called *The Life and Death of Mrs. Mary Frith*, published in 1662, but it is not thought to be reliable. For a review of the play's dramatic and nondramatic sources, as well as references to the real Moll Frith, see Gomme, pp. xiii–xix; and Mulholland, pp. 18–31.

66. Mulholland, pp. 18–31, is the most recent example. Gomme, pp. xiii–xix, also sums up the attempts to date the play.

67. Mulholland, pp. 18–19. As Mulholland observes (pp. 20–21), the *Consistory of London Correction Book* record concerning Mary Frith, which he cites at length on pp. 30–31, provides an extraordinary account both of the actual Moll and of the vehement opposition in Jacobean society to women wearing male attire, which is one offense of hers that is reiterated in the *Correction Book* entry.

reader attached to the 1611 quarto, Middleton takes pains to distinguish the created character from the real person, hinting that the play will present an idealized interpretation of this odd figure: "'Tis the excellency of a writer to leave things better than he finds 'em."[68] In fact, the playwrights maintain an ambivalent attitude toward the outlaw status of their central character, in whom courageous moral and sexual principles combine with a marginal social identity, both of which are symbolized in the play by her male attire.

The address to the reader and ensuing prologue clarify immediately the controversial nature of the title character and the fact that the major dramatic and symbolic issue of the play calls for a joint creative effort by audience and playwrights to assess her identity:

> Thus her character lies—
> Yet what need characters, when to give a guess
> Is better than the person to express?
> But would you know who 'tis? Would you hear her name?
> She's called mad Moll; her life our acts proclaim.
> [Prologue, 26–30]

In their introduction of Moll Frith, the playwrights evoke themes identical to those surrounding Hic Mulier in the *Hic Mulier/Haec-Vir* debate. First, they associate Moll's male apparel with erotic appeal and illicit sexuality: "For venery, you shall find enough for sixpence, but well couched and you mark it; for Venus being a woman, passes through the play in doublet and breeches; a brave disguise and a safe one, if the statute untie not her codpiece point" ("To the Comic Play-Readers"). Second, as in *Epicoene* and in the debate, erotic questions are less preoccupying than social ones: the entire prologue attempts to assign Moll a specific class and rank, "to know what girl this roaring girl should be / For of that tribe are many" (Prologue, 15–16). While the dramatists assure us confidently that their Moll is neither criminal, brawler, whore, nor city wife, the question of her actual social status is left unanswered. As

68. Thomas Middleton, "To the Comic Play-Readers, Venery and Laughter," in Middleton and Dekker, *The Roaring Girl*. All quotations from the play, identified in the text by act, scene, and line numbers, are from Fraser and Rabkin, pp. 334–68.

the action unfolds, the playwrights' vision of the controversial "roaring girl's" exact position in the Jacobean social hierarchy gradually assumes its distinct and complicated shape; and other characters are defined as social and moral beings according to their responses to her.

The play has a traditional New Comedy plot. A young man, Sebastian Wengrave, outwits his snobbish, greedy father, Sir Alexander Wengrave, who has threatened to disinherit Sebastian if he marries the woman he loves, all because of her relatively meager dowry. The subplot involves a theme equally characteristic of the Jacobean dramatic satirist: the attempt of lazy, poor, arrogant, upper-class "gallants" to cheat and seduce the wives of middle-class shopkeepers. Like the prologue and the *Hic Mulier/Haec-Vir* debate, the main plot stresses social issues and the secondary plot focuses on erotic complications. The conservative faction in the play is most strikingly represented by the father, Sir Alexander, and the lecherous, misogynistic gallant, Laxton, whose negative attitudes toward Moll resemble those of Jonson's *Epicoene* toward women in general and of the *Hic Mulier* author's toward women in men's clothing.

Moll enters the play for the first time during the subplot, as Laxton and cohorts are busily seeking to form illicit liaisons with shopkeepers' wives, chuckling privately over their erotic cunning and prowess. In this Renaissance equivalent of the locker room, Moll, who will smoke and swear, is greeted enthusiastically by the men, although with considerably less relish by the women, one of whom screams, "Get you from my shop!" (2.1.248). Both men and women, however, associate her mannishness with deformed and illicit sexuality:

> Mrs. G. Some will not stick to say she is a man, and some, both man and woman.
>
> Lax. That were excellent: she might first cuckold the husband, and then make him do as much for the wife.
>
> [2.1.219–22]

Like the author of *Hic Mulier,* Laxton finds this mannish woman sexy ("Heart, I would give but too much money to be nibbling with that wench" [2.1.193–94]); he also automatically assumes from her unconventional sexual behavior that she is a whore: "I'll lay hard siege to her; money is that aqua fortis that eats into many a maidenhead; where the walls are flesh and blood, I'll ever pierce through with a golden augur" (2.1.203–5). Complacently, Laxton secures an assignation with Moll, to which he travels overcome with self-pleasure and a thrilling sense of his own power in arranging a forbidden encounter.

Laxton is unpleasantly surprised. In his confrontation with Moll, which takes the appropriate form of a duel, Moll emerges as a defiant champion of female freedom from male sexual dominion, a role symbolized by her male attire. Laxton arrives on the scene searching for a woman in a "shag ruff, a frieze jerkin, a short sword, and a safeguard [i.e., a petticoat]" (3.1.34–35); Moll appears instead in male clothes, the significance of which she underscores: when Laxton, who takes a few moments to recognize her, remarks, "I'll swear I knew thee not," Moll replies meaningfully, "I'll swear you did not; but you shall know me now." Laxton, who is not at all clever, mistakes this response for an erotic overture: "No, not here; we shall be spied" (3.1.58–61). Discarding subtlety as hopeless, Moll beats Laxton up while delivering a stirring oration on the sexual injustices suffered by women at the hands of arrogant, slanderous men:

> Thou'rt one of those
> That thinks each woman thy fond flexible whore . . .
> How many of our sex, by such as thou,
> Have their good thoughts paid with a blasted name
> That never deserved loosely . . .
> There is no mercy in't.
> [3.1.77–93]

Furthermore, Moll attributes female sexual vulnerability specifically to the superior social power of male seducers, which she defies:

> In thee I defy all men, their worst hates
> And their best flatteries, all their golden witchcrafts,
> With which they entangle the poor spirits of fools,
> Distressed needle-women and tradefallen wives;

Fish that must needs bite, or themselves be bitten.
Such hungry things as these may soon be took
With a worm fastened on a golden hook.
Those are the lecher's food, his prey; he watches
For quarreling wedlocks and poor shifting sisters.

[3.1.97–105]

Finally, she does not simply dwell on female victimization, but asserts positively the capacity of women for full sexual responsibility, authority, and independence:

I scorn to prostitute myself to a man,
I that can prostitute a man to me . . .
. . . She that has wit and spirit,
May scorn to live beholding to her body for meat;
Or for apparel, like your common dame,
That makes shame get her clothes to cover shame.

[3.1.116–46]

Like the sympathetic *Hic Mulier* figure in the debate, Moll takes upon herself the defense and justification of all women. Indeed Laxton's attempted violation of Moll's chastity connects her with, rather than distinguishes her from, the shopkeepers' wives, most of whom are willingly engaged in sexual collusion with the gallants when the play begins. As a result we perceive that the "man-clothed" Moll,[69] the notorious roaring girl and *Hic Mulier* figure, is actually a sexual innocent compared to the conventional middle-class wives. More important than the wives' hypocrisy, however, is their eventual reform; at the end of the play they see through the schemes of their would-be seducers and choose to reject them in favor of their husbands, just as Moll's defeat of Laxton has portended that they would. The seducing gallants, who represent illicit sexuality, therefore turn out not to constitute a real threat to the social order at all. Moll herself recognizes this fact immediately: "Oh, the gallants of these times are shallow lechers. . . . 'Tis impossible to know what woman is throughly honest, because she's ne'er thoroughly tried" (2.1.336–40).

As Moll's defeat of Laxton makes clear, free-floating, amoral

69. The phrase is from Fitz, p. 16.

eros is stripped of its socially destructive power when women decide to take responsibility for themselves. The aborted sexual encounter between Moll and Laxton also dramatizes the specious logic involved in connecting Moll's unconventional male attire automatically with whorish behavior. In their depiction of Laxton's complacence, the playwrights clearly associate lechery and misogyny with obtuse, unobservant social conformity.[70] As we have seen, the idea of mindlessly adhering to social custom is the principal target of the sympathetic *Hic Mulier* figure when she defends her freedom in the debate. In *The Roaring Girl* this theme is amplified in the main plot through the representation of the censorious attitudes and actions that Sir Alexander Wengrave takes toward Moll Frith.

In his self-righteousness, self-deception, and self-pity, Sir Alexander is all self, incapable of distinguishing his emotional attachments from virtue. Proud of what he thinks is his shrewd observation of social life, he in fact continually misapprehends the realities that confront him in his passionate effort to conform to a preconceived ideal. Sebastian recognizes that his father's vulnerability to the opinion of others exceeds even his greed, and he forms a plan to gain both his inheritance and his true love, Mary Fitzallard, by telling his father that he plans to marry Moll Frith, the outrageous roaring girl who fights, smokes, swears, and wears men's clothes. Like Laxton, Sir Alexander assumes from Moll's masculine attire that she is both a whore and a thief, who can be entrapped into stealing money, exposed, and safely removed from the proximity of his son. Like Laxton, he fails repeatedly in his assaults on her integrity.

Sir Alexander labels Moll in his tirades against her a monster (1.2.130–36; 2.2.81–83), a siren (2.1.219–20), a thief (1.2.175; 4.1.201–6; 2.2.139), and a whore (1.2.137; 2.2.160). One funny scene shows him spying on her, appalled, as her tailor fits her for breeches. Like the conservative author of *Hic Mulier*, Sir Alexander perceives in Moll's male clothing a symbol not only of perverse sexuality, but also of the inevitable disintegration of stable marital

70. Laxton expresses his general view of women in 3.2.266–69: "That wile / By which the serpent did the first woman beguile / Did ever since all women's bosoms fill; / You're apple-eaters all, deceivers still."

relations: "Hoyda, breeches? What, will he marry a monster with two trinkets [i.e., testicles]? What age is this? If the wife go in breeches, the man must wear long coats, like a fool" (2.2.81–84). At the end of the play, before a nearly reformed Sir Alexander has discovered his son's true marital intentions, Moll's urbane teasing exposes his desire to maintain rigid gender roles as a regressive anxiety:

> *Moll:* [referring to herself]. Methinks you should be proud of
>   such a daughter,
>   As good a man as your son . . .
>   You do not know the benefits I bring with me;
>   No cheat dares work upon you with thumb or knife,
>   While you've a roaring girl to your son's wife.
>   [5.2.153–62]

More than any of the specific evils he attributes to her, Sir Alexander fears Moll's conspicuousness, her unconventionality, her social aberrance; the sheer *embarrassment* of having such a daughter-in-law is equivalent to ruin. "Why, wouldst thou fain marry to be pointed at?" he asks his son. "Why, as good marry a beacon on a hill, / Which all the country fix their eyes upon, / As her thy folly dotes on" (2.2.142–46). It is Sir Alexander's shallow, malicious willingness to accept received opinion without observing for himself, his bourgeois horror of nonconformity, that moves Sebastian to a rousing defense of Moll, the clearest articulation of her honesty in the play:

> He hates unworthily that by rote contemns . . .
> Here's her worst,
> Sh'as a bold spirit that mingles with mankind,
> But nothing else comes near it; and often-times
> Through her apparel somewhat shames her birth;
> But she is loose in nothing but in mirth.
> Would all Molls were no worse!
>   [2.2.176–86]

And it is precisely this thoughtless social conformity, dramatized by his malignant intolerance of Moll, that Sir Alexander abjures at the end, thereby making possible the formation of a new comic society that will be both flexible and just:

> Forgive me; now I cast the world's eyes from me,
> And look upon thee [i.e., Moll] freely with mine own . . .
>   I'll never more
> Condemn by common voice, for that's the whore,
> That deceives man's opinion, mocks his trust,
> Cozens his love, and makes his heart unjust.
>   [5.2.244–51]

In "The Place of Laughter in Tudor and Stuart England," Keith Thomas analyzes the ways in which comedy functioned conservatively, affirming the status quo by revealing, mocking, and containing social tensions; yet, Thomas points out, "there was also a current of radical, critical laughter which, instead of reinforcing accepted norms, sought to give the world a nudge in a new direction."[71] Given the heavy emphasis that the majority of English Renaissance society placed on gender-polarized sexual decorum and subdued, modest female behavior, it is evident that, with their idealized comic portrait of the *Hic Mulier* figure Moll Frith, Dekker and Middleton were joining those who, like the author of *Haec-Vir*, were beginning to call for greater freedom for women and equality between the sexes. Serious opposition to Moll is represented in the play as mindless conformity. Not only do the playwrights decline to link Moll's freewheeling, immodest habits and appearance with perverse or dishonest behavior, they also give her ample opportunity to acquit herself from her reputation as a criminal (5.1.323–73). Furthermore, Dekker and Middleton portray as noble Moll's integrity in refusing Sebastian Wengrave's proposal of marriage, made before she knows it is only a sham to deceive his father. Like the sympathetic, eloquent *Hic Mulier* figure, Moll refuses the conventional subordination required of a wife: "I have no humor to marry. . . . I have the head now of myself, and am man enough for a woman. Marriage is but a chopping and changing, where a maiden loses one head, and has a worse i' th' place."

71. Keith Thomas, "The Place of Laughter in Tudor and Stuart England," *Times Literary Supplement*, 21 January 1977, p. 78.

(2.2.38–48). Moll's virginity represents the particular condition of independence that Carolyn Heilbrun defines as "that fierce autonomy which separates the individual from the literal history of his sexual acts":[72] "Base is that mind that kneels unto her body . . . / My spirit shall be mistress of this house / As long as I have time in't" (3.1.149–52).

How far does *The Roaring Girl* go in its sympathetic imaginative vision of sexual nonconformity, female independence, and equality between the sexes, all conditions embodied in the title character? Clearly Laxton's humorous stupidity and Sir Alexander's petty malice are no match for Moll's integrity, vitality, intelligence, and courage. Yet a more subtle countermovement in the play resists the absorption of Moll into the tolerant new society that forms in the final scene.

Far from direct disapproval, this strand of qualified feeling can be discerned as an ambiguous undercurrent in the primarily positive attitude with which Moll is regarded by Sebastian and his fiancée, Mary Fitzallard, the couple whose relationship and opinions represent the desirable social norm in the play. For example, when Sebastian reveals to Mary his scheme of pretending to court Moll, he describes the roaring girl as "a creature / so strange in quality" (1.1.100–101) that Mary could not possibly doubt his love. As noted, Sebastian provides the major defense of Moll in the play; but the defense, though eloquent and just, is delivered to his father in the course of a deception and is couched entirely in terms of existing standards of sexual decorum, the basis of which Sebastian never questions: "and often-times / Through her apparel [she] somewhat shames her birth; / But she is loose in nothing but in mirth" (2.2.183–85). Is Sebastian referring to Moll's gender, social status, or both in his reference to her birth? This point is never clarified, nor is the rather odd remark that Mary makes when Sebastian introduces her to Moll:

> *Seb.*   This is the roaring wench must do us good.
> *Mary.* No poison, sir, but serves us for some use;
>   Which is confirmed in her.
>   [4.1.148–50]

72. Carolyn G. Heilbrun, *Toward a Recognition of Androgyny* (New York: Harper & Row, Colophon, 1973), p. 39.

Furthermore, Moll herself seems to acquiesce in the view that regards her as aberrant, thereby indirectly affirming existing sexual values: when Sebastian proposes to her she responds, "A wife you know ought to be obedient, but I fear me I am too headstrong to obey. . . . You see, sir, I speak against myself" (2.2.40–41, 62). These and similar remarks are too infrequent and undeveloped to undercut the predominant theme of approval and admiration that surrounds Moll in the play; but they do qualify the potential for any radical change in sexual values implicit in full social acceptance of Moll Frith.

The play makes clear that if the stifling, malignant conformity that unjustly opposes Moll is one thing, incorporation of her into society is quite another. Full social acceptance is no more the destiny of the *Hic Mulier* figure in this play, no matter how benevolent, than it is the fate of the sympathetic Hic Mulier in the debate, no matter how reasonable, eloquent, or bold. Earlier I observed that the playwrights' ambivalence toward Moll can be discerned as a disjunction between thematic content and dramatic form. The dominant content of *The Roaring Girl* elicits but does not clarify this issue; formal analysis of the function of disguise in the play, however, makes its subtlety more readily perceptible.

Although Moll Frith wears male clothing, she makes no attempt to conceal her identity, and all the other characters know she is a woman: in short, she is not in disguise. When used simply to denote a costume, worn in a play or festival, for example, "disguise" could be used as a morally neutral term in Jacobean England. But discussions of apparel in the moral and religious literature more often use "disguise" as an inclusive, censorious term, meaning, roughly, "deformity of nature" and comprehending in the range of disapproval not only the player, but the fop, the dandy, the overdressed woman, and of course, the *Hic Mulier* figure.[73] According to this conservative mentality, the roaring girl would be in disguise; but the play rejects precisely this negative interpretation of Moll's apparel. More illuminating for present

73. See, e.g., *Hic Mulier*, sig. C3: "Doe you make it the utter losse of your fauour and bounty, to have brought into your Family, any new fashion or disguise, that might either deforme Nature, or bee an iniury to modestie." Cf. Harrison, p. 123: "You shall not see any so disguised as are my countrymen of England"; and Nashe, p. 125: "England, the players' stage of gorgeous attire,

purposes is a brief comparison between Moll and the disguised heroines of Shakespearean romantic comedy.

In contrast to Moll, who insists on being recognized as a woman, heroines like Rosalind and Viola seek to conceal their identities and to protect themselves by masquerading as men. Modern criticism has been particularly adept at recognizing the symbolic, structural, and psychological functions of these romantic disguises. On the psychological level, the male disguise allows the Shakespearean heroine the social freedom to extend her personality and expand her identity by exploring the possibilities inherent in male sexual roles.[74] This opportunity for heightened awareness and personal growth incorporates into the desirable comic society formed at the end of the play an androgynous vision, recently defined as "a psychic striving for an ideal state of personal wholeness, a microcosmic attempt to imitate a mythic macrocosm," in which "being a human being entails more than one's sex identification and attendant gender development."[75]

The romantic comic form, however, represents neither a mythical nor a revolutionary society, but a renewed traditional society, whose stability and coherence is symbolized by marriage and is based on the maintenance of traditional sexual roles.[76] It is the temporary nature of the heroine's male disguise that contains the formal solution to the potential psychological and social problems it raises: that is, the heroine gladly sheds her disguise with its accompanying freedoms at the end of the play, in order to accept

---

the ape of all nations' superfluities, the continual masquer in outlandish habiliments, great plenty-scanting calamities art thou to await, for wanton disguising thyself against kind, and digressing from the plainness of thy ancestors."

74. See Alexander Leggatt, *Shakespeare's Comedy of Love* (London: Methuen, 1974), p. 202; Helen Gardner, *"As You Like It,"* in *Modern Shakespearean Criticism: Essays on Style, Dramaturgy, and the Major Plays,* ed. Alvin B. Kernan (New York: Harcourt, Brace & World, 1970), pp. 199, 202; Helene Moglen, "Disguise and Development: The Self and Society in *Twelfth Night,"* *Literature and Psychology,* 23 (1973), 13–19; and Dusinberre, p. 257.

75. Robert Kimbrough, "Androgyny Seen through Shakespeare's Disguise," *Shakespeare Quarterly,* 33 (Spring 1982), 20, 19. Cf. Margaret Boerner Beckman, "The Figure of Rosalind in *As You Like It,"* *Shakespeare Quarterly,* 29 (Winter 1978), 44–51.

76. Cf. Gardner, pp. 190–203; and Northrop Frye, "The Argument of Comedy," in Kernan, *Modern Shakespearean Criticism,* pp. 165–73.

the customary social role of wife, thereby allowing the play's androgynous vision to remain spiritual and symbolic without awakening the audience's dissatisfaction or desire for social change.[77] Northrop Frye has shown that the resolution of comedy, which is usually erotic, is often brought about by a bisexual eros figure who, like Puck, "is in himself sexually self-contained, being in a sense both male and female, and needing no expression of love beyond himself." In Shakespeare's later comedies, this structural role is taken over by the disguised female; but when the eros figure is no longer supernatural, "his" character must break down, as Viola's does into Viola and Sebastian in *Twelfth Night*, or be superseded, as Rosalind's is by the figure of Hymen in *As You Like It*.[78] As another critic puts it, "The temporary nature of the male disguise is of course essential, since the very nature of Shakespearean comedy is to affirm that disruption is temporary, that what has turned topsy-turvy will be restored."[79]

Like Shakespearean comedy, *The Roaring Girl* concludes festively with the re-formation of a flexible and tolerant society, whose stability and integration are symbolized in marriage. But in *The Roaring Girl* the functions performed by the disguised heroine in Shakespeare are structurally divided and displaced. Moll clearly answers to much of Frye's analysis of the comic eros figure: first, with her self-imposed virginity, refusal to marry, and men's clothes, she is "in a sense both male and female" and needs "no expression of love beyond [her]self"; second, it is she who brings about the benevolent and satisfactory resolution of the action when

---

77. Cf. C. L. Barber, *Shakespeare's Festive Comedy: A Study of Dramatic Form and Its Relation to Social Custom* (Princeton, N.J.: Princeton University Press, 1959), pp. 245–47; Leggatt, *Shakespeare's Comedy of Love*, p. 211; F. H. Mares, "Viola and Other Transvestist Heroines in Shakespeare's Comedies," in *Stratford Papers on Shakespeare*, ed. B. A. W. Jackson (Hamilton, Ont.: McMaster University Library Press, 1969), pp. 96–109; and Nancy K. Hayles, "Sexual Disguise in *As You Like It* and *Twelfth Night*," *Shakespeare Survey*, 32 (1979), 63–72.

78. Northrop Frye, *A Natural Perspective* (New York: Columbia University Press, 1965), pp. 82–83.

79. Clara Claiborne Park, "As We Like It: How a Girl Can Be Smart and Still Popular," in *The Woman's Part,* ed. Carolyn Ruth Swift Lenz, Gayle Greene, and Carol Thomas Neely (Urbana: University of Illinois Press, 1980), p. 108.

she actively helps Sebastian to gain Mary. Sebastian recognizes her function as the play's eros figure when he says, "Twixt lovers' hearts she's a fit instrument / And has the art to help them to their own" (2.2.204–5). In Frye's terms, Moll is a figure in whom eros "is a condition, not a desire."[80] But unlike Puck, Moll is not supernatural; she is human and will not disappear from social life. She is neither on an odyssey toward sexual and social integration, as Rosalind and Viola are, nor can she be said to grow psychologically, happily internalizing the discovery of love and freedom in the way that they do. She has no intention of marrying, no intention of relinquishing either her outfit or the unconventional principles and behavior it represents. She therefore assumes the social and psychological freedom of the traditional disguised heroine without providing the corresponding reassurance implicit in that heroine's eventual erotic transformation. These functions are instead displaced onto Mary Fitzallard, who, disguised as a page, joyously sheds the disguise to take her place as Sebastian's wife in the final scene. Moll, on the other hand, having served as the instrument who brings about the happy ending, is nevertheless excluded from the renewed comic society of married couples that forms on the stage at the end of the play. Sir Alexander makes this clear when he defines the new society by addressing "You kind gentlewomen, whose sparkling presence / Are glories set in marriage, beams of society / For all your loves give luster to my joys" (5.2.260–62). The playwrights conclude *The Roaring Girl* with an epilogue in which they emphasize the strangeness of the fictional, and the criminality of the real, Moll Frith.

In a sense the dramatists call attention to both a structural and social ambiguity in the world of the play by refusing to conflate Moll and Mary into a single figure.[81] Because they exclude Moll from the traditional, rejuvenated society demanded by the comic form, Middleton and Dekker never quite succeed in separating her from her outlaw status, despite the approval and admiration with which they have depicted her integrity, courage, and freedom in the play. It is true that Moll herself displays nothing but a benign

---

80. Frye, *A Natural Perspective*, p. 83.

81. See Gomme, who points out (p. xxiii) that Mary and Moll have the same name, and that Moll "impersonates" Mary in the final scene "in order to complete the trick which secures Mary's happiness."

indifference toward acceptance by established society: "I pursue no pity; / Follow the law and you can cuck me, spare not; / Hang up my viol by me, and I care not" (5.2.253–55). Moll's good-natured indifference allows the predominant tone of the ending of the play to remain festive. Yet her definition of herself as antisocial (5.1.362–63) and her exclusion by others combine to render unsettling the fact that her sexual independence has left her isolated from the very social structure that her courage and vitality have done so much to enliven and renew. The question of her social identity, raised at the beginning of the play, therefore remains unresolved at the end. It is because she has helped to create a society from which she is both excluded and excludes herself that Moll's status remains unclear; insofar as it is ambiguous, marginal, and problematic, Moll's social identity can be seen as a metaphor for the changing condition of women in early modern England.

Both *The Roaring Girl* and the *Hic Mulier/Haec-Vir* debate represent the figure of the woman in men's clothing as the symbolic focus of concern about sexual freedom and equality in Jacobean society. Each text depicts this unconventional figure as attractive and virtuous, while those who regard her as socially and sexually disruptive are represented in contrast as hostile, anxious, and self-deceived. When confronting the irrationality of her enemies, the *Hic Mulier* figure emerges as the voice of reason and common sense. In both play and debate it is she who possesses imagination, insight, and courage; she who embodies the promise of freedom and even of happiness. Nevertheless, this hopeful, likable figure fails in each context to gain full social acceptance. Not only is she excluded by others, but she herself acquiesces in her own defeat: in the debate she retreats completely, surrendering to the very values she has arisen to oppose; in the play she remains pleasantly isolated from society, a lovable outlaw whose eccentricity ensures that she will not constitute a social threat. Although these formal resolutions of debate and play are both agreeably festive in tone, however, neither effort to adhere to the comic purpose of reconciling social tensions is entirely convincing. The powerfully rendered *Hic Mulier* figure continues in each case to tower over the less compelling society that endeavors unsuccessfully to absorb her; viewed in terms of aesthetic logic, the *Hic Mulier* figure becomes content that cannot (illogically) be contained by form.

With their similarly ambivalent visions of Hic Mulier and Moll Frith as necessary but disruptive, benevolent but antisocial, both the debate and the play present an image of Jacobean society as unable to absorb one of its most vital and complex creations into the existing social and sexual hierarchies. The mixed approval and exclusion of the *Hic Mulier* figure evident in artistic representation and social commentary indicate a simultaneous search for and rejection of greater flexibility in sexual values. The parallel treatments of the controversy surrounding women in men's clothing in the dramatic and moral literature therefore combine to illuminate a particularly heightened time of groping for resolutions: in both *The Roaring Girl* and the *Hic Mulier/Haec-Vir* debate, the moral ambiguity and social challenge of sexual identity and equality as they were perceived in Renaissance England stand sharply before us.

3

A Waste of Shame:
The Heroics of Marriage in
English Renaissance Tragedy

i

"The Stage is more beholding to Love, then the Life of Man," Francis Bacon asserts in a typically bald and direct observation added to his essay "Of Love" in 1625. "For as to the Stage," he continues, "*Love* is ever matter of Comedies, and now and then of Tragedies: But in Life, it doth much mischiefe: Sometimes like a *Syren*; Sometimes like a *Fury*. . . . For whosoever esteemeth too much of Amorous Affection, quitteth both *Riches* and *Wise-dome*. . . . They doe best, who, if they cannot but admit *Love*, yet make it keepe Quarter: And sever it wholly, from their serious Affaires, and Actions of life."[1] Connecting a contemptuous view of erotic love as destructive and frivolous with a negative view of the stage as illusory, by implication properly divorced, like love, from "the serious affairs and actions of life," Bacon conjoins two characteristic Renaissance conceptions of sexuality and the the-

1. Sir Francis Bacon, "Of Love," in his *The Essayes or Counsels, Civill and Moral*, ed. with introduction and commentary by Michael Kiernan (Cambridge, Mass.: Harvard University Press, 1985), pp. 31–33. As Kiernan explains (pp. vii, xix), thirteen printed editions of *The Essayes* were published during Bacon's lifetime, and he continued to revise them for almost thirty years, from 1597 to 1625. "Of Love" was first published in 1612, although the passage quoted is from the 1625 edition, the last to appear in Bacon's lifetime. Though the second and third sections I have quoted (indicated by ellipses) received little revision, the opening part of the passage (3–24, p. 31) has been substantially revised and augmented. The original read as follows: "*Love* is the argument alwaies of *Comedies*, and many times of *Tragedies*. Which sheweth well, that it is a passion generally light, and sometimes extreme." Inter-

93

ater.[2] But in remarking on the relative frequency with which love is represented in comedies ("ever"—i.e., always) and in tragedies ("now and then"), the brilliant observer of actuality has uncharacteristically erred. The history of English Renaissance drama shows that by the time Bacon revised his essay to include its analogies among love, life, and the stage, eros, with increasing and discernible frequency, had in fact become the subject of tragedy. The opening arguments in his case against love confirm that Bacon, like Renaissance literary theorists, would find eros utterly inadequate to the serious action and heroic endeavor proper to the tragic form: "You may observe, that amongst all the great and worthy Persons, (whereof the memory remaineth, either Ancient or Recent) there is not One, that hath beene transported, to the mad degree of *Love*: which shewes that great Spirits, and great Businesse doe keepe out this weake Passion."[3] Yet in Jacobean England not only the public lives, but the sexual lives of "great Spirits" are commanding the attention of tragic playwrights, and with growing frequency eros is equated with the "great Businesse" that generates a tragic action and assumes the center of the stage.[4]

Bacon's observations in fact correspond accurately to the ori-

---

estingly, Bacon's change in emphasis from "many times of Tragedies" to the later "now and then of Tragedies," reflecting an increased desire to underscore the unsuitability of love as a tragic subject, is precisely what makes his observation wrong.

2. As Jonas Barish points out in *The Antitheatrical Prejudice* (Berkeley: University of California Press, 1981), p. 66, "outbursts of antitheatrical sentiment tend to coincide with the flourishing of the theater itself." See especially his chaps. 4, 5, and 6 for accounts of antitheatricalism in the Renaissance.

3. Bacon, pp. 31–32. Bacon does go on to concede, "You must except, neverthelesse, *Marcus Antonius* the halfe Partner of the Émpire of *Rome;* and *Appius Claudius* the *Decemvir*, and Law-giver: Whereof the former, was indeed a Voluptuous Man, and Inordinate; but the latter, was an Austere, and wise man: And therefore it seemes (though rarely) that *Love* can finde entrance, not only into an open Heart; but also into a Heart well fortified; if watch be not well kept."

4. See Madeleine Doran, *Endeavors of Art: A Study of Form in Elizabethan Drama* (Madison: University of Wisconsin Press, 1954), pp. 105–11, for the best account of traditional theories of tragedy and comedy in the sixteenth century. These stem primarily from two essays: the first, "De tragoedia et comoedia," is attributed to the fourth-century grammarian Donatus; and the second, also by an early grammarian, Diomedes, appears in a miscellaneous

gins, rather than the development, of English tragedy; as such their anachronistic quality recalls the extraordinary changes that that development comprised. English Renaissance tragedy can be characterized throughout its career by a relentless scrutiny of heroic energy; but that interrogation includes a major alteration in the conception of the heroic. Rooted in the connection between tragedy and history, the Elizabethan conception that Bacon shares focuses on a heroism of public action, emphasizing the protagonist's will to power.[5] Centered on political and military struggles, tragic action consigns women, eros, and sexuality to the periphery of its concerns. In striking contrast, Jacobean plays emphasize a heroism of personal endurance, creating tragedies of private life that often focus on the consequences of corrupt or unorthodox sexuality in a dark and narrow world increasingly devoid of possibility. The prominence of women as tragic heroes and/or of eros as a tragic subject increases remarkably in Jacobean plays.

---

collection of grammatical treatises published in 1478. Doran argues that these standard accounts of the forms were widely familiar and accessible. Although narrow, schematic, and notoriously inadequate as explanations of the drama that in fact burgeoned in England, the grammarians' treatises continued to hold sway in the sixteenth century, when, as even Sidney's *Defense* makes clear, there was no well-worked-out theory or "critical treatment" of the English drama. Doran demonstrates (pp. 107–8) that, reversing the probable origins of the forms, the grammarians' theories emerge in contrast to comic theory and center on the relative status of the persons ("leaders, heroes, kings"), the subject (tragedy: "conflicts, exiles; violent death" vs. comedy: "love affairs and the seizure of maidens"), and the ending ("a change of fortune for the worse.") Interestingly, in the Renaissance "the difference in subject was taken for granted," and theoretical disputes focused primarily on the persons and the ending proper to tragedy. See also Rosalie Colie, *The Resources of Kind: Genre-Theory in the Renaissance* (Berkeley: University of California Press, 1973). Colie argues for the acknowledgment of mixed genres and inclusiveness of genre theory in the Renaissance.

5. For the emergence of tragedy from history, see Doran, pp. 112–47; J. M. R. Margeson, *The Origins of English Tragedy* (Oxford: Clarendon, 1967), p. 117; and Martin Mueller, *Children of Oedipus and Other Essays on the Imitation of Greek Tragedy, 1550–1800* (Toronto: University of Toronto Press, 1980), pp. 8, 15, 20, 25, 46, 58. Mueller argues (p. 18) that Renaissance tragedy comprises "a shift from a collective to a private vision of tragedy" and from an emphasis on the fate of the community to an emphasis on individual psychology.

In the following discussion I attempt to show that, far from creating illusions divorced in emphasis and importance from "the life of man," Jacobean tragedy participates in a process of transformation in which the private life is beginning to be assigned a prestige and centrality that Bacon either refuses or fails to apprehend.[6] By connecting the altering attitudes toward love and sexuality expressed in English Renaissance moral and religious writing to shifting conceptions of tragic heroism, this chapter explores the discursive conditions that make such a transformation possible. Just as they can in romantic comedy, two salient modes of conceptualizing women, love, and marriage can be identified in tragedy. The first, the dualistic, polarizing discourse that either idealizes or degrades women and eros and regards marriage as a necessary evil, often emerges in tragedy as an irreconcilable conflict between desire and purity, love and duty, and can be associated with a heroism of public action. The second, the more multifaceted sensibility specifically articulated in Protestant moral literature, retains much of the sexual skepticism of the former outlook while at the same time regarding marriage with great respect as the basis of an ordered society. It is this sensibility that grants women and eros the kind of importance that allows them to become primary subjects of a tragic action. By focusing on *Othello* and *The Duchess of Malfi* as particularly illuminating examples of this process, I demonstrate that Protestant sexual discourse takes tragic form as a fatal deconstruction of the contradictions and paradoxes inherent in the Protestant marriage ideal itself and can be associated with the private (often female) heroism of endurance.

This chapter also attempts to reassess the historical significance of these altering tragic conceptions of the prestige and centrality of women, eros, and marriage. Commentators frequently have

6. See Lawrence Stone, *The Family, Sex and Marriage in England, 1500–1800* (New York: Harper & Row, 1977); and Gordon J. Schochet, *Patriarchalism in Political Thought: The Authoritarian Family and Political Speculation and Attitudes, Especially in Seventeenth-Century England* (Oxford: Basil Blackwell, 1975). Schochet argues (p. 54) that although the family was an established and frequently employed category in political philosophy prior to the seventeenth century, the family was never consciously recognized as a standard category in political argument and did not acquire an overtly important status in the centuries before the Stuart period. See also Edward Shorter, *The Making of the Modern Family* (New York: Basic, 1977).

viewed the shift in emphasis toward the erotic in Jacobean tragedy as a pessimistic diminishment, expressing a lack of confidence in public life and leading to sensationalism and the decadence of the form.[7] Less concerned with moral judgment, those sympathetic to what is often termed the "tragedy of intrigue" nevertheless persist in viewing these plays as a falling-off: their insistent, exclusive emphasis on the private life, it is assumed, leaves them devoid of political significance.[8] In contrast, new historicist approaches to this problem argue forcefully for the central political significance of sexuality in Jacobean tragedy. Yet these analyses tend to treat the representation of women and eros exclusively as a metaphor for what are viewed as "larger" social and political issues, perceiving the former as an allegory (often a disguise) of and for the latter, rather than regarding politics and sexuality as analogously related but distinctively important realms of experience. Thus new historicist approaches retain a hierarchical bias in which private experience remains subordinate to (i.e., less serious than) the concerns of public life.[9] In contrast, I argue that Jacobean tragedies of love and

7. See, e.g., Una Ellis-Fermor, *The Jacobean Drama: An Interpretation* (London: Methuen, 1936); Irving Ribner, *Jacobean Tragedy: The Quest for Moral Order* (Methuen, 1936); Robert Ornstein, *The Moral Vision of Jacobean Tragedy* (Madison: University of Wisconsin Press, 1960); T. B. Tomlinson, *A Study of Elizabethan and Jacobean Tragedy* (Cambridge: Cambridge University Press, 1964); Eugene M. Waith, *Ideas of Greatness: Heroic Drama in England* (New York: Barnes & Noble, 1971), pp. 141–46; and Arthur C. Kirsch, *Jacobean Dramatic Perspectives* (Charlottesville: University Press of Virginia, 1972).

8. See, e.g., Walter Cohen, *Drama of a Nation: Public Theater in Renaissance England and Spain* (Ithaca, N.Y.: Cornell University Press, 1985), pp. 357–84. See also Doran, pp. 137, 139; Margeson, p. 84; Northrop Frye, *Fools of Time: Studies in Shakespearean Tragedy* (Toronto: University of Toronto Press, 1967), p. 61; and Paula S. Berggren, "'Womanish' Mankind: Four Jacobean Heroines," *International Journal of Women's Studies*, 1, no. 4 (1978), 349–62.

9. See, e.g., Stephen Orgel and Roy Strong, *Inigo Jones: The Theatre of the Stuart Court*, vol. 1 (London: Sotheby Park Bernet; Berkeley: University of California Press, 1973), pp. 62–63; Arthur Marotti, "'Love Is Not Love': Elizabethan Sonnet Sequences and the Social Order," *ELH*, 49 (1982), 396–428; Louis Adrian Montrose, "Celebration and Insinuation: Sir Philip Sidney and the Motives of Elizabethan Courtship," *Renaissance Drama*, N.S. 8 (1977), 3–35, and "'Shaping Fantasies': Figurations of Gender and Power in Elizabethan Culture," *Representations*, 1 (Spring 1983), 61–94; Frank

marriage bear witness to a particular historical moment when private life was beginning to be assigned as much dignity and significance as public life and to be related analogously, rather than hierarchically, to public affairs; yet, because public and private domains were simultaneously perceived as distinct, they were consequently viewed with great anxiety as being in the process of pulling apart. In its creation of a heroism of marriage, Jacobean tragedy, like much of English Renaissance sexual discourse, attempts not only to articulate this moment of separation, but also to arrest it. Viewed as a historical process (rather than a fixed product of the conscious intentions of playwrights), tragedy can be seen to represent and mourn the failure of the endeavor to prevent social, moral, and sexual change; but in naming and giving significance to a previously unrecognized process of transformation, tragic discourse also itself participates in the dissolution of a prior system of meaning.

ii

Between approximately 1620 and 1630 John Donne delivered three sermons at weddings in which he meditates at length on the nature of marriage.[10] Donne's position as the Dean of St. Pauls, which established the official authority of his pronouncements on moral and religious matters, would lend central importance to his views of marriage in any case; but his choice of subject matter, his

---

Whigham, "Sexual and Social Mobility in *The Duchess of Malfi*," *PMLA*, 100 (March 1985), 167–86, esp. n. 21, p. 184, where Whigham argues that "the Duchess's actions should not be seen as erotic (a common male reduction of women's issues) but as political"; and Margot Heinemann, *Puritanism and Theatre: Thomas Middleton and Opposition Drama under the Early Stuarts* (Cambridge: Cambridge University Press, 1980), pp. 24, 46, where Heinemann argues that the increasing emphasis on private life in Jacobean tragedy represents the playwrights' attempt to escape the censor's greater concern with political issues.

10. All quotations, identified in the text by volume, sermon, and page numbers, are from *The Sermons of John Donne*, ed. George R. Potter and Evelyn M. Simpson, 10 vols. (Berkeley: University of California Press, 1953–62).

mode of reasoning, and the very structure of his marriage sermons combine to give these documents a special relevance to the development of tragedy. The fact that he delivered them at weddings makes Donne's sermons startling, for in them he develops a consistent view of marriage as at best a necessary evil, an institution based in human inadequacy and characterized by its associations with death and sin.[11] It is not that Donne finds nothing positive to say about marriage. It is rather that he subverts any arguments he makes about the importance of the institution by developing them in unpredictably negative ways, by undermining his praise with contradictions, or by changing the subject entirely.

Unlike that of the Puritans, Donne's style is scholastic, not only in its concentration on precise textual exegesis, but in its frame of reference, selection of issues, and citation of authority. Rather than relying, as the Puritans do, on Saint Paul and (often) the Old Testament, Donne builds his case on patristic insights, the wisdom of Tertullian, Ambrose, and Jerome. It is interesting to note his anachronistic preoccupation with celibacy. "There is no man nowe so dull, as to thynke that it is synne to marry," the reformer Heinrich Bullinger had observed confidently in 1543, dismissing the issue altogether as obsolete.[12] Yet in the 1620s we find Donne still preoccupied with defending a change in sexual values long accepted in the mainstream of Protestant marital discourse. "We depart absolutely from those old Heretiks who did absolutely condemn Mariage," he declares stoutly in 1627, "and wee must have leave too, (*which we are alwaies loath to doe* [my italics]) to depart from the rigidness of some of those blessed *Fathers* of the *Primitive Church*, who found some necessities in their times, to speak so very highly in praise of Continency and Chastity" (8.3.102). Donne's rhetorical dependence on patristic authority, as well as his belated

11. In their edition of the sermons Potter and Simpson point out (vol. 1, pp. 47–48) that many of Donne's published sermons probably are not as they were when he preached them. Most of them were delivered from notes, with the expectation that they would later be revised and polished for publication. No amount of polishing, however, would be likely to alter substantially the intense and persistent negativity about marriage that is expressed in these three sermons.

12. Heinrich Bullinger, *The golden boke of christen matrimonye*, trans. Miles Coverdale, with a preface by Thomas Becon (London, 1543), chap. 3.

need to join issue with celibacy in the first place, render this assertion dubious. "When men have made vows to abstain from mariage, I would they would be content to try a little longer then they doe, whether they could keep that vow or no; and when men have consecrated themselves to the service of God in his Church, I would they would be content to try a little farther then they doe, whether they could abstain or no," he remarks wistfully (3.11.243). [13] Donne's lingering, if reluctant, attachment to celibacy stems from the tacitly and subtly reiterated belief that sexual desire is evil; although this idea is present to some extent in many Protestant sermons, including those that are most idealistic about marriage, Donne's hostility toward eros differs in degree and intensity. [14] Most Puritan preachers stress the dangers of sexual immoderation, even within marriage. But Donne regards desire as the inherently dangerous product of sin: "The Devil hath advan-

13. Cf. "An Epistle to perswade a yong Gentleman to Mariage, devised by Erasmus in the behalfe of his frende," in Thomas Wilson, *The Arte of Rhetorique* (1580), pp. 40–64. Erasmus goes on quite a diatribe against celibacy, asking (p. 61), "Doe we praise so muche virginitie above all other? Why manne, there will bee neither single men, nor virgines alive, if menne leave to marrie, and mynde not procreation. Why doe you then preferre virginitie so muche . . . if it bee the undoing of all the whole worlde?" The argument is of course familiar from many sources, particularly Shakespeare's sonnets. But Erasmus is witty and vehement, clearly feeling that he must defend against the traditional prestige of celibacy: "Let the Swarmes of Monkes and Nunnes set forthe their order never so much, let them boaste and bragge their bealies full . . . yet is Wedlocke (beeying well and truely kepte) a moste holie kinde of life" (p. 52). Interestingly, by the time Donne was writing, such a defense had become completely unnecessary.

14. Cf. Stephen Greenblatt, *Renaissance Self-Fashioning: From More to Shakespeare* (Chicago: University of Chicago Press, 1980), pp. 241–52. Again Erasmus provides an interesting contrast by insisting (pp. 50–51) that sex was instituted in Paradise before sin: "We make that filthie by our owne imagination, whiche of the owne Nature is good and godlie . . . how chanceth it, that we thinke it lesse filthie to eate, to chewe, to digest, to emptie the bodie and to slepe, then it is to use carnall Copulation, suche as is lawfull and permitted?" Cf. Michaell de Montaigne, "Upon some verses of Virgil," in *The Essayes*, trans. John Florio (London, 1603), bk. 3, pp. 508–9: "Why was the acte of generation made so naturall, so necessary and so ivst, seeing we feare to speake of it without shame, & exclude it from our serious and reguler discourses? We pronounce boldly, to rob, to murther, to betray; and this we dare not but betweene our teeth."

tages enow against us, in bringing men and women together"
(3.11.242).

Not surprisingly, Donne's attachment to patristic sexual values
also includes an unmitigated misogyny. In the sermon preached at
Sir Francis Nethersole's marriage (1619/20), Donne spends the
majority of his time lecturing "the other sexe" on their inferiority:
"that they will be content . . . to be remembred that *they are the
weaker vessell,* and *that Adam was not deceived* but *the woman was.* . . .
Take it any way, and it implies a weaknesse in the woman, and an
occasion of soupling her to that just estimation of herself, *That she
will be content to learn in silence with all subjection*" (2.17.344–45).
Like Vives, Donne sees women's purpose not as *doing* anything,
performing any action ("for such vertues as may be had, and yet
the possessor not the better for them, as *wit, learning, eloquence,
musick, memory, cunning,* and such, these make her never the fitter"
[2.17.346]), but rather as *being* chaste ("for without that, *Matri-
monium jurato fornicatio,* Mariage is but a continuall fornication,
sealed with an oath" [2.17.346]).[15]

"Mariage is but a continuall fornication, sealed with an oath." A
glance at the devious way in which Donne develops his arguments
about marriage, changing the subject and subverting his own
praise, justifies the conclusion that this pithy reflection sums up his
predominant view of that institution. That marriage should be
rooted in the companionship between husband and wife, or that its
organization should resemble that of the nation-state and the
church, drawing together by means of analogy the family and the
social and spiritual orders, are two arguments that had been developed elaborately in Protestant sexual discourse for decades. But
Donne glances at the idea of marital companionship only in order

15. Cf. John Louis Vives, *Instruction of a christen woman,* trans. Richard
Hyrde, (1529; rpt. London, 1557), "Of the kepyng of virginitee and
chastitee": "For as for a man nedeth manye thynges, as wisdome, eloquence,
knowledge of things, with remembraunce, some crafte to lyue by, Justice,
Lyberalytee, lustye stomacke, and other thynges moe . . . but in a woman no
manne wyll loke for eloquence, greate wytte, or prudence, or crafte to lyve
by, or orderynge of the commen weale, or justice or lyberalitee: finally no
man wyll loke for any other thinge of a woman, but hir honestee . . . for in a
woman the honestee is in stede of all. . . . Take frome a woman hir beauty,
take from hir kynred, riches comelynes, eloquence, sharpenes of witte, coun-
nynge in hir crafte: geue hir chastitee, and thou haste geuen hir all thynges."

to dismiss it (see 2.17.346). And he introduces the concept of public and private domains not to relate them analogously, granting each domain its importance, but rather to subordinate one to the other in a hierarchy of relative spiritual value. In a curious twist on traditional Protestant arguments, he concedes that the family is the basis of the kingdom and the church; but, he insists, only "in regard of the *publique* good, God pretermits private respects," by which he means that the sole purpose of marriage is procreation and the perpetuation of society. Otherwise, "man might have done well enough in that state, so, as his *solitarinesse* might have been supplied with a farther creation of more men . . . might not man have been abundantly rich in friends, without this addition of a woman? . . . how much more conveniently might two friends live together, then a man and a woman?" (2.17.336–39).

Even more surprising than Donne's evasive dismissal of passionately valued and elaborately developed beliefs is his striking lack of interest in the relationship of marriage. As we will see, the Puritans devote abundant energy to constituting and examining this relationship, imagining in detail the probable pitfalls and possible joys of the interaction between husband and wife, and providing copious lists of roles, duties, and remedies for marital conduct.[16] In contrast, Donne changes the subject of the daily drama of marriage as soon as he can. He argues that Christian marriage is distinguished not by its emphasis on companionship, but by its status as a sacred mystery. Denying that marriage is a sacrament, as every Protestant was compelled to do, Donne nevertheless succeeds in restoring its sacramental quality in the conclusion of the very paragraph containing his denial (8.3.103–4). Similarly, having stated in the same text that the purpose of a marriage sermon is to dwell upon the couple, "the *parties* that are to be united," he has (again by the end of the paragraph) found reasons to avoid this focus, with its emphases on individual conduct and relevance to daily life. "I shall the lesse need to apply my selfe *to them*, for their particular instructions, but may have leave to extend my selfe upon con-

---

16. See Michel Foucault, *The History of Sexuality*, vol. 1: *An Introduction* (New York: Pantheon, 1978), pp. 3–17 and passim. Foucault dates from the seventeenth century what he terms (p. 22) "the great process of transforming sex into discourse."

siderations more general" (8.3.95–96), he says, and he moves quickly to his real—and decidedly otherworldly—concerns. The relationship, as opposed to the institution, of marriage, then, is for Donne of peripheral interest and importance.

Donne's views of marriage are articulated with the greatest concision and intensity in "A Sermon Preached At the Earl of Bridgewater's house in London at the mariage of his daughter, the Lady Mary, to the eldest sonne of the Lord Herbert of Castleiland" (1627). Most startling, particularly if one imagines being the bride or groom on such an occasion, is the text Donne chose to explore before this aristocratic gathering: "For, in the Ressurection, they Neither Mary Nor Are Given In Mariage, But Are As The Angels Of God in Heaven" (Matt. 22:30).[17] After dismissing the couple, as we have seen, Donne goes on to develop a compelling case against marriage as a lesser evil, for which angels after the Resurrection have transcended the need: "*Till then we must not look for this Angellical state*, but, as in all other states and conditions of life, so in all mariages there will be some encumbrances, betwixt all maried persons, there will arise some unkindnesses, some misinterpretations: . . . Then they mary not, till then they may; then their state shall be perfect as the Angels, till then it shall not" (8.3.97). In this sermon Donne, not tacitly and implicitly but clearly and completely, attributes the inevitable, because human, inferiority of marriage to its origins in sin and death. Referring again to resurrected angels, he explains:

> They shall not mary, because they shall have none of the uses of mariage; not as mariage is *physicke* against inordinate affections; for, every soule shall be a Consort in itselfe, and never out of tune: not as mariage is ordained for *mutuall helpe* of one another; for God himself shall be intirely in every soul; And what can that soul lack, that hath all God? Not as mariage is a *second* and a *suppletory eternity*, in the continuation and propagation of Chil-

17. Cf. Luke 20:34–36: "And Jesus answering said unto them, The children of this world marry, and are given in marriage: But they which shall be accounted worthy to obtain that world, and the resurrection from the dead, neither marry, nor are given in marriage: Neither can they die any more: for they are equal unto the angels: and are the children of God, being the children of the resurrection."

dren; for they shall have the first *Eternity*, individuall eternity in themselves. Therefore does S. *Luke* assigne that reason why they shall not mary, *Because they cannot dy.*

[8.3.99]

In this extraordinary passage Donne one by one discards the traditional purposes of marriage articulated in the Elizabethan *Book of Common Prayer* in 1549: the legitimation of desire, the procreation of children, and mutual companionship. The best one can say about marriage, it seems, is that in heaven it will not exist. Is this the John Donne who risked career, reputation, and solvency to marry for love?[18] Actually, the connection is not surprising; to a man so passionately obsessed with the body as was Donne, sexuality must have appeared first as an overwhelming, later as a dangerous force, associated with suffering and the destruction of hopes.[19] Donne's stress on desire as human inadequacy, originating in sin and leading to death, his emphasis on the inevitability of this process and the simultaneous need to transcend it ("till then we must not look for this Angellical state"), and his preoccupation with individual self-sufficiency and isolation ("for God himself shall be intirely in every soul; And what can that soul lack, that hath all God?") all clarify the tragic nature of his conception of eros and marriage and its consequent relevance to the representation of sexuality in Renaissance drama.[20]

Earlier I observed that the sexual values Donne expresses in the 1620s were anachronistic in their departure from what had been for decades accepted Protestant emphases and concerns.[21] The dis-

18. See John Carey, *John Donne: Life, Mind and Art* (London: Faber & Faber, 1981), pp. 71–76, for a discussion of Donne's marriage.

19. Donne's special preoccupation with the resurrection of the body is well known. A good example of his vivid imagining of the body's destiny in his marriage sermons appears in 8.3.98: "But the Resurrection of the *Body* is discernible by no other light, but that of *Faith*, nor could be fixed by any lesse assurance then an *Article* of the *Creed*. Where be all the splinters of that Bone, which a shot hath shivered and scattered in the Ayre? Where be all the Atoms of that flesh, which a *Corrasive* hath eat away, or a *Consumption* hath breath'd, and exhal'd away from our arms, and other Limbs?"

20. The conception of desire as lack of course both precedes Donne and follows him as well, receiving a thorough theoretical formulation in twentieth-century psychoanalytic discourse, particularly in Freud and Lacan.

21. In *The Development of the Family and Marriage in Europe* (Cambridge:

placement of one sexual discourse by another is an important process to which I will return later in this chapter. Here it will suffice to observe that Donne's marriage sermons present an example of the way in which one discourse never wholly superseded another, but rather absorbed and transformed it. The public importance of Donne's position (along with his superior eloquence) can serve to recall that his sexual sensibility still counted as a significant factor in the early seventeenth-century formation of marriage. Nevertheless, the dramatic representation of that sensibility is at its most commanding and pristine in Elizabethan, rather than in Jacobean, tragedy.

In creating *Tamburlaine* (1587), a shocking and revolutionary play, Marlowe treats sexuality with recognizable conservatism.[22] As is well known, one of Marlowe's brilliant innovations consists in endowing his warrior-hero with an aesthetic dimension, which adds to the complexity of his character; Tamburlaine's superb eloquence and sensitivity to beauty and desire are what prevent him from becoming a mindless and mediocre gangster. As Eugene Waith has pointed out, "the inclusion in [Tamburlaine's] nature of the capacity to love is a characteristic Renaissance addition to the classical model of the Herculean hero."[23] Unlike many Renaissance portrayals of soldiers, *Tamburlaine* does not at first appear obsessively misogynistic. As many critics have observed, the slaughter of the Damascus virgins (I.5.1)[24] is among the hero's most heinous deeds; but in his personal relation with his love, Zenocrate, Tamburlaine is caught up in adoration, rather than in active hatred, of eros:

> Zenocrate, the loveliest maid alive,
> Fairer than rocks of pearl and precious stone,

Cambridge University Press, 1983), Jack Goody traces the origins of Protestant sexual ideology back far beyond the Reformation. As I explain later in this chapter, however, I am interested in the present study not so much in the origins of these values as in the way they were grouped together and the degree to which they were emphasized in Tudor and Stuart England.

22. Cf. G. K. Hunter, "The Beginnings of Elizabethan Drama: Revolution and Continuity," *Renaissance Drama*, N.S. 17 (1986), 29–52.

23. Eugene M. Waith, "Tamburlaine," in *Marlowe: A Collection of Critical Essays*, ed. Clifford Leech (Englewood Cliffs, N.J.: Prentice-Hall, 1964), p. 77.

24. All *Tamburlaine* references identified in the text by part, act, scene, and

The only paragon of Tamburlaine,
Whose eyes are brighter than the lamps of heaven,
And speech more pleasant than sweet harmony!
[I.3.3.117–21]

It is true that he wins Zenocrate by kidnapping and raping her, a little-noticed fact that associates him with Truewit in *Epicoene*.[25] Unlike Ben Jonson, Marlowe recognizes that this method of courtship might be considered problematic; like Ben Jonson, however, he decides that women would probably have liked it and that Zenocrate must have been pleased. Marlowe confronts the situation by having one of Zenocrate's courtiers, Agydas, bring up the awful event. Agydas, who cannot understand her complaisance, receives the following response from the kidnapped, raped princess:

> *Agyd.* 'Tis more than pity such a heavenly face
> Should by heart's sorrow wax so wan and pale,
> When your offensive rape by Tamburlaine,
> (Which of your whole displeasures should be most),
> Hath seemed to be digested long ago.
> *Zenoc.* Although it be digested long ago,
> As his exceeding favors have deserved,
> And might content the Queen of heaven, as well
> As it hath changed my first conceived disdain.
> [I.3.2.5–12]

Zenocrate's acceptance of her rape, then, comprises a revision of past disdain. It is not surprising that Tamburlaine's worship of Zenocrate should rest on a foundation of hostility and violence: as is shown repeatedly throughout this book, whatever may be the relative emphasis of each component, the extreme elements coex-

---

line numbers, are to *Drama of the English Renaissance*, vol. 1: *The Tudor Period* ed. Russell A. Fraser and Norman Rabkin (New York: Macmillan, 1976), pp. 207–61.

25. Although it may very well be remarked upon somewhere, I have not yet encountered any discussion of the fact that Tamburlaine "wins" Zenocrate by raping her. In contrast, most scholars, like Joel Altman in *The Tudor Play of Mind: Rhetorical Inquiry and the Development of Elizabethan Drama* (Berkeley: University of California Press, 1978), p. 329, emphasize Tamburlaine as "a tender suitor" to Zenocrate.

ist, forming an intractable partnership in a dualizing mentality that either degrades women and eros on the one hand or idealizes them on the other.[26] In *Tamburlaine* we can witness this sensibility in the dramatic process of its formation and can perceive its connection with tragic heroism.

Tamburlaine comes to terms with his sexual desire in the only soliloquy—the one private moment—in either part of the play (I.5.1.100–190). Like Donne, Marlowe makes a very clear distinction between private and public domains. Indeed, Tamburlaine's problem with eros consists in his need to reconcile what he perceives as conflicting claims: the dramatic conflict is construed in terms of an inevitable antagonism between love and duty. Specifically, when Zenocrate begs Tamburlaine to refrain from savaging her country and murdering her father, he agrees to save her father but immediately refuses to call off his slaughter and conquest of the remaining territory and population, explaining, "Were Egypt Jove's own Land, / Yet would I with my sword make Jove to stoop" (I.4.4.78–79). In his later soliloquy, however, Tamburlaine acknowledges for the first and only time in his career that he has experienced some conflict about this situation:

> A doubtful battle with my tempted thoughts
> For Egypt's freedom, and the Soldan's life;
> His life that so consumes Zenocrate,
> Whose sorrows lay more siege unto my soul,
> Than all my army to Damascus' walls:
> And neither Persia's sovereign, nor the Turk
> Troubled my senses with conceit of foil
> So much by much as doth Zenocrate.
> [I.5.1.152–58]

In his love for Zenocrate, then, Tamburlaine recognizes the dangerous potential for the defeat of his heroic military ambitions. His

26. Cf. Theseus to Hippolyta in Act 1, Scene 1, of *A Midsummer Night's Dream* (ll.17–18): "I wooed thee with my sword / And won thy love doing thee injuries," in the edition by Louis B. Wright and Virginia A. LaMar, Folger Library General Reader's Shakespeare (New York: Washington Square, 1958); and Madelon Gohlke, "'I wooed thee with my sword': Shakespeare's Tragic Paradigms," in *Representing Shakespeare: New Psychoanalytic Essays*, ed. Murray M. Schwartz and Coppélia Kahn (Baltimore, Md.: Johns Hopkins University Press, 1980), pp. 170–87.

immediate, defensive reaction is to abstract from the individual and personal, to move rhetorically, as Donne does, to "considerations more general." "What is beauty, saith my sufferings then?" (I.3.1.160), he ponders, setting up the problem in broad aesthetic terms in an effort to find a "solution" to his potentially disruptive love for his wife. In a second variation on this movement, the warrior who conquers the world through his transforming eloquence acknowledges in one uncharacteristically vulnerable moment the inexpressibility of beauty ("One thought, one grace, one wonder, at the least, / Which into words no virtue can digest" [I.5.1.172–73]); yet he retreats immediately from the possible domestic consequences of this insight, stoutly declaring its inappropriateness to heroic endeavor: "But how unseemly is it for my sex, / My discipline of arms and chivalry, / My nature, and the terror of my name, / To harbor thoughts effeminate and faint!" (I.5.1.174–77). Tamburlaine's solution to the dilemma he perceives is to bring beauty into the service of heroism by the repression of desire: "And every warrior that is rapt with love / Of fame, of valor, and of victory, / Must needs have beauty beat on his conceits: / I thus conceiving and subduing both . . . " (I.5.1.180–83). It is the same solution proposed by Bacon with brittle and prosaic force: "They doe best, who, if they cannot but admit *Love*, yet make it keepe Quarter." Tamburlaine is able to conclude his soliloquy by returning to the—now psychologically unimpeded— issue of military glory.

Tamburlaine's repression of sexuality takes the form not of total denial (he is "conceiving and subduing" *both*), but of the segregation of eros into a separate and unequal realm. It is the solution of the medieval chivalric warrior-hero, the knight.[27] The effects of such a procedure are strikingly evident in Marlowe's conception of Zenocrate. Along with enhancing Tamburlaine's status by loving him and helping to define and sharpen the nature of his heroism by presenting a potentially opposing psychological principle that must be overcome, Zenocrate's other function in the play (stemming from those already mentioned) is to add a moral dimension completely absent in the hero himself that at least partially qualifies his magnificence. As Tamburlaine's slaughters increase and multi-

27. Cf. Waith, *Ideas of Greatness*, p. 148.

ply throughout Parts I and II (including the murder of one of his own sons, who, like his mother, dislikes carnage), Zenocrate's antiwar, anticruelty sentiments assume more rhetorical conviction in the play (e.g., in II.1.3). Yet—and this is the crucial point— while she adds a moral and symbolic emphasis to the play, affecting its tone, Zenocrate has no dramatic power. She is incapable of engendering any action.[28] She is unable to deter Tamburlaine from undertaking the bloody siege of Egypt or Damascus, a failure to restrain her husband that continues into the second part of the play. Just as in Donne's marriage sermons eros and women become peripheral, removed from the enactment of serious concerns, so in *Tamburlaine* the nature of the hero's repression of sexual desire ensures that Zenocrate's values and the feelings she engenders will remain crucial but marginal; symbolically powerful but dramatically ineffectual, lame. Thus Zenocrate functions not as a dramatic subject, generating action, but as an object of Tamburlaine's desire and contemplation; consequently, her role is a static and decorative one, to "sit up, and rest thee like a lovely queen" (II.1.3.16). Tamburlaine's tendency to aestheticize Zenocrate, to construe her as a beautiful object, is evident from a very early point in the play (e.g., I.3.3.118–21); that her final appearance in Part II is as a portrait decorating the coffin that contains her corpse—no matter how bizarre—merely constitutes the final step in Tamburlaine's project of preserving her permanently by rendering her immobile, freezing her in time.

Tamburlaine's idealization of Zenocrate therefore becomes a devious tribute: it is precisely because she is so powerful that she must be rendered static, inert. But the play makes clear that the constituting of Zenocrate as a monument is both necessary and heroic. For it is Zenocrate (or Tamburlaine's conception of her, which, I am arguing, is the same thing) who brings death into Tamburlaine's world and all his woe. As we have seen, Tamburlaine's desire for Zenocrate causes his only moment of internal conflict in the play. It is perfectly clear to him, in contrast, that he should murder his weakling son. And despite the fatal havoc Tam-

---

28. For contrasting views of Zenocrate's function and effectiveness in the play, cf. Altman, esp. pp. 333–36; and Richard A. Martin, "Marlowe's *Tamburlaine* and the Language of Romance," *PMLA*, 93 (March 1978), 248–64.

burlaine wreaks upon the world, the death of Zenocrate becomes his first actual experience (i.e., recognition) of mortality, introducing the final movement of Part II, in which the hero faces his only defeat in the form of his own death. It should be stressed that in examining Zenocrate's role in Tamburlaine's destiny, I am not arguing in terms of moral sympathy; as we have seen, Zenocrate's presence in the play symbolically enhances the hero and commands a significant quotient of sympathy, as well as respect. My concern, however, is with modes of conceptualization and the formation of belief, discernible not in terms of audience response but in terms of dramatic structure. Seen from this vantage point, Zenocrate's dramatic (as distinct from her symbolic) role is to oppose Tamburlaine's heroism and present a prologue to his doom. Like Donne constructing a marriage sermon, Marlowe constructing a tragic action construes the relationship between sexuality and death as one of (symptomatic) cause and (inevitable) effect, requiring heroic resistance in order to be transcended and overcome.[29]

iii

I hope by now it is apparent that a sensibility which views the nearly absolute repression of desire as necessary for the fulfillment of social and political obligation, requiring that eros be severed from the "serious affairs and actions of life," precludes the possibility of love as the central subject of tragedy in the Renaissance and entails by definition a dissociation between heroism and the private life. Marlowe's *Dido, Queen of Carthage*, probably written with Thomas Nashe in the same year as Tamburlaine (c. 1587), presents a final illustration of this point.

As Renaissance poets adapted it from Virgil, the legend of Dido and Aeneas is the classic Western allegory of civilization and its discontents. The hero's repression of erotic passion in pious, if sorrowful, submission to public duty and obligation creates the

29. Cf. Gohlke; and Madelon [Gohlke] Sprengnether, "Annihilating Intimacy in *Coriolanus*," in *Women in the Middle Ages and the Renaissance: Literary and Historical Perspectives*, ed. Mary Beth Rose (Syracuse, N.Y.: Syracuse University Press, 1986), pp. 89–111. See also my analysis of Lyly's heroes in Chapter 1.

female martyr to love.[30] During the Renaissance, however commentators viewed Dido, Aeneas was a favorite hero, adding an
inward moral and religious dimension to the Homeric military
drive toward conquest and glory.[31] Thus it becomes particularly
interesting that, in their attempt to represent the Dido legend as
tragic, Marlowe and Nashe succeed only in rendering it degrading
and ridiculous. Their conflicted Aeneas is weak, self-pitying, and
ambivalent (2.1; 5.1);[32] their Dido, imperious, fickle, and
capricious (4.4). Neither is courageous; both are the pettiest of liars
(e.g., 3.4 and 4.4). The characters and subplots Marlowe and
Nashe add also function to subvert the dignity of the principal
characters and undermine the importance of their love. For example, the loyal Anna, pursuing Dido's disappointed suitor, Iarbas, is
transformed to Dido's rival in love; and the playwrights include
comic scenes that steal the show by reminding the audience of the
predominantly grotesque and anarchic properties of desire. Providing a gloss on the humiliating relationship of Dido and Aeneas,
Act 4 ends when a withered crone falls in love with a boy (Cupid,
of course, disguised as Aeneas's son Ascanius). "My veins are
wither'd and my sinews dry; / Why do I think of love, now I
should die?" she moralizes (4.4.33–34). The play concludes with
the triple suicide of Dido, Anna, and Iarbas, detracting from the
potentially noble and traditionally solitary passion of the queen and
focusing instead on the self-destructive communal disasters engendered by sexual desire.

Thus while *Dido, Queen of Carthage* includes some of the characteristically idealizing love themes (e.g., transformation and self-
sacrifice), Marlowe and Nashe simply cannot take these issues se-

30. See D. C. Allen, "Marlowe's Dido and the Tradition," in *Essays on
Shakespeare and Elizabethan Drama in Honour of Hardin Craig*, ed. Richard
Hosley (Columbia: University of Missouri Press, 1962), pp. 55–68; and
Mueller, esp. pp. 230–48. Mueller points out (p. 233) that in Virgil, "the
tragedy of Dido is based on a separation of public and private values that is
unknown in Greek tragedy."

31. See Reuben A. Brower, *Hero and Saint: Shakespeare and the Graeco-
Roman Heroic Tradition* (New York: Oxford University Press, 1971), pp. 55–
58.

32. All citations and quotations identified in the text by act, scene, and line
numbers, are from *The Tragedie of Dido Queene of Carthage*, ed. H. J. Oliver
(Cambridge, Mass.: Harvard University Press, 1968).

riously enough to grant them the stature and centrality of a tragic subject. Just as Donne's sermons construe eros as potentially dangerous, unavoidably imperfect and humiliating, but also as irrelevant and peripheral to humanity's transcendent, heavenly destiny, so the dramatists' *Dido* represents love as anarchic and self-destructive, but also as frivolous and absurd. The whimsical Ovidian prologue, in which eros is introduced in the form of Jupiter's capricious dalliance with Ganymede, is by no means irrelevant, as some scholars have argued, but consistent with the representation of eros throughout the play.[33] Some scholars have noticed the similarity of this play to the brittle, charming, and misogynistic comedies of Lyly, which, as we have seen, also deny the seriousness and dignity of desire.[34] Far from being a critique of heroic energy, then, Marlowe's *Dido* avoids any treatment of the heroic and clarifies instead the dissociation between public heroism and private life.

Although sexual desire in *Tamburlaine* is idealized and exalted, it is also rendered dramatically inert, consigned to subordinate status, and viewed as potentially destructive of public enterprise. As Eugene Waith observes, one of the major properties of Tamburlaine's heroism, like that of Castiglione's ideal courtier and the chivalric warrior-knight, is his ability to treat "beauty as the handmaid of valour." Waith argues that in *Tamburlaine* Marlowe provides "the definition of a hero." Transcending his Scythian-shepherd origins, Tamburlaine, a type of Hercules, adds to "the intrinsic kingliness of the hero, associated with the ideal of freedom" a magnificent physical stature, towering wrath and cruelty, inflexible will, incomparable, transforming rhetorical power, delicate, idealizing aesthetic sensitivity conjoined with the ability to love, and uncompromising valor, ambition, and pride: "he does not belong entirely to either earth or heaven." While stressing Tamburlaine's "incorporeal spirit," Waith does not deny either "the tensions between his egotism and altruism, his cruelties and benefactions, his human limitations and his divine potentialities"

---

33. See, e.g., *The Tragedie of Dido Queene of Carthage*, p. 4, nn. 1–2. Brower comments at length (pp. 120–41) on the Elizabethan use of Ovidian material specifically as a denial of the heroic mode.

34. Cf. Allen, p. 64; and my analysis of Lyly's plays, above.

or his enactment of the tragic hero's characteristic "collaboration with death and fate in the destruction of his physical being."[35]

Tamburlaine, then, is the complete hero of Renaissance humanist idealism, combining military proficiency with rhetorical ability and devoting himself to public action. Indeed, his lowly origins, conjoined with his transforming eloquence, connect him optimistically and confidently with the increasing social mobility of the sixteenth century, when education and verbal skill were rapidly becoming as important to advancement in the bureaucratic nation-state as aristocratic birth and military competence.[36] Yet Tamburlaine's heroism, like Elizabethan social mobility, contains its own implicit obsolescence. Although they remained greatly indebted to *Tamburlaine*, exploiting and refining many aspects of the play, English Renaissance tragic dramatists—including Marlowe himself in subsequent plays—never sought to duplicate the conjunction of military competence with the ability to engage and suppress the private life that constitutes Tamburlaine's greatness.[37] The happy combination of transcending birth, demonstrating prowess, and cultivating repression apparently seemed more appropriate to the transient figures of history—Henry V, for example, who manages to escape the taint of his father's usurpation. In contrast, tragic playwrights increasingly insisted on the importance of the private life, weighing its fatal demands and scrutinizing the price, even the whole idea, of public success.[38] Referring specifically to Chapman and Shakespeare, Reuben A. Brower describes this shift in the tragic sensibility: "Both English writers share the tendency to replace physical by moral heroism, to make

35. Waith, "Tamburlaine," pp. 78, 70, 74, and passim. See also Harry Levin, *The Overreacher: A Study of Christopher Marlowe* (Cambridge, Mass.: Harvard University Press, 1952). For the complicity of the tragic hero with death, see Frye, esp. pp. 3–9, 33, 39.

36. See Frank Whigham, *Ambition and Privilege: The Social Tropes of Elizabethan Courtesy Theory* (Berkeley: University of California Press, 1984), pp. 12–18 and passim; Maurice Keen, *Chivalry* (New Haven, Conn.: Yale University Press, 1984), esp. pp. 238–53; and Lawrence Stone, "Social Mobility in England, 1500–1700," *Past and Present*, 33 (1966), 16–55.

37. Cf. Hunter.

38. See G. K. Hunter, "The Heroism of *Hamlet*," in *Hamlet,* Stratford-upon-Avon Studies, no. 5, ed. J. R. Brown and B. Harris (London: Edward Arnold, 1963), pp. 90–109, esp. p. 96.

the great battle the inner one of the soul or of reason against passion, to regard the heroic career as humane education or as a tragic failure to achieve it. The increased self-consciousness of Chapman's heroes as compared with Homer's, their penchant for reflection and meditative analysis is equally typical of the heroes of Shakespeare. . . . This image, combining the ancient heroic ethos with the Renaissance ideal of passion governed by reason, had immense possibilities for a practising dramatist."[39] It is in the dramatists' increasing concern for "the private life of the soul," rather than horrors, madness, and revenge, that Brower locates the major influence of Seneca on Renaissance tragic heroism,[40] "a version of heroism," G. K. Hunter adds in a discussion of *Hamlet*, "which depends less upon acting or even upon knowing than upon *being* . . . *Hamlet* represents an enormous and convulsive effort to move forward to the heroism of the individual, without abandoning the older social and religious framework of external action."[41]

Transforming conceptions of tragic heroism inevitably generated a shift in emphasis in the representation of heroic qualities. Specifically, a dramatic focus on physical action and self-assertion diminished, and the exploration of heroic endurance, self-denial, and suffering increased. This shift was in turn accompanied by a greater emphasis on the private life. It is often argued that Shakespearean tragic heroes combine in their dramatic identities both action and suffering, internalized victor and victim.[42] Yet scholars have also tended to polarize these conceptions of tragic action as opposed, viewing the emphasis on suffering and endurance in the latter dynamic as leading away from the idea of the heroic, which

39. Brower, pp. 80–81.

40. Brower, p. 168. See also G. K. Hunter, "Seneca and the Elizabethans: A Case Study in 'Influence,'" pp. 159–73, and "Seneca and English Tragedy," pp. 174–213, both in his *Dramatic Identities and Cultural Tradition: Studies in Shakespeare and His Contemporaries* (Liverpool: Liverpool University Press, 1978); and T. S. Eliot, "Seneca in Elizabethan Translation," in his *Selected Essays* (London: Faber & Faber, 1932), pp. 65–105.

41. Hunter, "The Heroism of *Hamlet*," pp. 105–8, italics his.

42. See, e.g., Waith, *Ideas of Greatness*, p. 126; Hunter, "The Heroism of *Hamlet*," p. 108; and Maynard Mack, "The Jacobean Shakespeare: Some Observations on the Constructions of the Tragedies," in *Modern Shakespearean Criticism: Essays on Style, Dramaturgy, and the Major Plays*, ed. Alvin B. Kernan (New York: Harcourt, Brace & World, 1970), pp. 323–50.

is construed in turn as the energetic pursuit of "some ideal which stretches human capacities to the utmost, whether the ideal is impossibly remote and therefore self-destructive . . . or attainable."[43] Brower, for example, constructs a dichotomy between the heroic and the "saintly"; and Eugene Waith strongly argues against the heroism of a figure like the Duchess of Malfi: "Nothing could make clearer the distinction between this play and what can properly be called heroic drama than the ironic fact that alive, the heroine is a victim, and only begins to exert a powerful influence over others after her death."[44] In summary of this viewpoint, then, the logic of the increasing emphasis on private life, with its corollary focus on suffering and endurance, inevitably leads away from tragic and heroic representation in Renaissance drama.

Although these arguments provide a partial description of a result, they do not constitute an analysis of a historical process. Once again they are based on the equation of history with political and military action, and they depend on distinguishing public from private life and privileging the former domain. As I hope to show, however, the culmination of Jacobean tragedy has to do both with changing ideas of what constitutes heroic experience and with the purpose of tragedy as a genre. In the following chapter I return to these developments, exploring their causes in sociohistorical terms. Here I am arguing that many of the most important Jacobean tragedies focusing on love and sexuality develop a new conception of heroism that depends not on an ideally imagined separation between public and private life, but on the assumption that the two domains should and must be united. Representing public and private spheres as analogous realms of experience and granting them equal significance, these plays are not concerned with conflicting allegiances between love and duty per se; they focus instead on the contradictions and paradoxes inherent in sexuality itself. In what follows I demonstrate the way in which Jacobean tragedies construct a heroics of private life, centered on the relationship of marriage. As noted above, such an endeavor is precluded by the

43. Waith, *Ideas of Greatness*, p. 169. Cf. Frye, esp. pp. 3–39; and Norman Rabkin, *Shakespeare and the Problem of Meaning* (Chicago: University of Chicago Press, 1981), pp. 81–89.
44. Brower, pp. 416–20; Waith, *Ideas of Greatness*, p. 146.

conception of eros, women, and marriage as either idealized and transcendent or degraded and peripheral that is dramatized in *Tamburlaine* and *Dido*. The heroics of marriage requires a different sensibility for its articulation, one in which private life is viewed as central, women are perceived as active and complex, and marriage has gained in stature and prestige. That sensibility can be located precisely in Protestant (largely Puritan) sexual discourse.

iv

Recent research on the history of marriage, the family, and sexuality has demonstrated that privacy in the modern sense was at best a newly emerging and in many cases completely unrecognized phenomenon in the Renaissance. In her studies of such peasant rituals as the charivari, for example, Natalie Davis explores the ways in which the community could exert public pressure on a married couple, articulating their views of that couple's intimacy through a cruelly mocking, but acceptable ritual.[45] Lawrence Stone and Edward Shorter show that physical privacy was rare, even in the most aristocratic households,[46] an argument for which literary evidence abounds: in Beaumont and Fletcher's *The Maid's Tragedy*, the scene at the beginning of Act 3 (ll. 1–120) in which Evadne and Amintor's wedding night is assumed to require the communal attention of the court provides one example; the account of a raucous crew surrounding the bed of a newly married couple during consummation, separated from the bride and groom only by a curtain, provides another.[47]

45. Natalie Zemon Davis, "The Reasons of Misrule," in her *Society and Culture in Early Modern France* (Stanford, Calif.: Stanford University Press, 1979), pp. 97–123, and *The Return of Martin Guerre* (Cambridge, Mass.: Harvard University Press, 1983), pp. 20–21.

46. See Stone, *Family, Sex, and Marriage*, pp. 4, 6–7, 256, 484, 605; and Shorter, pp. 39–53.

47. Francis Beaumont and John Fletcher, *The Maid's Tragedy*, in *Stuart Plays*, ed. Arthur H. Nethercot, Charles R. Baskervill, and Virgil B. Heltzel; rev. Arthur H. Nethercot (New York: Holt, Rinehart & Winston, 1971). For an account of the raucous crew, see George Puttenham, *The Arte of English Poesie*, facsimile reproduction of 1906 reprint, ed. Edward Arber (Kent, Ohio: Kent State University Press, 1970), pp. 64–68. Although Puttenham relates

This fluid relation between public and private life, which assumes their continuity rather than their disjunction, can be construed in political terms as the incursion of authority in its attempts to regulate behavior.[48] *Certain Sermons or Homilies Appointed to Be Read in Churches in the Time of Queen Elizabeth* clearly represents such an endeavor. The queen's abundantly expressed displeasure at her courtiers' marriages is well known; and in a similar vein of establishing the assumption of royal dominion over the intimate lives of subjects, Jonathan Goldberg tells the less familiar tale of James I interrogating his daughter about the minute details of her wedding night.[49] Extending the logic behind such incidents to the modern centuries, Michel Foucault has argued that our assumptions of privacy in sexual matters constitute a collective delusion. We have, he believes, surrendered our claims to sexual autonomy to the manipulative, self-interested ideological control of the helping professions, replacing the church's confession box and monarchical scrutiny with the supervision of the social worker and the analyst's couch.[50]

Foucault's argument, if extreme, is trenchant and compelling. His analysis functions as an exposé, stripping away illusions and forcing acknowledgment of the hidden mechanisms of power, reg-

---

this story as an account of epithalamia in ancient times, asking pardon (p. 65) "of the chaste and honorable eares," he adds that the custom is "(in my simple opinion) nothing reproueable."

48. The best study of the ways in which relations of power constitute individuality in Renaissance literature is Greenblatt's *Renaissance Self-Fashioning*. Also see Natalie Zemon Davis, "Boundaries and the Sense of Self in Sixteenth-Century France," in *Reconstructing Individualism: Autonomy, Individuality, and the Self in Western Thought*, ed. Thomas C. Heller, Morton Sosna, and David E. Wellbery (Stanford, Calif.: Stanford University Press, 1986), pp. 53–63. Davis is less concerned with the incursions of authority against the individual. Indeed, she sees autonomy as a nineteenth-century value and provides a very useful discussion of the "embeddedness" of the self in the family and other social structures and networks of relationship, as well as stressing the fluid boundaries between the individual and the social body in the Renaissance. See also Jonathan Goldberg, *James I and the Politics of Literature* (Baltimore, Md.: Johns Hopkins University Press, 1983), pp. 86–89.

49. Goldberg, p. 107.

50. Foucault, passim. See also the discussion of René Girard in Tony Tanner, *Adultery in the Novel: Contract and Transgression* (Baltimore, Md.: Johns Hopkins University Press, 1979), pp. 89–91.

ulatory mechanisms of the sort that were open and acceptable in the Renaissance. The peculiarly modern cultural illusion about the individuality and independence of sexual relations, then, like the many problems of the modern family, is coincident with an ideology that, mystifying privacy, was not characteristic of the Renaissance. As Jonathan Goldberg observes: "Even as it withdrew from public life, cutting itself off from the world it once replicated, the modern family opened itself to a continual surveillance from the outside world. . . . Modern parents worry endlessly about childrearing; a whole structure of society is brought into the home in manuals and in a pervasive support system that includes doctors, psychiatrists, social scientists, therapists of all sorts, judges when children prove delinquent, teachers. . . . In this ideological structure lies the crucial difference between the modern, post-Freudian family, and the family in the seventeenth century. The family of the past did not regard its relationship to society as problematic."[51]

Although the basic distinction Goldberg makes is eloquent and illuminating, an understanding of Jacobean tragedy requires that it be refined. Evidence from the drama and from Renaissance sexual discourse indicates clearly both an emerging awareness of an increased sense of conflict between the demands of public and private domains and a profoundly anxious cultural perception of that disjunction as problematic. Jacobean tragedy centering on private life can be understood as an attempt to define and articulate this process of change, as well as an endeavor to arrest it.

This dramatic attempt at the definition and control of private life finds its discursive analogue in Puritan sexual discourse. Historians have questioned the originality of the post-Reformation ideal of marriage, as well as its relevance to actual behavior.[52] Although my analysis assumes a complex interrelationship between ideology and conduct, it is primarily concerned with the parallel construction of sexual values and dramatic forms; connections with the actual sexual behavior of Renaissance men and women are meant to be suggestive. Second, whereas many of the Puritan marital

51. Goldberg, pp. 88–89.
52. See, e.g., Goody, pp. 23–26; and Kathleen M. Davies, "Continuity and Change in Literary Advice on Marriage," in *Marriage and Society: Studies in the Social History of Marriage*, ed. R. B. Outhwaite (London: Europa, 1981), pp. 58–80.

themes may be derivative, the emphasis, elaboration, and wide distribution they receive in the Puritan tracts are completely new. Indeed, no one has questioned the existence of the Puritan view of marriage as a pervasive ideal of central importance; it is the power, popularity, and wide accessibility of this sensibility that establishes its relevance to the drama, an equally popular and accessible means of communication.[53]

In their ideological campaign to promote the importance of the family, the Puritans continually define the family as a private institution that is nevertheless distinguished by its connections to political and spiritual life. With urgent solemnity all the Puritans argue—indeed, insist upon—the public dignity and cosmic significance of marriage, viewing it as the arena in which salvation and damnation are determined for husband and wife. "*The priuate vocations of a family, and functions appertaining thereto, are such as Christians are called unto by God, and in the exercising whereof, they may and must imploy some part of their time*," declares William Gouge, not untypically.[54] Although the Puritan preachers express a wider variety of views and approaches than is commonly recognized, the crucial configuration on which all their arguments depend is their careful, fervent elaboration of the ancient analogy connecting the family, society, and the spiritual realm.[55] "Commonwealths I say," Alexander Niccholes declares of marriages, joining his colleagues in explaining that the husband is to the wife as the magistrate is to the subject, as Christ is to the church.[56] One of the most

53. See Davies, pp. 79–80, for statistics about the frequent publication of some of the Puritan marriage tracts.

54. William Gouge, *Of Domesticall Duties* (London, 1622), p. 17, italics his.

55. See, e.g., Gouge, pp. 2, 17, 219–20, 260–61, 410; William Perkins, *Christian Oeconomie; or, Houshold Government* (London, 1631), in *Workes,* vol. 3, p. 669; John Dod and Robert Cleaver, *A Godlie forme of householde Government* (London, 1598), sig. A⁴; Samuell Hieron, *The Sermons of Master Samuell Hieron* (London, 1635), p. 469; and William Whately, *A Care-cloth* (London, 1624), p. 38. The Puritan analogies among the family, the state, and the church are discussed in William Haller and Malleville Haller, "The Puritan Art of Love," *Huntington Library Quarterly,* 5 (1941–42), 235–72; and in Christopher Hill, "The Spiritualization of the Household," in his *Society and Puritanism in Pre-Revolutionary England* (New York: Schocken, 1964), pp. 443–81.

56. Alexander Niccholes, *A Discourse of Marriage and Wiving* (London, 1615), p. 178, in *Harleian Miscellany,* ed. William Oldys, vol. 2 (1808–13).

resonant constructions of this critical link between public and private life occurs in Gouge's enumeration of the multiple victims created by one couples' adultery. The sin of adultery is committed against

> *each person in the holy Trinitie* . . . one's neighbour, as the partie with whom the sinne is committed . . . the *husband* and *wife* of each partie . . . the *children* borne in adulterie . . . the *alliance* and *friends* of each partie (to whom the griefe and disgrace of this foule sinne reacheth) the *whole family* appertaining to either of them . . . the *towne, citie, and nation* where such vncleane birds roost (for all they lie open to the vengeance of God for this sinne) and the very *Church of God* (the holy seed whereof is by this sinne hindred) . . . against the *parties* themselues that commit this sinne, and that against their soules, bodies, name, goods, and all that appertaineth to them.[57]

Extending the idea of the family as a model of the church and the state, Gouge, in this vision of the inexorably escalating communal violence resulting from a single adultery, assigns a new, public significance to the actions of private individuals. The other Puritans share Gouge's sense that the cosmic and political, as well as the individual, stakes involved in marriage are momentous indeed. Choosing "a good Wife from a bad," Niccholes warns his readers, "is to cut by a Thread, betweene the greatest Good or Evil in the World." John Dod and Robert Cleaver assert that an irresponsible father who neglects the little commonwealth of his family is nothing less than the "murtherer of their souls, and cutthroats of their salvation."[58]

As these emphases on the communal consequences of individual actions and on the connections between individual choice and public responsibility indicate, the Puritans develop from their idea of the family as a model of the church and state, containing within its private sphere multiple levels of significance and possibility, a conception of marriage as a heroic endeavor. To some, marriage presents the opportunity for self-knowledge and the glory of happiness: "the very name . . . should portend unto thee *merryage* . . . for

---

57. Gouge, p. 220, italics his.
58. Niccholes, p. 156; Dod and Cleaver, sig. A⁴.

marriage awaketh the understanding as out of a dream."[59] Others, more pronounced in their distrust of sexuality, view marriage as a solemn duty but happiness as a dangerous delusion. "Likely none doe meete with more crosses in marriage, or beare their crosses more vntowardly, then those that most dreame of finding it a very Paradise," remarks William Whately, the Jacobean vicar of Banbury.[60] Yet whether the Puritans stress the obstacles or the rewards inherent in marriage, the crucial point becomes their consensus that this relationship constitutes the arena in which the individual can struggle and meet death or defeat, triumph or salvation: "for marriage is an adventure, for whosoever marries, adventures; he adventures his peace, his freedom, his liberty, his body; yea, and sometimes his soul too." Furthermore, undertaking this quest, "the means either to exalt on high to preferment, or cast down headlong to destruction," becomes "this one and absolutely greatest action of a man's whole life," requiring the unwavering commitment characteristic of the hero and assuming the properties of inevitable destiny: "as thereon depending the future good or evil of a man's whole after-time and days." Marriage is a perilous odyssey, a voyage on a dangerous sea, "wherein so many shipwreck for want of better knowledge and advice upon a rock."[61]

Describing the perils involved in the heroic marriage and suggesting their remedies, commentators rely frequently on military metaphors of conquest and self-defense: "for it is in this action as in a strategem of war: 'Wherein he that errs can err but once, perisheth unrecoverably to all after-advice and relief'";[62] "a valiant souldier doth neuer repent of the battaile, because he meetes with strong enemies; he resolues to be conquerour, and then the more and stronger his foes, the greater his honour";[63] "[domestic] au-

59. Niccholes, p. 160. Cf. Dod and Cleaver, sig. K³; Gouge, pp. 225, 227; John Wing, *The Crowne Conjvgall, or, The Spouse Royal* (London, 1632), pp. 85, 98; and Henry Smith, "A Preparative to Marriage," in *The Works of Henry Smith*, vol. 1, ed. Thomas Fuller (Edinburgh, 1866), pp. 1–40.

60. Whately, sig. A4v.

61. Niccholes, pp. 162, 159, 164, 159, 161. For the absolute, unwavering nature of the tragic hero's commitment, see references in notes 42 and 43, above.

62. Niccholes, pp. 159–60.

63. Whately, p. 80.

thoritie is like a sword, which with ouer much vsing will be blunted, and so faile to doe that seruice which otherwise it might when there is most need. A wise, graue, peaceable man, may alwayes have his sword in readiness, and that also very bright, keene, and sharpe: but he will not be very ready to plucke it out of his scabberd."[64] It should be stressed that the Puritans' use of military metaphors to construct the heroism of marriage is qualitatively different from poets' use of Petrarchan conceits that image love as the war between Venus and Mars. These tracts do not employ the vocabulary of the battle of the sexes—often frivolous, always self-defeating. Theirs is instead the language of epic endeavor, the intensely serious vocabulary of Tamburlaine the Great. But the Puritans' use of "high astounding terms" to construe marriage does not function to clarify conflicting allegiances between duty and desire, between public and private life, and to favor the former; rather, their urgent insight is that private life *is* public; love *is* a duty and marriage the conquest that must be achieved.

Indeed, the Puritans have not so much duplicated the military idiom in their idealization of marriage as absorbed and transformed it. Referring to bullying husbands, for example, Gouge observes, "Their authoritie is like a swaggerers sword, which cannot long rest in the sheath, but vpon euery small occasion is drawne forth. This frequent vse of commanding, maketh their commandements nought regarded."[65] If applied to Tamburlaine, this image of a restrained commander constitutes not praise, but a critique. The virtues required by the heroics of marriage are not those of magnificence—physical prowess and imperial will—but of the inner strength and courage required to act when necessary, but also to refrain from direct action, to suffer and endure. Husband and wife are frequently viewed as "yokefellows" in a struggle in which the inevitability of trouble must be acknowledged and prepared for: "Expectation of an enemie," warns Whately, "is halfe an arming; but suddennesse addes terriblenesse vnto a crosse, and makes it insupportable."[66] The well-prepared soldier-spouse of either sex

64. Gouge, p. 378.

65. Gouge, p. 378. For other uses of the heroic/military idiom in constructing marriage, see Wing, "To the Reader" and pp. 63, 74, 125–33; and Whately, pp. 25–26, 42, 46–48, 58–59, 68, 72, 74, 76–77, 80.

66. Whately, p. 74.

must be armed above all with patience. With a shrewd sense of the dynamics of daily life bordering on psychological insight, Gouge explains that "if either of them be cholericke or prone to be angry on a sudden, the other must endeuour to take away all occasions of offence: and if both should be testie and hastie to wrath, when the one seeth the other first moued, the partie whose passion is not yet stirred, ought the rather to be setled and composed to all meeknesse and patience, lest, if both together be prouoked, the whole houshold be set on fire."[67] In his slightly more apocalyptic account, Whately also emphasizes the need to suffer and endure: "So must the husband and wife resolue to conquer the troubles of marriage, and vse the buckler of patience against the blowes of aduersitie, that they may conquer. . . . O, let me be strengthened with all might, according to thy glorious power, vnto all long-suffering and patience with ioyfulnesse. Lord, strengthen me against all infirme and impotent fallings of heart, against all furious and violent risings of spirit: and seeing thou hast brought me into marriage, inable mee to beare the burdens of marriage."[68] As the rhetoric of armed struggle in this context makes clear, virtuous suffering, the extreme of which is victimization, is not conceived as passive but as a kind of action, requiring perhaps above all a dynamic obedience to God: "The Lord that now doth exercise mee with these trials, will afford mee so much the more glorie in Heauen. . . . Not onely troubles suffered for righteousnesse sake, doe make the Crowne of glorie more bright and weightie, but all troubles patiently suffered, are the seede of great rewards to come. . . . O, therefore make me more obedient to thee."[69]

Patience in the face of inevitable affliction; the moral prestige such affliction grants the sufferer, who is personally chosen by God to endure; obedience, humility, fortitude—the heroism of endurance has a multiplicity of sources, including Seneca and the stoics, the lives of the Catholic saints, the continuing popularity of medieval treatises on the art of dying, Patient Griselda stories, and the careers and tribulations of both Protestant and Jesuit martyrs related to Renaissance audiences.[70] The eclectic background of this

67. Gouge, p. 241.
68. Whately, pp. 80–82.
69. Whately, pp. 83, 85.
70. See references in notes 23, 27, 31, 35, and 37–44, above. Also see Nancy Lee Beaty, *The Craft of Dying: A Study in the Literary Tradition of the ars*

tradition makes clear that it comprises a conception of heroism that includes both sexes among its protagonists. Yet the relevance that this construction of goodness and greatness has for women is peculiarly striking. For the terms that constitute the heroism of endurance are precisely those terms used to construct the Renaissance idealization of woman: patient suffering, mildness, humility, chastity, loyalty, and obedience.[71]

As Catherine Belsey has shown, in both Puritan sexual discourse and English Renaissance tragedy, women begin to emerge as subjects. Basing the identity of the subject in language and action, Belsey defines subjectivity as "the destination of meaning. . . . To be a subject is to have access to signifying practice, to identify with the 'I' of utterance and the 'I' who speaks. . . . Subjects as agents act in accordance with what they are, 'work by themselves' to produce and reproduce the social formation of which they are a product."[72] Women by no means assume this status uniformly in the Puritan tracts, any more than they do in tragedy. In Niccholes's contribution to the heroics of marriage, for example, entitled "A Discourse of Marriage and Wiving" (1615), woman remains the unaddressed and objective other, the goal to be achieved by the hero-quester, man. Similarly, in John Wing's *The Crowne Conjugall, or The Spouse Royal* (1632), a rhapsodic aria, the pursuit of happiness finds its destination in "the worth of a gracious wife"; thus Wing clearly establishes happiness as a male prerogative. Ecstatically grateful, Wing does address woman, but, again as a distinct other and only to assure her that as "the *weaker creature*," both "fraile, and in-

---

moriendi in England, Yale Studies in English 175 (New Haven, Conn.: Yale University Press, 1970).

71. For accounts of the association of female heroism with patient suffering, endurance, and martyrdom, see Marina Warner, *Alone of All Her Sex: The Myth and the Cult of the Virgin Mary* (New York: Random House, Vintage, 1983), esp. pp. 68–78. Also see Jane Tibbetts Schulenburg, "The Heroics of Virginity: Brides of Christ and Sacrificial Mutilation," pp. 29–72, Mary Ellen Lamb, "The Countess of Pembroke and the Art of Dying," pp. 207–26, and Mary Beth Rose, "Gender, Genre, and History: Seventeenth-Century English Women and the Art of Autobiography," esp. pp. 259–67, all in Rose, *Women in the Middle Ages and the Renaissance.*

72. Catherine Belsey, *The Subject of Tragedy: Identity and Difference in Renaissance Drama* (London: Methuen, 1985), pp. 5–6.

feriour," she should possess even greater happiness in marriage than man: "If a *piece of man* (*a rib*) could make you so *rare a favor to us, our whole man* must needs *be a much more rich mercy to you.* All this, (and much more which I could adde) is *on our side*, and shewes you to be more happy *in us*, then it is possible *for us* to be in you."[73]

In contrast to the misogyny of Niccholes and Wing, the prominence women assume in other Protestant tracts becomes more striking. Edmund Tilney's *Flower of Friendship* (1568), a dialogue clearly modeled after *The Courtier*, distinguishes itself from its predecessor by including women not merely as mediators, but as protagonists in the debate. Rather than concentrating solely on the need for female chastity, Gouge's *Of Domesticall Duties* (1622) inveighs against the sexual double standard, insisting that both partners in a marriage must remain chaste and arguing for equality of sexual desire: "Their power also ouer one another in this respect is alike." Gouge spends a virtually equal amount of time enumerating husbands' and wives' duties and responsibilities in marriage.[74] Of the tracts I have studied, however, Whately's *A Care-cloth* (1624) treats women with the greatest interest and imagination. Whately not only gives women equal time in his considerations of marriage, but also recognizes a distinctly female point of view and attempts to enter into it. Clearly, Whately has tried to imagine what it is like to *be* a woman: "What if he lye thus by me groning, and tossing, many dayes, weekes, moneths, and some yeeres?" he asks, taking on the role of a dreadfully unhappy wife. "What if breeding be troublesome, so that I scarce enjoy an healthie day from conception to quickning, from quickning to trauel? What if bringing forth be so tedious and painefull, that I neuer become a mother, but by going thorow the torment of an hundred deaths in one, besides a long weakenesse after? . . . How shall I beare head-ach, heart-ach, back-ach, stomack-ach, retching, casting, longing, loathing, quawines, pangs, swoundings, and twentie deaths a day?"[75]

This imaginative apprehension of female consciousness, projected into a soliloquy, brings us very close to the capabilities of the

---

73. Wing, pp. 128, 129, 133, italics his.
74. Gouge, p. 219.
75. Whately, pp. 48–49.

drama. Given the fact that the properties of the heroism of endurance as established in the Puritan tracts coincide with the Renaissance idealization of women, it becomes clearer why women
are able to assume a place of central importance in the drama of
marriage, as well as to find a voice in which distinctly female
experiences can be articulated. It is, perhaps, more accurate to state
that this place and voice begin to be imagined in Puritan sexual
discourse, which, like the drama, is produced almost exclusively
by men.[76]

Throughout the heroics of marriage the conceptualization of
women is riddled with ironies and paradoxes that are continually
inscribed but inconsistently acknowledged. Although they are ev-
erywhere present, most of these unresolved logical discrepancies
center on the issue of equality between spouses and the corollary
tenet of wifely obedience and subordination. As is well known, the
Puritans believed in a kind of spiritual autonomy that led them to
assert an equality before God between the sexes. In his discussion
of marriage, for example, Calvin includes both versions of the
creation story found in Genesis.[77] Dod and Cleaver acknowledge
that men and women will be equals in eternity, and Wing comments that "what wee read of *man*, or *the Sonne of man*, is generally
to be taken, as intended of both *sexes*, the words (and their meaning) being as true of *women*, as men."[78] This valued spiritual equality becomes the basis of the companionship between man and
woman that the Puritans agree is fundamental to marriage. The
problems come not when the preachers are formulating their vision of sexual equality, but when they turn to consider conduct,
action. As we have seen, rather than dwelling exclusively on
female chastity, many of them argue against the sexual double
standard, with some explicitly asserting equality of rights, expec-

76. The first English play known to be by a woman is Elizabeth Cary's
The Tragedy of Mariam (1603–4? published 1613), ed. W. W. Greg (Oxford:
Oxford University Press, 1914).

77. John Calvin, "The Form and Manner of Celebrating Marriage," in his
Tracts and Treatises on the Doctrine and Worship of the Church, trans. Henry
Beveridge, vol. 2 (Grand Rapids, Mich.: Wm. B. Eerdmans, 1958), pp. 123,
125.

78. Dod and Cleaver (rpt. London, 1630), sig. K8; Wing, p. 25, italics
his. See also Calvin, pp. 123–25.

tations, and feelings in relation to sexual desire.[79] But having articulated that men and women have identical power in the realm of desire, Gouge, for example, immediately subverts this argument by declaring that the husband's power, and therefore his responsibility, are in fact greater in sexual as in other relations: "the more it appertaineth to them [i.e., husbands] to excell in vertue, and to gouerne their wiues by example."[80]

Along with that of the spirit, the other conception of domestic equality that the Puritans urge, and with blithe inconsistency undermine, centers on class, status, age, and money, all areas in which, notably, private and public domains are linked by marriage in an affirmation of existing hierarchies. "An equall yoke-fellow would be taken, of due proportion in state, birth, age, education, and the like, not much under, not much ouer, but fit and correspondent. . . . The rich and noble will likely despise, or set light by the poorer and meaner: so will the younger doe the aged," observes Whately, suggesting potential conflicts that do in fact become crucial in Jacobean tragedy.[81] When a marriage is socially unequal, however, it is always the husband's identity that determines the social status of the couple. If a man "of meane place be maried to a woman of eminent place," she must nevertheless acknowledge him as her superior: "It booteth nothing what either of them were before mariage . . . for in giuing her selfe to be his wife, and taking him to be her husband, she aduanceth him aboue her selfe, and subiecteth her selfe unto him."[82] This merging and transforming of a woman's identity into her husband's finds its correlative in the legal status of Renaissance wives, who lost all property, rights, and power upon marrying. As Lawrence Stone summarily reminds us, "By marriage, the husband and wife became one person in law—and that person was the husband."[83]

79. See, e.g., Perkins, p. 680; Calvin, p. 124; Gouge, pp. 217–19, 356, 425; and Whately, pp. 25–26, 73.

80. Gouge, p. 219. Also see Keith Thomas, "The Double Standard," *Journal of the History of Ideas*, 20 (1959), 195–216.

81. Whately, p. 73.

82. Gouge, p. 272.

83. Stone, *Family, Sex and Marriage*, p. 195. Also see Barbara J. Todd, "The Remarrying Widow: A Stereotype Reconsidered," in *Women in English Society, 1500–1800*, ed. Mary Prior (London: Methuen, 1985), p. 55; and T.

This comment suggests that the surrender of female identity demanded by patriarchal absolutism, which denied wives any status as individual actors, also denied them the status and power of subjects, or protagonists in the drama. Such a syndrome does in fact help to account for one notable development in English Renaissance drama, namely, the relative absence of mothers as protagonists.[84] Yet as Stone himself shows, the legal construction and cultural ideology of marriage in the Renaissance, including the status of wives, was far from being definite and clear. Nowhere do these inconsistencies manifest themselves more openly than in the Puritan doctrine of wifely subordination and obedience.

Like the analogy connecting family, church, and state, the requirement that wives be obedient commands the absolute consensus of these domestic idealists. "By nature woman was made man's subject," Dod and Cleaver state baldly.[85] Wives who fail to obey their husbands, pronounces Gouge in a stricture reiterated throughout the tracts, "thwart Gods ordinance, peruert the order of nature, deface the image of Christ, ouerthrow the ground of all dutie, hinder the good of the family, become an ill patterne to children and seruants, lay themselues open to Satan, and incurre many other mischiefes which cannot but follow vpon the violating of this maine duty of Obedience."[86] To obey does, henceforth, seem best. Yet, while fervently proclaiming and defining the subjection of women, the Puritans provide the necessary material for its subversion. After lionizing obedience, for example ("*Let wiues be subject to their husbands in euerie thing*"), Gouge urges women never to obey husbands who want them to do what "is forbidden by God."[87] In a similar vein, after demanding obedience and subjection (rising against husbands is the equivalent of rising against God), writers including Gouge, Dod and Cleaver, and Hieron urge women not only to disobey, but actively to seek to correct

E., *The Lawes Resolutions of Womens Rights; or, The Lawes Provision for Woemen* (London, 1632), p. 119, according to which the husband and wife "are but one person in Law, and the Feme taketh nothing but by agreement of the husband." Also see pp. 129–30.

84. See Belsey, pp. 155–60.
85. Dod and Cleaver (1598), p. 149.
86. Gouge, p. 287, italics his.
87. Gouge, pp. 295 (italics his), 328.

erring husbands.[88] Furthermore, they define wives' subjection as merely temporal, temporary. "Her *place* is indeed a place of inferiority and subiection, yet the neerest to equality that may be," Gouge sums up, unhelpfully.[89]

Absolute spiritual and social equality between the sexes, coexisting with the equally absolute subjection of women that is decreed and then subverted—the logical inconsistencies that now appear so glaring, particularly given their consequences, seem never to have occurred to the Puritans. These contradictions and paradoxes permeate not only the conceptualization of women, but all matters concerning love, marriage, and sexuality in Puritan discourse. The moral ambivalence of sexual desire, for example, is fully documented yet only dimly perceived by the preachers, who in the same tracts treat eros variously as a solemn duty and a dangerous trap, the God-given, potentially joyful foundation of society and a necessary evil to be shunned except in procreation.[90] Individual choice of a spouse and the often contradictory need for parental consent in marriage present a final example of the issues that are treated with distinct double-mindedness, in which reverence for hierarchy and obedience to authority clash with a growing middle-class distaste for property-based marriage and an as yet incompletely formulated notion of individual autonomy.[91] Whately's declaration that a couple need not obey their parents—"in not suffering them to marrie in the Lord, but offering to force them marrie against the will of God . . . for no man can passe away anothers right, without his liking"—followed immediately by his equally adamant assertion that a couple marrying without parental consent lives in sin until "they haue procured an after-consent, to

88. Gouge, pp. 295, 328; Dod and Cleaver (1630), sig. o6ʳ; Hieron, p. 411.

89. Gouge, p. 356, italics his.

90. On the equation of married love (sometimes eros is specifically meant) with happiness, see, e.g., Dod and Cleaver (1630), sig. K3; Gouge, pp. 225, 227, 415; Wing, pp. 85, 98, 100; and Smith, pp. 1–40. For the (often ambivalent) association of sexual love with sin, see Gouge, p. 223; Dod and Cleaver (1598), p. 98; and Whately, pp. 25–26, 36, 41, 44, 66. Cf. Perkins, e.g., p. 671; he disavows these associations.

91. See, e.g., Hieron, who speaks strongly (p. 405) against "the buying & selling of children among parents," the "forced marriages, which mostly have the same issue of extreme loathing," and the unequal yoking "of an ox and an ass together."

ratifie that, which ought not to haue been done before the consent" is typical.[92]

Belsey has stated that "marriage becomes in the sixteenth and seventeenth centuries the site of a paradoxical struggle to create a private realm and to take control of it in the interests of the public good."[93] Indeed, it could be argued that the eager urgency of the Puritan analogies among family, church, and state, the very insistence on these relationships and the equal importance of the terms that constitute them, itself articulates a conflict between public and private realms and a profound anxiety about the need to draw them together. Similarly, the equation of marriage with love and happiness and the glimmering awareness of individual psychology and particular personality that some writers display indicate a dawning conception of privacy—that is, of autonomy or interiority—that involves a problematic notion of an individual self separate from the self manifested in society at large. That the Puritans should glimpse these ideas to the point of admitting them into their domestic discourse and then fail to develop their logic has seemed to some scholars to be evasive and self-interested (i.e., an indication that the Puritans were seeking to establish their own spiritual authority and to profit from the publication of their sermons) and to others to thrust the Puritan idealization of marriage into incoherence.[94] I do not believe that the Puritans, busily seeking to separate the present from the past and participating in the

---

92. Whately, pp. 33–34. Cf. T.E., *Lawes Resolutions*, p. 53, italics mine: "It is now received a generall opinion that the good will of parents is required, *in regard of honestie, not of necessitie,* according to the Canons which exact necessarily, none other consent but only of the parties themselves, whose Conjunction is in hand, without which the conclusion of parents is of none effect." T.E.'s separation of the moral and legal burdens constituting parental consent points to the moral ambiguity encompassing the whole issue. See also Goody, who argues (pp. 24–25) that the emphasis on consent in marriage "was not limited to countries of a particular demographic structure or historical destiny; it was a characteristic of the Christian Church as a whole, in principle from earliest times, and was in no way peculiar to the English. Indeed, the English Protestants reestablished the requirement of parental agreement in the sixteenth century although it was absent in Catholic doctrine, even though laymen often insisted on their veto."

93. Belsey, p. 130.

94. See, e.g., Belsey, p. 155; and Davies.

abstract and visionary formation of an ideology, were aware of the contradictions they were articulating. The value of their discourse does not lie in its self-consciousness or its prescience.[95] Rather, because of its historical position, Puritan marriage ideology in the Renaissance provides a remarkable index of the ways in which modern sexual values were being created, terms were being constructed, and conflicts were taking shape. The apprehension and exploitation of ideological inconsistencies became the task not of sermons, but of the drama, in which a greater attachment to the concrete, an obligation to action, and a dependence on conflict brought paradox into the light of representation, giving visibility and significance to contradiction and seeking to resolve it through the operations of form.

V

In *Othello* the two predominant modes of English Renaissance sexual discourse meet and clash tragically. As we will see, the two sensibilities and styles overlap as well as conflict throughout the play. But in the complex exploration of sexuality that *Othello* comprises, the dualizing mentality that simultaneously exalts and degrades women and eros also is clearly distinguished from the heroics of marriage, which comes painfully into being, defined and comprehended as a failed achievement. It is not simply the competition between distinctive modes of sexual apprehension that issues in violence, however; the heroics of marriage also collapses from within, dissolving inevitably from its own unresolved contradictions.

We can begin by focusing on Act 1, Scene 3, of the play, in which Desdemona and Othello seek to justify their marriage be-

95. For this reason the debate on whether or not Puritan marriage sermons and tracts are "feminist" is largely irrelevant. See, e.g., Juliet Dusinberre, *Shakespeare and the Nature of Women* (London: Macmillan, 1975); and Linda T. Fitz, "What Says the Married Woman: Marriage Theory and Feminism in the English Renaissance," *Mosaic*, 13 (Winter 1980), 1–22. The liveliest and most thorough summation/entry in this debate is Linda [Fitz] Woodbridge, *Women and the English Renaissance: Literature and the Nature of Womankind, 1540–1620* (Urbana: University of Illinois Press, 1984).

fore the Venetian Senate in response to Brabantio's outraged accusations of abduction and witchcraft. The materials that constitute the drama of this scene involve those in power demanding in a public forum to hear a detailed account of the intimate relationship of a newly married couple, much as King James demanded a narration of his daughter's wedding night. The two salient modes of sexual discourse, which are fully articulated and distinguished in the Senate scene, consequently take dramatic form as competing views of the relationship between private and public life.

As is noted often in commentaries on the play, Othello, a stranger and alien, founds his identity and assesses his own value in terms of his relationship to the Venetian state that has granted him membership in the community because of his exceptional abilities as a military leader.[96] His self-confidence that his marriage will be politically sanctioned despite the honored insider Brabantio's objections is based on his sense of worthiness as a public servant ("Let him do his spite; / My services, which I have done the signiory, / Shall out-tongue his complaints" [1.2.17–19]).[97] Similarly, he mourns his eventual loss of Desdemona as a surrender of professional status ("Farewell, Othello's occupation's gone!" [3.3 363]); in attempting to recover his identity after discovering his fatal misapprehensions, he looks to his deeds of public service ("I have done the state some service, and they know't" [5.2.340]); finally, he construes his suicide as an act of justice against an enemy of Venice and, characterizing himself as "a malignant and a turban'd Turk" (5.2.354), assumes the dual role of criminal-outsider and state executioner in taking his own life. Othello's relationship to the state, forged through public service, is also personal and intimate, in that it permeates every aspect of his life and identity.

How can a man formed by and so devoted to public life integrate marriage as a source of primary meaning and value into his self-conception and experience? Othello, of course, is the hero of action par excellence. Like Tamburlaine's, his heroism combines superb

96. Cf. Helen Gardner, *The Noble Moor* (London: Oxford University Press, 1955), p. 192.

97. All quotations from *Othello*, identified in the text by act, scene, and line numbers, are from the Arden edition, ed. M. R. Ridley (London: Methuen, 1958).

military prowess with rhetorical magnificence and the status of an outsider whose merits and services "shall out-tongue . . . complaints" (1.2.19). Again like Tamburlaine, Othello makes clear that he views private life not only as separate from public action, but also as subordinate to, and even potentially subversive of, public service. These beliefs are hinted at very early in the play, when Othello makes clear to Iago that he perceives marriage as opposed to freedom and the heroic style: "But that I love the gentle Desdemona, / I would not my unhoused free condition / Put into circumscription and confine / For the sea's worth" (1.2.25–28). It is the exception of love, then, that provokes Othello to marry; yet in persuading the Senate to allow Desdemona to accompany him to Cyprus, he elaborates a contempt for both eros and domesticity, characterizing each as trivial and idle:

> And heaven defend your good souls that you think
> I will your serious and great business scant,
> For she is with me; . . . no, when lightwing'd toys
> And feather'd Cupid, foils with wanton dullness
> My speculative and active instruments
> That my disports corrupt and taint my business,
> Let housewives make a skillet of my helm.
> [1.3.266–72]

In short, Othello feels that he must, in Bacon's terms, make love "keepe Quarter" by severing it "wholly, from . . . serious Affaires and Actions of life." Just as in *Tamburlaine*, then, the heroism of action accompanies a view of the private life as subordinate and subversive, and it is consequently associated with the necessary repression of sexuality. Othello makes this association clear when he characterizes his desire for his wife's company as follows:

> . . . I therefore beg it not
> To please the palate of my appetite,
> Nor to comply with heat, the young affects
> In my defunct, and proper satisfaction,
> But to be free and bounteous of her mind.
> [1.3.261–65]

Though the precise meaning of these extraordinary lines is contro-

versial,[98] their purport is clear: sexual desire is degrading and potentially dangerous; marriage should involve a dignified separation
between public and private life, in which the latter is clearly subordinate to the former. Like Tamburlaine, then, Othello confidently
asserts his ability to subdue eros to public service. From the point
of view of the heroism of action, his tragedy emerges from unsuccessful repression: desire proves more central to him, marriage
more necessary, than such heroism will allow.[99]

Scholars have examined in depth, both in psychoanalytic and in
sociocultural terms, the complex ways in which *Othello* associates
sexual desire with fear, hatred, evil, sin, and finally death. Exploring Freud's theoretical formulations of "the ultimate incapacity of
erotic instincts to be fully satisfied or harmonized," Arthur Kirsch
views Othello's sexual tragedy as emerging from a striving after
unconditional love that, rooted in the primary narcissism of a
child's original attachment to its mother, is ultimately doomed to
unfulfillment. Arguing that "the awesome energy of Othello's
jealousy, its primitive and superstitious vindictiveness, is a function of the same primal forces that animated his earlier exaltation
and love," Kirsch concludes that "Othello's jealous anguish suggests the tragic vulnerability of a love so absolutely rooted in, and
dependent upon, the exaltation of symbiotic union." Citing
Freud's analysis of "the dissociation of affection and sensuality . . .
[that] are rarely completely fused in civilized man," Kirsch aptly
describes the mentality that either degrades or idealizes women and
desire as "the polarization of erotic love."[100] That the two instincts

98. See Arden edition, pp. 36–37.

99. See Richard S. Ide, *Possessed with Greatness: The Heroic Tragedies of
Chapman and Shakespeare* (Chapel Hill: University of North Carolina Press,
1980), esp. pp. 50–74. Ide deals with the ways in which Othello's attachment
to the military/heroic ethic dooms him to domestic tragedy. Cf. Matthew N.
Proser, *The Heroic Image in Five Shakespearean Tragedies* (Princeton, N.J.:
Princeton University Press, 1965), p. 110; Proser makes a similar point. Both
critics, however, regard this as a moral failing of Othello's, a judgement that
does not correspond to my purpose and that seems beside the point when
considering significance in tragedy.

100. Arthur Kirsch, *Shakespeare and the Experience of Love* (Cambridge:
Cambridge University Press, 1981), pp. 33, 37, 39. Also see Peter Erickson,
Patriarchal Structures in Shakespeare's Drama (Berkeley: University of California
Press, 1984), pp. 80–103; Marianne Novy, *Love's Argument: Gender Relations*

inevitably coexist as a dichotomy in the play can be perceived in an exchange about Desdemona that takes place between Cassio and Iago in Act 2, Scene 3, where it becomes ominously clear how readily Cassio's idiom of sentimental exaltation can be translated into Iago's idiom of misogynistic contempt:

Iago. He [i.e., Othello] hath not yet made wanton the night with her; and she is sport for Jove.

Cas. She is a most exquisite lady.

Iago. And I'll warrant her full of game.

Cas. Indeed she is a most fresh and delicate creature.

Iago. What an eye she has! methinks it sounds a parley of provocation.

Cas. An inviting eye, and yet methinks right modest.

Iago. And when she speaks, 'tis an alarm to love.

Cas. It is indeed perfection.

Iago. Well, happiness to their sheets!

[2.3.15–25][101]

Relating *Othello* to Protestant sexual discourse, Stephen Greenblatt adds to Kirsch's insights by emphasizing the negative view of desire embedded in Christian orthodoxy. The conjunction of sexual pleasure with sin and death, an association that persists—when pleasure is pursued immoderately—even within marriage, constitutes a tradition, Greenblatt argues, that leaves Othello vulnerable to Iago's unbearable equation of erotic love with inevitable adultery. Analyzing the blissful reunion between Othello and

---

in *Shakespeare* (Chapel Hill: University of North Carolina Press, 1985), pp. 125–49; Sprengnether p. 93; Gohlke, pp. 170–87; Richard Wheeler, "Since First We Were Dissevered: Trust and Autonomy in Shakespearean Tragedy and Romance," in Schwartz and Kahn, pp. 150–69; Irene G. Dash, *Wooing, Wedding, and Power: Women in Shakespeare's Plays* (New York: Columbia University Press, 1981), pp. 103–30; and Carol Thomas Neely, *Broken Nuptials in Shakespeare's Plays* (New Haven, Conn.: Yale University Press, 1985), pp. 105–35.

101. Cf. Kirsch, *Shakespeare and the Experience of Love*, p. 36: "Cassio idolizes Desdemona and at the same time is capable of a sexual relationship only with a whore of whom he is essentially contemptuous." See also Neely, whose view of Bianca (pp. 122, 134) is considerably more sympathetic than that of Kirsch or of Cassio.

Desdemona on Cyprus after the storm (2.1), Greenblatt explores the ways in which Othello's expressions of ecstatic love, intimately intertwined with thoughts of death (i.e., "If it were now to die, / 'Twere now to be most happy" [2.1.189–90]), convey not only gratified desire but "the longing for a final *release* from desire, from the dangerous violence, the sense of extremes, the laborious climbing and falling out of control that is experienced in the tempest."[102] We have seen a similarly pressing need to render inert the tumultuous, anarchic motions of desire in *Tamburlaine*, another play in which the simultaneous exaltation and degradation of women and eros combines with the heroism of action to constitute a hierarchical relationship between a privileged public and a subordinate private life.

But the conjoined repression and idealization of eros, with its accompanying consignment of women and marriage to the periphery of serious endeavor, is by no means the only possible relationship between public and private life that the play represents; nor does this polarizing sensibility fully account for Othello's experience. Indeed, in the Senate scene, the moment when competing conceptions of marriage and sexuality are articulated, Othello's stated view that the two domains must remain rigorously separate is echoed, oddly, only by Brabantio. "Neither my place, nor aught I heard of business, / Hath rais'd me from my bed, nor doth the general care / Take any hold of me, for my particular grief / Is of so flood-gate and o'erbearing nature / That it engluts and swallows other sorrows, / And it is still itself," Brabantio insists hysterically, distinguishing personal from political concerns as he bursts into the Senate, interrupting a war council in an endeavor to recover his daughter (1.3.53–58). Attempting to reestablish self-control throughout his subsequent speeches, Brabantio persists in making this distinction: "Please it your grace, on to the state affairs; / I had rather to adopt a child than get it; . . . Beseech you now, to the affairs of state" (1.3.190–91, 220). On the issue of segregating public and private life, then, Brabantio and Othello are in agree-

---

102. Greenblatt, p. 243, his italics. See also Denis de Rougemont, *Love in the Western World*, trans. Montgomery Belgion (New York: Harcourt, Brace, 1940); and Sigmund Freud, *Beyond the Pleasure Principle*, trans. James Strachey (New York: Norton, 1961).

ment instead of conflict in the Senate scene. This tacit emotional alliance between them, rather than the nonexistent truth-value of the assertion, lends Brabantio's warning to Othello an eerie clairvoyance: "Look to her, Moor, have a quick eye to see: / She has deceived her father, may do thee" (1.3.292–93).

Desdemona, not Brabantio, unwittingly articulates a conception of sexuality and its relation to public life that is antagonistic to Othello's. Openly and proudly acknowledging her love for her husband, Desdemona characterizes herself as a soldier-spouse, adopting the vocabulary of the epic quest:

> That I did love the Moor, to live with him,
> My downright violence, and scorn of fortunes,
> May trumpet to the world: my heart's subdued
> Even to the utmost pleasure of my lord:
> I saw Othello's visage in his mind,
> And to his honours, and his valiant parts
> Did I my soul and fortunes consecrate:
> So that, dear lords, if I be left behind,
> A moth of peace, and he go to the war,
> The rites for which I love him are bereft me.
> [1.3.248–57][103]

In contrast to Othello's emphatic severance of body and mind (1.3.261–65), Desdemona's definition of marriage conjoins physical and mental life. As has been suggested, the radical distinction between her experience of desire and Othello's is clarified during their reunion on Cyprus. Where Othello seeks release and inertia ("It stops me here, it is too much of joy" [2.1.197]), Desdemona anticipates growth and fruition ("The heavens forbid / But that our loves and comforts should increase, / Even as our days do grow" [2.1.193–95]).[104] Furthermore, by using a quasi-military idiom to insist that separation between spouses makes non-sense of marriage, and by associating herself with the Turkish wars, she also

---

103. Ridley's choice of the Quarto's (Q₁) "utmost pleasure," rather than the Folio's "very quality," in line 151 of this passage in the Arden edition, which I accept, obviously serves to highlight Desdemona's eroticism.

104. Cf. Greenblatt, pp. 240–44; and Kirsch, *Shakespeare and the Experience of Love,* pp. 25–27.

emphatically draws together public and private domains. In the paradoxically active submission that Desdemona describes herself as undertaking in her marriage, expressed in military terms, we can recognize the dynamic obedience and devotion idealized in the Puritan tracts. In short, Desdemona presents herself to the Senate as a hero of marriage.

In defining marriage as a heroic endeavor, Desdemona, like the Puritans, analogizes public and private life, drawing them together and granting them equal distinction, rather than establishing a hierarchy in which the latter is clearly subordinated to the former in dignity, interest, and importance. And her visionary construction of marriage is borne out by the structure of the play. The action of the Senate scene, in which the Senators dispatch their decisions about the Turkish enemy with quick, acute rationality, changes rapidly to focus on Othello's private life, revealing the general's marriage not as a peripheral matter, but as an event of the most decided political significance.[105] That Othello's intimate being is directly connected to affairs of state is, again, an assumption basic to his identity, revealing his insistence on the separation between love and duty as an unrecognized contradiction that becomes a fatal delusion. Similarly, in the second act, the Turkish enemy is again introduced and then quickly dismissed as the significant component at issue; instead the focus of central dramatic meaning and conflict turns out to be love and marriage. In recalling the associations of the tempest that perilously escorts Desdemona and Othello to Cyprus with the unpredictability and dangers of eros, we can also recall the Puritan conception of marriage as a heroic voyage on a dangerous sea: "such a continual storm and tempest to those that launch not forth in a prosperous gale . . . it is such a sea, wherein so many shipwreck for want of better knowledge and advice upon a rock."[106]

Viewed from the perspective of transforming conceptions of heroic experience, the first and second acts of *Othello* can be seen to represent the process of the heroism of action giving way to the heroism of endurance associated with marriage. The conflict of

105. Cf. Alvin B. Kernan, "*Othello*: An Introduction," in his *Modern Shakespearean Criticism*, pp. 353–54; and Neely, p. 109.

106. Niccholes, pp. 160–61.

allegiances between eros and action, so precisely defined and resolved by Tamburlaine, who simply relegates private life to a peripheral and subordinate position, is in *Othello* obsolete. Differentiating between love and duty and subduing beauty to heroism are no longer the necessary tasks. Indeed, they are deluded efforts, for the play quickly makes clear that the hero's major task has become the conduct of marriage itself: "for marriage is an adventure, for whosoever marries, adventures; he adventures his peace, his freedom, his liberty, his body; yea, and sometimes his soul too."[107]

Othello's sexual tragedy therefore emerges not as insufficient repression, the criterion of the heroism of action, but as a misconstruction of his heroic quest. The ironies of his delusions are multiple, because the play makes clear that Othello is in many ways well equipped to undertake the heroics of marriage. As Greenblatt points out, he responds to love and marriage precisely as an adventure, "a supreme form of romantic narrative, a tale of risk and violence issuing forth at last in a happy and final tranquillity."[108] Indeed, despite his own disclaimers, Othello's embrace of marriage as a perilous quest duplicates, rather than contrasts with, his attitude toward public service. For example, in stark contrast to Tamburlaine's perpetually imperious vocabulary ("for *will* and *shall* best fitteth Tamburlaine" [I.3.3.41]), which the revolutionary shepherd uses to slaughter existing monarchs and to create a new society under his own rule, Othello's rhetoric is that of a humble suitor seeking recognition and acceptance by the established state ("Most potent, grave, and reverend signiors / My very noble and approv'd good masters"; "Rude am I in my speech"; "I do beseech you"; "Your voices, Lords: beseech you"; "With all my heart"; "Please your grace"; "We must obey the time" [1.3.76–77, 81, 114, 260, 278, 283, 300]—these are his typical modes of address).[109] The posture of dignified humility that Othello assumes toward the state resembles the dynamic obedience described in the Puritan tracts as an essential component for protagonists in the heroics of marriage. And the contrast between

107. Niccholes, p. 162.
108. Greenblatt, p. 243.
109. Cf. Gardner, pp. 193–94.

Othello and Tamburlaine is replicated in their methods of courtship. Where Tamburlaine rapes Zenocrate, establishing his dominion by force, Othello entertains and woos Desdemona in response to her desire, observing her closely and allowing her to take the lead (1.3.144–70). Interestingly, Othello also characterizes his heroism as much in terms of suffering as of action, or more precisely, in terms of the endurance that constitutes a dynamic combination of the two: "I spake of most disastrous chances, / Of moving accidents by flood and field; / Of hair-breadth scapes i'th'imminent deadly breach; / Of being taken by the insolent foe;/ and sold to slavery, and my redemption thence" (1.3.134–38).[110] His original attitude toward Desdemona conveys the same loving submission to a power that will enhance and complete his own; along with direct acknowledgment of the intimate connection between his love for her and his military prowess: "She lov'd me for the dangers I had pass'd, / And I lov'd her that she did pity them" (1.3.167–68).[111]

Freedom for Othello therefore would seem to lie in a commitment to the heroics of marriage, yet he is unable adequately to make the leap from the hierarchies of the heroism of action to the analogies of the heroism of marriage. Just as he unwittingly articulates a profound ambivalence toward the ecstasy and dangers of desire in his reunion with Desdemona on Cyprus, Othello in the Senate scene emphasizes the associations between eros and action that are crucial to him even as he denies them, vigorously insisting on the absolute separation between public and private life. In contrast, subordinating the private life without ambivalence, Tamburlaine is able to reconcile its established marginality with the polarization of erotic love that removes women and eros from the realm of significant action by exalting or degrading them: for Tamburlaine the heroics of marriage is not a possibility. But Othello, for whom marriage has become central, rather than peripheral, remains torn between the two perspectives, unable wholly to admit the claims of either. Like Niccholes, who views marriage as "this one and absolutely greatest action of a man's whole life," asserting that "there is in marriage an inevitable

110. Cf. Hunter, "The Heroism of *Hamlet*," p. 108.
111. Erickson, pp. 89–92.

destiny,"[112] Othello acknowledges the critical importance of his marriage to his identity and his fate, defining it as "there, where I have garner'd up my heart, / Where either I must live, or bear no life, / The fountain, from the which my current runs / Or else dries up" (4.2.58–61). Yet, along with being unable to absorb the centrality of his marriage into his conception of himself as a public servant, Othello is unable to master the one quality that is essential to the successful undertaking of the heroics of marriage, namely, patience. The possibility of Othello's submitting to his suffering with patient endurance is transformed insidiously by Iago into the humiliating picture of the oblivious cuckold that was the source of profound anxiety, reflected by endless, derisive jokes, in Jacobean society.[113] Significantly, when explaining why patience is impossible for him, Othello makes a distinct separation between the demands of public and private identity:

> Had it pleas'd heaven
> To try me with affliction, had he rain'd
> All kinds of sores and shames on my bare head,
> Steep'd me in poverty, to the very lips,
> Given to captivity me and my hopes,
> I should have found in some part of my soul
> A drop of patience; . . .
> *But there, where I have garner'd up my heart.* . . .
> [4.2.47–54, 58, italics mine]

112. Niccholes, pp. 164, 173.
113. See 4.1.61–89:

Iago. Would you would bear your fortunes like a man!
Oth. A horned man's a monster, and a beast.
Iago. There's many a beast then in a populous city,
   And many a civil monster . . .
   Think every bearded fellow that's but yok'd
   May draw with you . . .
   Confine yourself but in a patient list . . .
          . . . marry, patience,
   Or I shall say you are all in all in spleen,
   And nothing of a man.

See also Keith Thomas, "The Place of Laughter in Tudor and Stuart England," *Times Literary Supplement,* 21 January 1977, pp. 77–81.

In this context, Othello's tragic conflicts are strikingly defined in the magnificent speech that articulates his belief in Desdemona's infidelity: "O now for ever / Farewell the tranquil mind, farewell content: / Farewell the plumed troop, and the big wars, / That makes ambition virtue: . . . Farewell, Othello's occupation's gone!" (3.3.353–64). In this moving elegy to the heroism of action, three points are salient. First, Othello acknowledges the indissoluble link between his public and his personal life by describing the loss of the one as the loss of the other. Yet he has leaped over the construction of a comparison between the two domains. By absorbing Desdemona entirely into the terms of his professional identity he denies the analogous connection between the two that prompted him to make the speech in the first place. Consequently, though he acknowledges the centrality of his marriage, he apprehends desire as a loss, a sign of human inadequacy and subversion of identity. Othello's erotic ambivalence, together with his inability to accept the emotional consequences of the connections he recognizes between public and private life, combine to disqualify him as a protagonist in the heroics of marriage. Unable to embrace the humility and patience that marriage requires, he construes his murder of Desdemona as an execution of justice and revenge undertaken (dispassionately) as a public service, thus misapplying to his marriage the criteria of the heroism of action that he himself has dimly perceived as obsolete (eg., 5.2.6 and 5.2.65–66): "Even so my bloody thoughts with violent pace / Shall ne'er look back, ne'er ebb to humble love, / Till that a capable and wide revenge / Swallow them up" (3.3.464–67).

The thrust of this analysis has implied that the heroics of marriage is the liberating, progressive discourse in *Othello*. A commitment to its assumption of the prestige and centrality of the private life and to its terms of patient endurance might indeed have averted tragedy. Yet it is not simply that such a commitment proves impossible for Othello and would require either a sermon or another play; more important, the heroics of marriage itself constitutes a tragic discourse. As noted above, the requirements of the heroics of marriage resemble those of the Renaissance idealization of women; thus, although this discourse is concerned with both sexes, its materials have a particular relevance to women, allowing them a mode in which they can define themselves and be perceived as heroes.[114] Accordingly in *Othello* the articulation and break-down of the idealization of marriage are dramatized in the career of Desdemona.

As recent studies of the fashioning of identity in the Renaissance make clear, verbal mastery becomes one of the primary character-istics of the hero, essential for the maintenance of power as well as the achievement of social mobility.[115] Much of the action in *Othello* depends upon the characters' submission to and creation of narrative. Othello's account to the Senate of his courtship of Desdemona becomes a metanarrative, a successful act of persua-sion in which is embedded the story of another successful act of persuasion. He has won his wife by telling his tale: "She lov'd me for the dangers I had pass'd / And I lov'd her that she did pity them" (1.3.163–68). "I think this tale would win my daughter too," says the Duke, as a way of sanctioning the marriage when Othello has finished his account (1.3.171). Confirming the centrality of narrative discourse to their courtship, Desdemona adds, "I saw Othello's visage in his mind" (1.3.252), implicitly equating her erotic responsiveness to her husband, which she ex-plicitly defines, with the act of listening to his life history. The love and marriage between Desdemona and Othello are therefore con-strued as the triumphant ability of language to constitute reality.

Terry Eagleton has argued that "when language is cut loose from reality, signifiers split from signifieds, the result is a radical fissure between consciousness and material life."[116] As is well known, such a fissure is necessary for Othello and Desdemona, who must absorb, or overcome, the material obstacles of Othello's age, his blackness, and his foreignness, which to varying degrees are perceived as impediments by every character in the play.[117] Thus at the start of the play Desdemona and Othello have experi-enced the power and independence of language as liberating and enabling; they equate language with desire and perceive their abil-ity to form and manipulate both as endlessly creative. But as Ea-gleton points out, the effects of linguistic autonomy, "a kind of

114. Cf. Lamb; and Rose, "Gender, Genre, and History," pp. 259–67.
115. See n. 36, above.
116. Terry Eagleton, *William Shakespeare* (Oxford: Basil Blackwell, 1986), p. 7.
117. Cf. Kirsch, *Shakespeare and the Experience of Love.*

discursive imperialism, in which words determine reality rather than the other way round," can be dangerously chaotic as well. When signs are detached from the material world, reality becomes flexible and manipulable on the one hand; but on the other, a vacuum can result in which "signs are now purely . . . dead letters emptied of all constraining content and so free to couple . . . in an orgy of inbreeding. . . . A sign can be roughly defined as anything which can be used for the purpose of lying."[118] The arch-liar of the play, Iago, of course proves time and again the power of words to triumph over visual and material reality; in this context Othello's vulnerability to Iago's fictions can be seen as paradoxically related to his own loving sensitivity to the claims of autonomous discourse. Eagleton's insight clarifies the ways in which the creative potential of language in *Othello* is inextricably intertwined with its destructive power. "All that's spoke is marr'd," comments Gratiano at the conclusion of the play (5.2.358), in an effort to characterize the defeated potential constituting the tragic situation.

Desdemona both creates and is enveloped by the tragic paradoxes of language. The untenable position that she occupies in the action can best be described by noting that she makes three remarkable attempts to save her marriage in the play, and that each attempt is a lie. In examining her three lies, we can see that each issues from the paradoxical, contradictory materials that compose the heroics of marriage.

Desdemona's first lie involves not telling her father about her marriage. Strictly speaking, this lie of omission precedes the action and is responsible for generating the preliminary conflicts in the play. Brabantio's superstitious horror at his daughter's secret elopement with an aging Moor clearly distinguishes him as the irrational contender in the Senate scene; no matter how ominously qualified, the lovers' happiness and confidence command greater sympathy than the racist torment of the shattered, deceived father. It immediately becomes clear that Brabantio's conception of his daughter as "a maiden never bold of spirit, / So still and quiet that her motion / Blush'd at her self" (1.3.94–96), couched in the traditional terms of the Renaissance idealization of women as silent,

---

118. Eagleton, pp. 6–9. Cf. Mueller, who argues (p. 6) in another context that in *Othello*, "the destructiveness and destruction of grand language are the subject matter of the play."

chaste, and obedient, is based fragilely on the most oblivious pater-
nal self-deception. In defending her marriage before the Senate,
Desdemona not only manifests courage and determination, she
defines herself as a full-fledged subject, who assumes the legitimacy and priority of her independent desires and actions: "*I did
love* the Moor to live with him . . . ; "*My heart's subdued /* Even to
the utmost pleasure of my lord"; "*I saw* Othello's visage in his
mind / And to his honours, and his valiant parts / *Did I my soul and
fortunes consecrate*"; "The rites for which *I love him* are bereft me"
(1.3.248–57, italics mine). It is important to stress that what commentators have seen as Othello's "male dream of female passivity"
is by no means presented unequivocally in this scene.[119] In contrast
to Brabantio's admiration for his daughter's alleged silence and
obedience, Othello responds with loving pleasure to Desdemona's
self-assertion:

> She gave me for my pains a world of sighs;
> She swore i' faith 'twas strange, 'twas passing strange;
> 'Twas pitiful, 'twas wondrous pitiful;
> She wish'd she had not heard it, yet she wish'd
> That heaven had made her such a man: she thank'd me,
> And bade me, if I had a friend that lov'd her,
> I should but teach him how to tell my story,
> And that would woo her. Upon this hint I spake.
>
> [1.3.159–66]

Indeed, Othello's lingering attachment to his view of Desdemona
as an active, separate person asserts itself in his last attempt against
succumbing to jealousy:

> 'Tis not to make me jealous
> To say my wife is fair, feeds well, loves company,
> Is free of speech, sings, plays, and dances well;
> Where virtue is, these are more virtuous:
> Nor from mine own weak merits will I draw
> The smallest fear, or doubt of her revolt,
> For she had eyes, and chose me.
>
> [3.3.187–93]

Scholars have demonstrated convincingly the ambivalence and

119. See, e.g., Greenblatt, p. 239.

narcissism of Othello's love for Desdemona, insights with which I
fully agree.[120] Here I wish to stress, however, that whatever illusions are involved in Desdemona and Othello's marriage,
Desdemona, like Juliet, Rosalind, Portia, Viola, and Olivia,
chooses freely to enter into them; at this point in the play she is not
merely a victim and object of Othello's desires and fears, but a
subject, with her own, distinctive set of actions and priorities.[121] It
is true that the terms in which Desdemona describes her own
conflict in the Senate scene, picturing herself as bound either to
father or to husband, seem to undermine her assertions of independence and subjectivity:

> My noble father,
> I do perceive here a divided duty: . . .
> My life and education both do learn me
> How to respect you, you are lord of all my duty,
> I am hitherto your daughter: but here's my husband:
> And so much duty as my mother show'd
> To you, preferring you before her father,
> So much I challenge, that I may profess,
> Due to the Moor my lord.
> [1. 3.180–89]

The unresolved paradoxes inherent in the ideals of female equality
and wifely obedience do contribute to her destruction. Although
the lines just quoted suggest the contradictions inherent in
Desdemona's assumption of autonomy, however, these potentially disturbing issues are deflected at the beginning of the play.

Like Othello's construction of a conflict between love and duty,

---

120. See Greenblatt; and the references in n. 100 above.

121. See Eagleton, who chastises (e.g., pp. 69–70) Othello's "wholly
'imaginary' relation to reality; his rotund, mouth-filling rhetoric signifies a
delusory completeness of being, in which the whole world becomes a sig-
nified obediently reflecting back the imperious signifier of the self. Even
Desdemona becomes his 'fair warrior,' as though he can grasp nothing which
he has not first translated into his own military idiom." Desdemona does not
simply accept such translations of her identity, however, but actively creates
them herself; further, the military idiom, absorbed and transformed by domestic idealism, is part of the larger cultural vocabulary of the heroics of
marriage.

Desdemona's description of a conflict of loyalties between husband and father turns out to be easily dealt with, obsolete. No one at this point in the play, including Brabantio, questions the well-established and accepted priority of wifely obedience or primary loyalty to a spouse. Brabantio's bitter grievance lies instead with Desdemona's failure to gain his consent for her marriage: it is this omission that constitutes her deception. Rather than finding, as he had assumed, that chaste modesty is the source of his daughter's opposition to marrying one of the "wealthy curled darlings of our nation" (1.2.68), he discovers that she has been "half the wooer," determined to love the man she wants to love and to choose a spouse for herself (1.3.176), a decision that she presents to her father as a fait accompli.

It is in the context of selecting her own mate that Desdemona inscribes herself in the heroics of marriage (1.3.248–59), and at this point it is useful to recall the paradoxical view of parental consent to marriage embedded in that discourse. Time and again the Protestant idealizers of marriage protest vehemently the common phenomenon of parents forcing children to marry against their will; inexplicably, they are equally resistant to the idea of children marrying without parental consent. "No man can passe away anothers right, without his liking," William Whately asserts in seeming defense of individual choice of a spouse; yet as we have seen, he immediately adds that a couple marrying without parental consent are living in sin until "they haue procured an after-consent, to ratifie that, which ought not to haue been done before the consent."[122] It is precisely this ambivalence in which Desdemona is trapped. Clearly, her father's superstitious abhorrence would have caused him to withhold his consent; Brabantio himself admits that had he known his daughter's inclinations, he would have gone to any lengths, including forcing her to marry the despised Roderigo, in order to impede them (1.2.176). Desdemona's marriage to Othello consequently requires elopement. Yet the fact that Brabantio remains permanently unreconciled to the match creates a lingering, negative resonance throughout the play that is never overcome: "If you have lost him, / Why, I have lost him too," Desdemona reminds Othello (4.2.47–48) ; and Gratiano's first re-

122. Whately, p. 34.

action to Desdemona's murder is to remark, "Poor Desdemona, I am glad thy father's dead; / Thy match was mortal to him, and pure grief / Shore his old thread atwain" (5.2.205–7). Thus the play keeps subtly alive the associations between Desdemona's independent act of choosing her own spouse with death and sin. These associations explain her otherwise illogical deathbed response, "They are loves I bear to you," to Othello's warning, "Think on thy sins" (5.2.39–40). Thus Shakespeare dramatizes the contradictions inherent in individual choice and parental consent in the heroics of marriage by establishing Desdemona's match as courageous and triumphant, while giving it the discursive status of a lie.

The unresolved dilemmas implied and hinted at in Desdemona's first lie explode into tragedy in the circumstances surrounding the second and third. Once again Desdemona's predicament can be located in the contradictory terms in which female identity is constructed in the heroics of marriage. To reiterate, the Puritans both assert and deny female equality and subjectivity. They consider women equal to men in the sight of God and value them for their domestic capabilities, as well as their spiritual and physical companionship; they often grant women's rights and desires in marital sexual relations, usually referred to as "mutual benevolence," as much validity as those of men. When focusing on the issue of individual choice of a spouse, the Puritans frequently ignore gender or, like Niccholes and Wing, address males exclusively. Yet many argue for the woman's need to choose and consent, as well as the man's. Dod and Cleaver, for example, insist that a couple should spend as much time as possible together during courtship, observing each other: "It must be a mutual promise, that is, either party must make it to other, not the man only, nor the woman only, but both the man and the woman"; otherwise, "it is no true and perfect contract."[123] Even as they argue for female equality in sexual relations and (occasionally) independence in choosing a mate, however, the Puritans are constantly establishing the well-known if ambiguous hierarchy of domestic power, recommending that women help and advise their husbands while insisting on

123. Dod and Cleaver (1598), pp. 108–9, 122.

wifely obedience, silence, and subjection: "Hee is her head, and shee his glorie."[124]

We can recall that in the Senate scene Desdemona defines herself precisely in terms of choice and desire: "I did love the Moor, to live with him" (1.3.248). Othello has responded to his wife's independence and self-conception during courtship with joyous pleasure, muted only by an ambivalence of which, at this point, he remains dimly aware. Yet it is precisely these qualities of self-assertion that combine with terrible irony to ruin Desdemona. As Kirsch and Greenblatt have demonstrated, her eroticism becomes for the deluded Othello the very source of his anguish, just as her autonomy in choosing him takes on the insidious characteristics of deception. Iago's fictions gradually coax Othello toward alienation, leading him to give credence to his hitherto unrecognized agreement with Brabantio:

> *Iago.* She did deceive her father, marrying you;
> And when she seem'd to shake and fear your looks,
> She lov'd them most.
> *Oth.* And so she did.
>
> [3.3.210–13]

In a similar vein, Desdemona's loyalty, liveliness, and self-assertion take a bitterly ironic and self-defeating form after her marriage, when she focuses on pleading for Cassio, her suspected partner in adultery. When, after succumbing to Iago's temptation, Othello begins to confront Desdemona with his suspicions, the heroics of marriage collapses into its irreconcilable contradictions, adding force to the unyielding claustrophobia of the play. This process reaches a climax at Desdemona's second lie, which involves her loss of the handkerchief that was Othello's first gift to her.

As noted, Desdemona's self-presentation in the Senate scene is couched in a quasi-military idiom, in which she identifies herself with Othello's profession of soldier, an association reiterated in descriptions of Desdemona by herself and others throughout the play. (e.g., 2.1.74; 2.1.75; and 3.4.149). In this same speech she establishes her identity as a wife in terms of the dynamic, chosen

---

124. Dod and Cleaver (1598), pp. 122–23.

submission defined in Protestant sexual discourse: "I saw Othello's visage in his mind, / And to his honours, and his valiant parts / Did I my soul and fortunes consecrate" (1.3.252–54). Desdemona's conflation of her desire and devotion with Othello's profession therefore unites public and private life in the analogous association idealized in Protestant sexual discourse. Othello's account of their courtship further clarifies his wife's identification with his heroic exploits; indeed, it is the "strangeness" of these endeavors, their legendary quality, that have enchanted her, thus making her self-assertion and their marriage possible. (1.3.128–70). When Desdemona lies to Othello about losing the handkerchief he gave her, however, it is precisely her allegiance to the exotic quality of his narrative reminiscences, the power of the discourse that won her love, which recoils to overwhelm and terrify her. The moment of the second lie is worth quoting at length:

Oth. I have a salt and sullen rheum offends me,
    Lend me thy handkerchief.
Des. Here, my lord.
Oth. That which I gave you.
Des. I have it not about me.
Oth. Not?
Des. No, faith, my lord.
Oth. That's a fault: that handkerchief
    Did an Egyptian to my mother give,
    She was a charmer, and could almost read
    The thoughts of people; . . .
    To lose, or give't away, were such perdition
    As nothing else could match.
Des. Is't possible?
Oth. 'Tis true, there's magic in the web of it;
    A sibyl, that had number'd in the world
    The sun to make two hundred compasses,
    In her prophetic fury sew'd the work;
    The worms were hallow'd that did breed the silk,
    And it was dyed in mummy, which the skillful
    Conserve of maidens' hearts.
Des. I' faith is't true?
Oth. Most veritable, therefore look to't well.

Des. Then would to God that I had never seen it!
Oth. Ha, wherefore?
Des. Why do you speak so startingly and rash?
Oth. Is't lost? is't gone? Speak, is it out o' the way?
Des. Heaven bless us!
Oth. Say you?
Des. It is not lost, but what an if it were?
Oth. Ha!
Des. I say it is not lost.
            [3.4.47–82]

Interestingly, Desdemona next attempts to respond to Othello's exotic tale of the handkerchief much as she did during the legends of his courtship, with an act of self-assertion:

Oth. Fetch't, let me see it.
Des. Why, so I can sir, but I will not now,
            This is a trick, to put me from my suit,
            I pray let Cassio be receiv'd again.
Oth. Fetch me that handkerchief, my mind misgives.
Des. Come, come,
            You'll never meet a more sufficient man.
Oth. The handkerchief!
            [3.4.83–89]

Aside from the fateful irony of her choice of subject, Desdemona's attempt to distract Othello, which persists for several more lines after the passage just quoted, now appears to him as willfulness, wifely disobedience. Endeavoring to declare her independence from Othello's discourse, she succeeds only in compounding the lie. Her identity as a subject, constituted by her active, chosen responsiveness to her husband's narrations, consequently begins to dissolve.

Initiated in the course of her second lie, this process of dissolution continues when Desdemona, overwhelmed by Othello's anguish, retreats from efforts to understand to fragile rationalizations of his behavior. Significantly, these rationalizations are expressed as an acknowledged division between public and private life, in which the latter is regarded as subordinate and inferior to the former:

> Something sure of state,
> Either from Venice, or some unhatch'd practice,
> Made demonstrable here in Cyprus to him,
> Hath puddled his clear spirit, and in such cases
> Men's natures wrangle with inferior things,
> Though great ones are the object.
>   [3.4.137–42]

In this speech, Desdemona reverses her conception of marriage as a heroic endeavor, uniting public and private domains and granting her status as a subject. As we have seen, this status is equivocal at best and is inscribed in a discourse that succumbs to its own contradictions. That wifely heroism is itself a contradiction becomes manifest in Desdemona's third lie. Attempting to protect Othello from being discovered as her murderer, Desdemona responds to Emilia's "O, who has done this deed?" with "Nobody, I myself, farewell" (5.2.124–25). Desdemona's final effort to identify with and absorb herself in her husband's actions (itself the definition of marriage in this play) becomes an act of self-assertion that is, simultaneously, an act of self-cancellation: "Myself" is the equivalent of "Nobody." Constituting the final dissolution of Desdemona's identity, the third lie is a dying voice. In this context Othello's outraged retort, "She's like a liar gone to burning hell, / 'Twas I that kill'd her" (5.2.130–31), could be read as a protest against his wife's destruction. But it is too late; the assertive and lively woman who "is fair, feeds well, loves company, / Is free of speech, sings, plays, and dances well" has disappeared, along with the troublesome contradictions of the heroics of marriage. Her chastity reestablished, Desdemona, like Zenocrate, is rendered inert, removed from the realm of significant action. Brabantio's fantasy of "a maiden . . . So still and quiet, that her motion / Blush'd at herself" is consummated in the figure of the dead Desdemona "as monumental alabaster . . . one entire and perfect chrysolite," the "heavenly sight" with which *Othello* concludes (5.2.5; 146; 279).

The resolution of the action can be understood by examining the conjoined mechanisms of the play's complex treatment of language and sexuality. In her martyrdom Desdemona returns, as it were, from the dead and lies in a self-sacrificing attempt to shield Othello. Both directly before and after the murder he idealizes her chastity as "whole," "entire," "perfect," and "alabaster," using terms that suggest virginity and stasis. Thus he denies her liveliness and wifehood and reveals both his longing and the desire to be released from that longing. In the process initiated by Desdemona's third lie, then, husband and wife in a sense conspire to retrieve the realm of autonomous discourse in which, discounting social and material circumstances, they originally constructed their courtship and defined their marriage. Yet the power to create reality through language has increasingly become identified in the play with lying. Itself a lie, Desdemona's final self-abnegation initiates the resolution of the action and is essential to it, though it is inadequate to bring the conflict to completion. What is needed to finish that process is not autonomous discourse, but "a material limit before which the power of discourse is disarmed."[125] It is not Desdemona's martyrdom that convinces Othello of her fidelity, but Emilia's defiant self-assertion, rooted as it is in narrating the actual circumstances of Iago's deceptions. In a small exchange with Othello that takes place after she discovers the murdered Desdemona, Emilia distinguishes herself precisely in these terms:

Oth. Why, how should she be murder'd?
Emil. Alas, who knows?
Oth. You heard her say, herself, it was not I.
Emil. She said so, I must needs report a truth.
[5.2.128–31]

It is significant that Emilia's revelations are all couched within the contradictory discourse of the heroics of marriage. Discovering that she has unwittingly contributed to her mistress's murder by adhering to wifely silence and obedience (i.e., in confidentially stealing Desdemona's handkerchief at her husband's request), she

125. Eagleton, p. 10.

now realizes that her only recourse is to speak and disobey: "I am bound to speak," she replies to Iago's attempts to silence her, "I hold my peace sir, no, / I'll be in speaking, liberal as the air, / Let heaven, and men, and devils, let 'em all, / All, all cry shame against me, yet I'll speak" (5.2.185, 220–24). Here Emilia's declarations summon the paradoxical associations of speech throughout the play both with truth and with the incipient violation of established order; specifically, her linkage of her own courage and self-assertion with possible shame evokes the contradictions of the heroics of marriage. When we recall the Puritans' ambiguous injunction that a wife must obey her husband absolutely unless he commands what "is forbidden by God," we can perceive Emilia's predicament as an irreconcilable conflict between the private obligations of a wife (loyalty, silence, and obedience) and the public duties of a citizen (revelation of a murder): "Good gentlemen, let me have leave to speak. / *'Tis proper I obey him, but not now*: / Perchance, Iago, I will ne'er go home" (5.2.196–98, italics mine).

Shakespeare thus distributes the components of female heroism between two characters. Although the destinies of both Desdemona and Emilia issue in martyrdom, their heroic styles are distinct. The waiting woman, subordinate in social status as well as integrity, at last courageously acknowledges and embraces through active conflict the contradictions of the status of wife that are inscribed in the heroics of marriage. The aristocratic Desdemona, on the other hand, dwindles, rather than grows, from a lively and courageous girl to a wife who is "half asleep," retreating with little choice to fragile explanations that subvert the basis of her marriage and to a naive, insistent, and unhelpful purity, and recovering her courage only in a final act of self-cancellation.[126]

Desdemona's unavoidable retreat to victimization, to passivity, and to the assumption of a kind of pre-marital chastity corresponds to Othello's final idealization of her as virginal, static, and inert. Removed from the heroics of marriage, she is also removed from action and conflict. The consignment of women and eros to inactivity is one of the solutions of the heroism of action. No longer distracted by the confusing, contradictory centrality that marriage has assumed in his identity, Othello ends his life by recalling his

126. Cf. Dash, pp. 103–30.

military achievements and devotion to public service. Thus the
beautiful, immobilized Desdemona combines with the neighing
steed, the plumed troop, the spirit-stirring fife, the royal banner,
and all quality, pride, pomp, and circumstance of glorious war to
evoke with unarguable lyric beauty the tremendous elegiac power
of the lost past.

vi

No Shakespearean tragedy focuses exclusively on a strong,
central female figure. That in *Othello* Shakespeare should diffuse
female heroism between two figures, distinguishing the sexual
styles of waiting woman and lady, has significant implications for
determining his interests, as well as for assessing the tragic representation of sexuality. Before turning to these crucial issues, however, I would like to introduce a comparison with *The Duchess of
Malfi* (c. 1613–14), written approximately ten years after *Othello*.
Here it suffices to note that it is, of course, Othello's heroism that
assumes central importance in the earlier play. Although Shakespeare clearly recognizes and explores the potential for female heroism in the qualities inscribed in the Protestant idealization of marriage, he remains primarily concerned to examine the decline of the
heroism of action by dramatizing its inadequacy when faced with
the challenges of private life. In his next tragedy of love, *Antony
and Cleopatra* (1607), rather than elaborating his insights into the
contradictions inherent in marriage itself, he chooses instead to
focus on the conflict between eros and public service, continuing
his intense scrutiny of the tragic obsolescence of the epic-chivalric
heroic style.

In *The Duchess of Malfi* the process of decline characterizing the
representation of the heroism of action in Jacobean tragedy is already complete, its logic manifest. As in *Othello*, the distinction
between public and private domains demands scrutiny and re-
definition. Conflicts centered on these issues are initiated by an
aristocratic woman's decision to disobey her male relatives and to
marry a man not her social equal, thus defying traditional social
and sexual hierarchies and opening the way for their dissolution.
But what is striking in comparing *Othello* and *The Duchess of Malfi*

is less the similarity of the elements constituting each play than the differences with which they are emphasized and arranged. For example, in *Othello* the state is both rational and just; the hero's harmonious relationship with the state involves rewarded merit and dignified gratitude. In need of Othello's services and respecting his abilities, the political hierarchy of Venice easily accepts his unusual marriage. The complex psychological and sociocultural factors that combine to undo Othello do not stem from political absolutism, then, but are more subtle and diffuse.

The Duchess of Malfi also begins with a picture of the state as traditionally conceived by humanist idealism: governed by a rational prince with the aid of learned and truthful counsellors, setting an example of judiciousness for the people, and inspiring the nobility to virtuous action (1.1.5–23).[127] But this idealized state is dislocated to France. It quickly becomes apparent that Italy, where the play takes place, has a decadent and corrupt court, dominated by a vicious, melancholy, and hypocritical Cardinal ("the spring in his face is nothing but the engendering of toads" [1.1.167–68]) and his pathological brother, Ferdinand ("a most perverse and turbulent nature; / What appears in him mirth is merely outside. / . . . He speaks with others' tongues, and hears men's suits / With others' ears: will seem to sleep o'th'bench / Only to entrap offenders in their answers; / Dooms men to death by information. / Rewards by hearsay" [1.1.179–85]). In a further perversion of the humanist political ideal, each brother surrounds himself with sycophants and "never pays debts, unless they be shrewd turns" (1.1.191). The profitable counsel to be exchanged between prince and advisers has degenerated into rigid, mindless, absolutism. "Methinks you that are courtiers should be my touchwood, take fire when I give fire; that is, laugh when I laugh, were the subject never so witty," advises Ferdinand, in one of his eeriest speeches (1.1.127–30). Given the diseased nature of the state, how can its defense be valued? Military heroism is evoked only in brief allusions and associated with the Cardinal, Ferdinand, and their savage, discontented henchman, Bosola (e.g., 1.1.76, 89–126; 3.3;

127. All references to *The Duchess of Malfi*, identified in the text by act, scene, and line numbers, are to Fraser and Rabkin, vol. 2, *The Stuart Period*, pp. 476–515.

3.4). The steward Antonio's victories at games become nostalgic exercises, staged by servant courtiers for the amusement of their betters. "When shall we leave this sportive action, and fall to action indeed?" asks Ferdinand, disingenuously (1.1.92–93).

Webster is dramatizing an anachronistic neofeudal regime in the process of decline: in short, to use Lawrence Stone's terms, a crisis of the aristocracy. Though scholars have noted this fact, until a short time ago analyses have subordinated the political and sociocultural issues that generate conflict in the play to moral assessments of guilt and innocence: shall we blame the Duchess or praise her for courageously compromising the demands of her position in order to marry her steward for love? How shall we assess the guilt and latter-day conversion of the dangerous, tortured, victimized Bosola?—itself a question that leads to assessments of the relevance of the play's fifth act, from which the Duchess has disappeared.[128] In a recent essay, however, Frank Whigham has forcefully redirected analysis, demonstrating that moral judgments of the characters are at best peripheral to an understanding of the play and locating the action precisely within Jacobean social processes.[129]

Whigham partially couches his arguments in the terms set down by Raymond Williams's conception of culture as a perpetually dynamic network of processes of change. In relation to a hegemonic dominant culture, Williams isolates several formative modes that "are significant both in themselves and in what they reveal of the characteristics of the 'dominant.'" His notions of "residual" and "emergent" processes are most illuminating in terms of *The Duchess*. Williams defines the "residual" as a process by which a culture relates to the elements of its own past: "thus certain experiences, meanings, and values which cannot be ex-

---

128. These questions indicate the principal directions of almost all of the scholarship on *The Duchess of Malfi*. Representative examples of different ways in which these issues are addressed include James L. Calderwood, "*The Duchess of Malfi*: Styles of Ceremony," *Essays in Criticism*, 12 (1962), 133–47; and Susan C. Baker, "The Static Protagonist in *The Duchess of Malfi*," *Texas Studies in Literature and Language*, vol. 22, no. 3 (Fall 1980), 343–57.

129. Whigham, "Sexual and Social Mobility." Whigham's essay includes a good bibliography of criticism of the play. See also Margaret L. Mikesell, "Matrimony and Change in Webster's *The Duchess of Malfi*," *Journal of the Rocky Mountain Medieval and Renaissance Association*, 2 (January 1981), 97–111.

pressed or substantially verified in terms of the dominant culture, are nevertheless lived and practiced on the basis of the residue . . . of some previous social and cultural institution or formation." Although this aspect of the residual can have an oppositional relation to the dominant culture, it is distinct from "that active manifestation of the residual . . . which has been wholly or largely incorporated into the dominant culture." Where the residual describes a culture's relation to its past, Williams's notion of "emergent" formations delineates a process by which a dominant culture confronts the present and future. "By emergent," he argues, "I mean . . . that new meanings and values, new practices, new relationships and kinds of relationship are continually being created."[130]

These concepts enable Whigham to explain mechanisms of cultural change that generate irreconcilable conflicts in *The Duchess of Malfi*. For example, he argues that Ferdinand is an embattled aristocrat, resisting an onslaught of upward mobility. Ferdinand's pathology is rooted in a residual exclusivity that now appears deranged, an obsessive pride in purity of blood that becomes the basis of an incestuous attachment to his sister. Antonio, on the other hand, participates in the (to Ferdinand) threatening emergent cultural forces. Whether Antonio's motives for marrying the Duchess are ambitious is arguable, but it is clear that his valuable skills are administrative rather than military; and that his managerial abilities match those that became increasingly important to upwardly mobile men in sixteenth-century England, men who sought and attained advancement at court through education and achievement, rather than assuming elite status as a birthright. The isolated, perplexed Bosola perceives the evil of the neofeudal regime of the Aragonian brothers but cannot imagine a place for himself within another political formation. A veteran soldier without an occupation in times of peace, the neglected henchman embodies the socioeconomic transition from a collectivist ethic of service to an ascribed aristocracy to a mobile bourgeois economy of wages, employment, and individualistic achievement. As

130. Raymond Williams, *Marxism and Literature* (Oxford: Oxford University Press, 1977), pp. 122–23.

Whigham explains, Bosola, losing his belief in rank, finds himself caught between residual and emergent cultural modes:

> As the human origin of rank was gradually revealed, it became clear that the power to confer it was freely available to those who could pull the strings of influence or purse. When ascriptive status emerged as a commodity, the king's sacred role as fount of identity began to decay, and with this shift came a change in the nature of identity itself. It became visible as something achieved, a human product contingent on wealth, connection, and labor. Later, when Marx described it theoretically, the notion could seem a conceptual liberation. . . . But in the Renaissance, when this insight began to be visible, it seemed a loss rather than a liberation. The obligation to found identity on one's actions seemed to sever the transindividual bonds that bound the polity together; it left one on one's own.[131]

Although he is describing Bosola, Whigham provides in this passage a cogent analysis of the historical conditions that make female heroism possible in Renaissance tragedy. Bosola, himself of "base descent," remains enmeshed in an unholy and dependent alliance with the corrupt and anachronistic past embodied in Ferdinand; for him the glimpse of a possible future, though poignant, is belated and brief. Yet it is not Bosola but the Duchess herself who is the hero of the play, precisely because it is she who most fully embodies the "coincidence of loss and possibility" located in the shifts of cultural identity taking place in the Renaissance.[132] Proud of her royal birth and stature, the widowed Duchess is also in love with her steward and determined to disobey her brothers, woo Antonio, and marry him. Thus she is caught between classes, between sexes, between tenses: as a young widow, she has a past and seeks a future; as an aristocrat who is also royal, she is independent, politically central, a ruler; but as a woman she is marginal, subordinate, and dependent—a status that her brothers' tyranny makes abundantly clear. With her conjoined, paradoxical attachments to present, future, and past, to status granted at birth as well

131. Whigham, "Sexual and Social Mobility," p. 177.
132. Ibid.

as status gained by achievement, to female independence and female subordination, the Duchess is in a position as fluid and anomalous as the social conditions of Jacobean England. Viewed in this context, it becomes clear why Webster chooses an aristocratic woman as the figure that could represent most fully the irreconcilable conflicts of tragedy.

Understanding the play's class and sexual conflicts in terms of emergent and residual cultural modes allows us to connect the two dominant types of Renaissance sexual discourse examined in this book more firmly with historical process, with the shifting relations among present, past, and future, than is possible to do when exploring *Othello*. Specifically, the polarizing mentality that idealizes or degrades women and eros is associated in the play with the decadent, tyrannical Ferdinand and the alienated, paralyzed Bosola. As Whigham shows, Ferdinand's obsessive attachment to his sister constitutes not a desire for sexual union, but a deranged purity, in which her absolute chastity becomes the equivalent of his exclusivist, aristocratic territoriality.[133] In his narcissistic identification with the Duchess as his twin, he insists that she remain unmarried, her life sexless. "And women like that part, which, like the lamprey, / Hath never a bone in't," he warns obscenely (1.1.343–44).[134] Ferdinand's association of sex with pollution is echoed by Bosola's misogyny, which is second only to Truewit's in its nauseated specificity and is distinct in intensity from that of the comic wit only by being completely gratuitous. "I would sooner eat a dead pigeon, taken from the soles of the feet of one sick of the plague, than kiss one of you fasting," Bosola tells an old lady, who at first appears to enter the play for the sole purpose of being abused by him (2.1.44–46).[135] The other character who

133. Whigham, "Sexual and Social Mobility," pp. 169–71.

134. For a discussion of erotic imagery in the play, see Dale Randall, "The Rank and Earthy Background of Certain Physical Symbols in *The Duchess of Malfi*," *Renaissance Drama*, N.S. 18 (1987).

135. Actually, like the character Julia, the Cardinal's mistress, the old lady seems to be in the play as a comment on and warning about the Duchess's marriage. Her odd appearances (see also 2.2.1–27) can be linked with the complex of witch imagery that pervades the play (see, e.g., 3.1.78, 3.2.140–41, 3.4.57–58, and 3.5.54–55) and the misogynistic connections of the Duchess with the lady-of-pleasure tradition, traced by Randall.

associates the Duchess with absolute purity is Antonio, who, in his role as obedient steward at the beginning of the play, construes her as divine, an unattainable ideal, associated with rebirth, an exception to her sex:

> Whilst she speaks,
> She throws upon a man so sweet a look
> That it were able to raise one to a galliard
> That lay in a dead palsy; and to dote
> On that sweet countenance: but in that look
> There speaketh so divine a continence
> As cut off all lascivious and vain hope.
> Her days are practiced in such noble virtue
> That, sure her nights, nay more, her very sleeps,
> Are more in heaven than other ladies' shrifts.
>
> [1.1.205–13]

The Duchess recognizes her brother's grotesque misogyny and Antonio's rapturous idealization as equally life-denying; indeed, she resists the dualizing sexual sensibility that would relegate her to aestheticized inactivity and permanent widowhood in terms and imagery that recall the destinies of Zenocrate and Desdemona. "Why should only I, / Of all the other princes of the world / Be cased up, like a holy relic? I have youth, / And a little beauty," she protests to Ferdinand (3.2.137–40). And she exhorts Antonio to marry her by resisting in a similar vein immobilization as an icon, associating the widow's enforced chastity with stasis and death: "This is flesh, and blood, sir, / 'Tis not the figure cut in alabaster / Kneels at my husband's tomb" (1.1.459–61).[136]

   Much of the scholarly debate about the Duchess's actions has centered on her sexuality. She has been blamed for being irresponsible, overly passionate, too bold, in analyses that often focus on the demands of her social position and/or on the conservative body of Renaissance thought that regarded a widow's remarriage as lustful and disloyal. Or she is praised for being both courageous and nurturing, in analyses that often pit the individual against society and, in post-romantic terms, privilege the former while

---

136. Cf. *Othello*, 5.2.3–5: "Yet I'll not shed her blood, / Nor scar that whiter skin of hers than snow, / And smooth, as monumental alabaster."

regarding the latter as oppressive.[137] In order to escape these terms, Whigham rejects entirely an analytic focus on the erotic, which he regards as moralistic and trivial: "the Duchess's actions should be seen not as erotic (a common male reduction of women's issues) but as political," he insists.[138]

Yet to view eros as a comparatively trivial, nonpolitical issue is also to miss the point. The Duchess repeatedly emphasizes her sexuality, indicating in precise and definite terms its centrality to her identity ("This is flesh, and blood, sir . . ."). Throughout the play Webster not only stresses the strength of her desire for Antonio, but also focuses on her pregnancies, her erotic playfulness, and her tender, nurturing motherhood. "I pray thee look thou givest my little boy / Some syrup for his cold, and let the girl / Say her prayers ere she sleep," she instructs her waiting-woman at the moment of her death (4.2.203–5).[139] The Duchess's erotic identity, then, is omnipresent in the play and central to it. The point is not that erotic issues are separate from, and/or less important than, political ones; to adopt this position is to accept the sexual stance of Bacon, Donne, Tamburlaine, Othello, and—what is decidedly less appealing—of Ferdinand. As we have seen, this point of view does not adequately account for the number of great Jacobean tragedies that center on private experience. Rather than representing public and private life as a hierarchy that subordinates the latter to the former, *The Duchess of Malfi* attempts to draw the two domains together and to confer upon them equal distinction. The point is a crucial one, because in this play, unlike *Othello*, the effort constitutes a central, rather than a subordinate action, and its failure provides the primary tragic material of the play.

The effort to unite public and private life and to confer upon them equal prestige is formulated in the Protestant idealization of marriage. This is the discourse in which the Duchess is inscribed. As we have seen, in the Protestant conception of marriage as a

137. See, e.g., Calderwood; and Baker.
138. Whigham, "Sexual and Social Mobility," p. 184.
139. See Alan Dessen, "Modern Productions and the Elizabethan Scholar," *Renaissance Drama*, n.s. (1987); Dessen points out the ways in which excluding these lines from a production of the play, as was done in the recent National Theatre production (1985–86), tends to alter the audience's view of the Duchess and to reduce the complexity of her character.

heroic endeavor, a military idiom is absorbed and transformed from the heroism of action, and this idiom, though sometimes applied exclusively to males, frequently ignores gender or explicitly includes women as subjects. It is precisely this military vocabulary of conquest and defeat that the Duchess uses to define her marriage to her steward. In response to her brothers' demand that she remain widowed, for example, she reflects:

> Shall this move me? If all my royal kindred
> Lay in my way unto this marriage,
> I'd make them my low foot-steps. And even now,
> Even in this hate, as men in some great battles
> By apprehending danger, have achieved
> Almost impossible actions: I have heard soldiers say so—
> So I, through frights and threatenings, will assay
> This dangerous venture. Let old wives report
> I winked, and chose a husband.
> [1.1.348–56]

"My laurel is all withered," she says, characterizing her eventual defeat; and she adds, "I am armed 'gainst misery" (3.5.90, 141). Finally, the Duchess's conception of her marriage as a dangerous but necessary venture also takes on the lonely, absolutist commitment shared by the tragic hero and the hero of marriage ("I am going into a wilderness, / Where I shall find nor path, nor friendly clue / To be my guide" [1.1.367–68]), leading her inevitably to ponder her own condition in universal terms, as Desdemona never could, and to her prolonged encounter with death. It has been argued correctly that the Duchess's confrontation with "ultimate universal hostilities" distinguishes her as "the first fully tragic woman in Renaissance drama."[140] I would add to this crucial point that it is the full recognition of the importance of private life, here claiming equal status with public concerns, that makes her tragic stature possible; in turn, the Duchess's heroism helps to define and clarify the heroics of marriage.

It has also been argued that the Duchess's metaphysical confrontation with the foundations of human identity contains "the kind of speculation familiar from Shakespearean tragedy, where the ele-

---

140. Whigham, "Sexual and Social Mobility," p. 174.

vated are crushed as they inaugurate new conceptual options."[141] Despite her disclaimers to Ferdinand ("Why might not I marry? / I have not gone about, in this, to create / Any new world, or custom" [3.2.110–27]), this argument continues, the Duchess is in fact thoroughly committed to constructing a revolutionary future, viewing herself, like Tamburlaine, as a pioneer who will ignore traditional class barriers and chart a course through the wilderness to discover and colonize a new world, disdainful of the past and independent of it.[142] "All her particular worth grows to this sum: / She stains the time past; lights the time to come," says Antonio; and keeping social history in mind, we can recall that this observation reflects the hopes of a steward who, whether he achieves greatness or has it thrust upon him, unquestionably becomes a protagonist of upward mobility in the play (1.1.218–19).

How revolutionary is the Duchess? Her assertiveness in wooing Antonio has been characterized as androgynous, an attempt to conjoin male and female modes.[143] This idea can lead us to compare the behavior of the Duchess and that of the disguised female comic hero, whose androgyny gives her the freedom actively to pursue her mate. As discussed earlier in this study, the female comic hero's androgynous disguise exists in a holiday world over which she reigns, but the holiday world functions solely to renew and perpetuate the orderly world of every day. At the end of a romantic comedy, therefore, the festive world is left behind; the female hero, who has been free from sexual constraint throughout the play, surrenders her disguise along with her control, in a gesture of commitment to her future as an obedient, subordinate wife. In romantic comedy the contradictions between the woman's present freedom and her future constraint are contained in the final, harmonious, comic focus on the present.

141. Whigham, "Sexual and Social Mobility," p. 174.
142. Cf. Berggren, p. 353; and Whigham, "Sexual and Social Mobility," p. 172.
143. See, e.g., Lois E. Bueler, "Webster's Excellent Hyena," *Philological Quarterly*, 59 (1980), 107–11. Bueler provides a fascinating account of the associations of sexual ambiguity with the hyena, alluding to Ferdinand's pathological fantasies of his sister's sexual relations: "Methinks I see her laughing— / Excellent hyena!—talk to me somewhat, quickly, / Or my imagination will carry me / To see her, in the shameful act of sin" (2.4.38–41). Also see 3.2.222 for an intriguing reference to Antonio as a hermaphrodite.

In *The Duchess of Malfi* the Duchess's widowhood, with its temporary and limited freedoms, can be viewed in aesthetic terms as the symbolic equivalent of an androgynous disguise. Unlike a married woman, a widow in Renaissance England had a distinct legal capacity that she was progressively consolidating in the late sixteenth century, and unlike a single woman, she had an acknowledged right to choose her own mate. Just as the female comic hero does, the widowed Duchess identifies her future mate and follows eros into an alternative world. But as scholars have demonstrated, the widow's freedom constituted an anomaly that was difficult for Jacobean culture to absorb. On the one hand, an independent woman running her own household presented a contradiction to English patriarchal ideology; on the other, a widow who did remarry was criticized as lustful and disloyal, particularly in the threat her remarriage posed to a family's retention of property.[144]

Like Moll Frith's male clothes, then, the Duchess's widowhood calls attention to the irreconcilable contradictions in Jacobean sexual values. But while, unlike the female hero of romantic comedy, Moll refuses to surrender her clothes, she also removes herself from participating in marriage. Thus her androgyny does not constitute a radical threat to the existing social structure. In contrast, the Duchess both marries and attempts to remain independent from the dominant culture, conceptualizing her marriage as autonomous: "All discord, without this circumference / Is only to be pitied and not feared" (1.1.472–73). There is, of course, no place within the absolutist state of the Aragonian brothers to absorb and contain the Duchess's unusual marriage. The vision of the future cannot be amalgamated, put off, or distanced, as it can in a comic structure. In tragedy the future has arrived, and it is unquestionably violent, revolutionary.

Webster, then, clearly recognizes the radical potential of female heroism in the process of cultural change. From this perspective, distinct conceptual alliances and antitheses begin to take shape in our consideration of the play. The dualizing mentality that either idealizes or degrades women and eros becomes associated with an embattled and declining aristocracy, tyrannical political absolutism, an obsolete heroism of action, a receding past. In contrast, the

144. See Todd, esp. p. 73.

heroics of marriage is associated with the bourgeois recognition of merit in determining status, rather than the aristocratic reliance on birth; with administrative rather than military skill; with upward social mobility and female independence; an impending future.

Yet the Duchess's identity and greatness—her heroism—are grounded in the past as well as projected into the future. Though on one level the dichotomy between a corrupt and decadent past and a more promising future is confidently formulated and supported in the play, on another the relation between past and future emerges in contrast as one of conflicting loyalties between two worthwhile modes of thought and being. This second, more subtle, syndrome, which assigns not only corrupt power but sympathy and value to the past, can be perceived by locating the Duchess precisely within the heroics of marriage, the discourse that she creates and adheres to and that defines her.

Like Desdemona, the Duchess is forced to defy male relatives (i.e., authorities) in order to marry the man she wants. Again like Desdemona, she becomes embroiled in the contradictory injunctions of the idealization of marriage that both do and do not encourage woman to have a say in selecting her spouse and do and do not demand familial consent to a match. Yet while Shakespeare dramatizes this issue as a subtle and significant but subordinate theme, Webster brings it to the very center of the action, embodying its consequences in the career of a female hero whose private life subverts the established order. Although Desdemona's marriage matters to the established political order, its primary public importance rests in the state's need for her husband's services; her elopement with Othello precedes the action and takes place offstage. In contrast, the Duchess is a ruler; it is *her* marriage that has crucial importance to the state and shakes its foundations, a fact that, conjoined with her brothers' tyranny, makes the radicalism of her action at once more apparent and more urgent than that of Desdemona. Because the marriage between the Duchess and Antonio is fully dramatized on stage, the ambivalences conjoining family consent and female independence, which are reduced in *Othello* to the receding residue of Brabantio's displeasure, constitute the major, irresolvable, tragic conflicts in the later play. The Duchess and Antonio's marriage contract *per verba de presenti* itself has an ambiguous status. As historians have demonstrated, clandestine marriage, or vows made between consenting adults with a witness present, constituted a perfectly legal union in England until marriage laws were clarified in the eighteenth century. But the social status of such a marriage, contracted without banns, solemnized outside the church, and associated with both poverty and illicit sexual activity, was at best marginal.[145] All throughout her wedding ceremony, the Duchess both abjures and affirms the need for legitimating institutions and traditions, thus unwittingly emphasizing the problematic vulnerability of her marriage. Citing the legality of the ceremony, she demands, "What can the Church force more?" adding insistently, "How can the Church build faster? / We now are man and wife, and 'tis the Church / That must but echo this" (1.1.489, 493–95). Later, when Ferdinand calls her children bastards, the Duchess counters angrily, "You violate a sacrament o'th'Church / Shall make you howl in hell for 't" (3.5.39–40).

But the most powerful contradictions that work to undermine the Duchess's marriage are those centered on status and rank. Though the inequalities that separate Othello and Desdemona (the Moor's age and blackness) are profound, they are nevertheless sufficiently intangible to be easily absorbed by the state: the marriage challenges prejudice, rather than established, class-based social and political hierarchy.[146] In contrast, the discrepancies in rank between the Duchess and Antonio comprise officially institutionalized boundaries, not to be crossed: "Of love, or marriage, between her and me, / They never dream of," Antonio realizes (3.1.36–37), referring not only to the ruling elite, but to the rest of the populace as well. By locating the foundation of identity in merit rather than birth, then, the Duchess drives a radical, irreconcilable wedge between the natural and social orders, previously regarded as identical. "If you will know where breathes a complete man, / I speak it without flattery," she tells Antonio, "turn your eyes, / And progress through yourself" (1.1.440–42).

Yet the Duchess does not adhere entirely to this commitment to

145. See Stone, *Family, Sex and Marriage*, pp. 35, 317, 629.

146. Interestingly, Othello justifies his marriage to Desdemona by alluding to his royal birth as well as his personal merit: "I fetch my life and being / From men of royal siege, and my demerits / May speak unbonneted to as proud a fortune / As this that I have reach'd" (1.2.21–4).

achieved rather than ascribed status. Although the greatest obstacles to her marriage take the form of the brothers' tyranny, an external impediment, it is important to note the extent to which the Duchess herself continues to rely on her royal birth. It is not simply that she takes the lead in the wedding scene ("The misery of us, that are born great, / We are forced to woo because none dare woo us" [1.1.445–46]); she also delivers a very mixed message on the question of rank. Thus she defines Antonio as a "complete man" and claims to "put off all vain ceremony," begging to be regarded not as a royal Duchess, but merely as "a young widow / That claims you for her husband" (1.1.460–62). At the same time, however, she reminds him "what a wealthy mine / I make you lord of" and adds, in what is probably the clearest example of the double bind created by her superior power, "Being now my steward, here upon your lips / I sign your *Quietus est.* This you should have begged now" (1.1.434–35, 467–68). As is often observed, the Duchess continues to take the lead throughout the play, whereas Antonio repeatedly demonstrates his helpless inability either to confront the dreaded brothers or to outwit their villainy: "I am lost in amazement: I know not what to think on 't," he says at one point, in what could stand as a summary statement of his position (2.1.182).[147]

Based in a problematic awareness of a wife's possible social superiority to her husband, the perception of a potentially severed relation between hierarchies of gender and power is also a central issue in the heroics of marriage. "But yet when it hapeneth, that a man marrieth a woman of so high a birth, he ought (not forgetting that hee is her husband) more to honour and esteeme of her, than

147. Cf. Whigham, "Sexual and Social Mobility," p. 176. Whigham remarks of Antonio that "he agreed to his wife's coercive marriage proposal with the deference of the subordinate he feels himself to be." Whigham notes several instances of Antonio's inability to keep up with the aristocratic world he has furtively and reluctantly embraced, including his remaining in hiding when Ferdinand approaches his wife with a dagger (3.2) and, finally, his futile journey in Act 5, when he attempts a reconciliation with the Aaragonian brothers: "Antonio's final action, the desperately naive journey to the Cardinal for reconciliation, freezes him for us, as one whose unsought elevation never brought much sense of how to navigate the webs of alliance and enmity."

of his equall, or of one of meaner parentage, and not onely to account her his companion in loue, and in his life, but (in diuers actions of publike apparance) to hold her his superior," advise Dod and Cleaver. Yet they contradict themselves by adding, "She ought to consider, that no distinction or difference of birth and nobility can be so great, *but that the league which both Gods ordinance and nature hath ordained betwixt men and women, farre exceedeth it: for by nature women was made man's subiect.*"[148] What bond is more "natural," birth or marriage? Dod and Cleaver lean toward the radical position of granting greater importance to marriage, but continue perplexed. Their perception of the problem, which comes from the thwarted attempt to unite not only gender and power, but public and private domains, is itself subversive, but it remains unresolved and, as such, sheds light on *The Duchess of Malfi.* "You are a lord of mis-rule," the Duchess teases Antonio, who counters playfully, "My rule is only in the night" (3.1.6–8). The fact that their marriage must remain exclusively private— within "this circumference"—does indeed become the sign of its doom.

The contradictions about rank, status, gender, and power that characterize the heroics of marriage perpetuate rather than resolve the conflicts between past and future. At the moment of the Duchess's death, the irreconcilable loyalties that are the source of tragic conflict become most clearly visible. On the one hand, the Duchess's rank plays a central role in the construction of her tragic heroism. "For know, whether I am doomed to live, or die, / I can do both like a prince," she tells Ferdinand (3.2.70–71). Later, when Bosola confronts her with chaos and destruction, she asserts her identity in the play's most famous line, "I am Duchess of Malfi still" (4.2.142). The Duchess's courage and dignity in facing death are indissolubly conjoined with her royal stature. On the other hand, the sociopolitical conditions that make heroism possible in the play unquestionably reside in the decay of and need to defy the order from which her stature derives. Antonio correctly defines the heroic response to the resulting untenable position as one of active, chosen suffering: "Though in our miseries fortunes have a

148. Dod and Cleaver (1630), sigs. K and K2v.

part / Yet in our noble sufferings she hath none: / Contempt of pain, that we may call our own" (5.3.55–57).

As I have tried to show, with its background in stoicism, religious martyrdom, and medieval treatises on the art of dying, the heroism of endurance that Antonio defines is connected in Protestant moral treatises with the idealization of marriage and the elevation of the private life, a combination of elements particularly amenable to the construction of female heroism. Much recent scholarship has demonstrated that unstable social conditions often generate female heroism and creativity, which in turn play a major role both in demolishing an old order and in constructing a future.[149] In this context, an interesting example of Shakespeare's relative conservatism in representing women emerges from contrasting the Duchess's death with Desdemona's. The two scenes offer a remarkable instance of a reverse parallel. Both women are unjustly strangled for misconceived sexual crimes; both die martyr's deaths, accompanied by loyal and loving waiting women. As we have seen, Desdemona's understanding of her own situation, along with her responsibility for it, recedes throughout *Othello*. At the moment of her murder, she begs for her life, an action that, however sensible it may appear in isolation, is definitely not characteristic of a tragic hero. Desdemona's final act is one of self-cancellation; courageous self-assertion is instead assigned to the waiting woman, Emilia, who is given the noble lines: "Thou hast not half the power to do me harm / As I have to be hurt" (5.2.163–64). By distributing the components of female heroism between the two women, Shakespeare confers independent selfhood on the subordinate character, while merging Desdemona's identity entirely with Othello's. Thus the stage is cleared for Othello's final, climactic consideration of his own, more active heroism, and the focus centers entirely on the lost past. The emphases in the Duch-

149. See Rose, "Gender, Genre, and History"; Lamb; and Schulenburg. See also Penny Schine Gold, *The Lady and the Virgin: Image, Attitude, and Experience in Twelfth-Century France* (Chicago: University of Chicago Press, 1985). For a very interesting treatment of female heroism in Restoration and eighteenth-century tragedy, see Laura Brown, "The Defenseless Woman and the Development of English Tragedy," *Studies in English Literature*, 22 (1982), 429–43.

ess's death scene are, of course, different. The most prolonged moment in the play, the Duchess's death is made to carry the full burden of tragic significance, as her debates with Bosola on the meaning of life and the effects of her death on the other characters make clear. Summoning all her princely dignity, the Duchess also dies thinking of her children's welfare, thus dissolving the distinction between "woman" and "greatness" that her waiting woman, Cariola, makes after her marriage (1.1.505). The Duchess's dual role as agent and sacrifice is never simplified to an emphasis on her victimization. Instead, her courage in facing death is emphasized ("Pull, and pull strongly, for your able strength / Must pull down heaven upon me," [4.2.230–31]), along with her acceptance of responsibility for her own actions. "Doth not death fright you," asks Bosola. "Who would be afraid on 't?" she replies, "Knowing to meet such excellent company / In th' other world" (4.2.211–14). A final contrast occurs when Cariola provides a foil to the Duchess's heroism by begging for her life, the exact reverse of the situation in *Othello* (4.2.231–55).

Despite the Duchess's greater prominence, however, she is assigned precisely the same fate as Desdemona and, for that matter, Zenocrate: she is removed from the active resolution of the conflicts of the play and granted instead the indirect role of inspiration. In one critic's useful terms, she ceases to be the maker, and becomes instead the bearer, of meaning.[150] A varied range of crucial activities occupies the stage for an entire act after the Duchess's murder, when, like Desdemona, she returns from the dead as a disembodied voice, an echo and "thing of sorrow" meant to protect her husband (5.3.24). In order to clarify her permanent status as an unattainable ideal, Webster specifically constructs her death as a work of art, relegating her value to the state of bodiless, aestheticized inactivity that she had heroically resisted in life: "This is flesh, and blood, sir, / 'Tis not the figure cut in alabaster / Kneels at my husband's tomb" (1.1.459–61). "Who do I look like now?" she asks Cariola in preparation for her death. "Like to your picture

150. Laura Mulvey, quoted in Nancy J. Vickers, "Diana Described: Scattered Woman and Scattered Rhyme," in *Writing and Sexual Difference*, ed. Elizabeth Abel (Chicago: University of Chicago Press, 1980), p. 109.

in the gallery, / A deal of life in show, but none in practice; / Or rather like some reverend monument / Whose ruins are even pitied." "Very proper," replies the Duchess, ready now for death (4.2.30–35).

As the hero of the play the Duchess embodies its major conflicts; thus in order to remove her from their active resolution, Webster has had, as it were, to rewrite her part. The Duchess is inscribed in the heroics of marriage, a discourse that inevitably breaks down from a combination of external opposition and its own internal contradictions, which emerge as an irresolvable conflict of loyalties between future and past. At the end of the play, Webster resolves the conflict by discarding the future and reinscribing the Duchess in the dualistic discourse that idealizes (or degrades) women, thus placing her above and beyond the action, in a position that she, pursuing the future, had specifically resisted and that is unambiguously associated in the play with death and the disappearing past. As Bosola seeks to avenge her murder and the Cardinal and Ferdinand die, leaving "no more fame behind 'em than should one / Fall in a frost, and leave his print in snow" (5.5.114–15), the associations of the past with pathology and corruption also recede, while the dead Duchess's elegiac role assumes greater prominence. Viewed in the context of the polarizing sexual discourse that defines her final position, the construction of the Duchess's death can be seen as reactionary: she is removed from the potentially radical conflicts of the heroics of marriage that have fully defined her, and the sympathy and value assigned to her life are unambiguously allied instead with a compelling tribute to the lost past.

vii

Webster's removal of the hero from the last act of the play is so striking and bold a move that it raises important questions about the nature of English Renaissance tragedy. Indeed, given its pointed critique of political absolutism (the form of government favored, if not enacted, by James I), its recognition of the centrality of the private life, and its profound exploration of female heroism, *The Duchess of Malfi* becomes an excellent text from which to assess the nature and extent of radicalism in Jacobean tragedy. By embodying major tragic stature exclusively in a woman, Webster acknowledges the female hero's pivotal role in the process of historical change, exploring the workings of the contradictory components of female identity in Renaissance sexual ideology as Shakespeare never does.[151] Recalling the comparison between Tamburlaine's revolutionary career and the Duchess's role as a social pioneer who courageously disregards traditional class and rank barriers, one can perceive the impossibility of finding either figure in Shakespeare's plays, where shepherds who gain power turn out to be princes in disguise; and powerful, central women preside exclusively over the comic world, not the more elevated and prestigious tragic one. The figures of Malvolio and Antonio provide a similarly telling contrast. A Renaissance playwright creating an upwardly mobile steward clearly had options in his representation of that figure. Should he be a pompous ass, a vain, deluded buffoon, easily outwitted and finally expelled by the aristocracy? Or should he be able, competent, appealing and, if perhaps also mediocre, nevertheless aware of his own limitations and capable of winning a Duchess's love?

My purpose in making these comparisons is not to find fault with Shakespeare, but to point out that, given the variety of conceptual options available in Jacobean culture, he often chooses the conservative ones, a pattern that becomes obvious when we view him not on his own, but in relation to his fellow playwrights. Because Shakespeare is indisputably the greatest writer of English tragedy, his conservatism relative to his contemporaries should have a great deal to tell us about the nature and purposes of that form of drama. Despite Webster's considerably greater interest in, and sympathy for the future, for example, he nevertheless ends *The Duchess of Malfi* by diminishing the future and paying a powerful tribute to the past. Recent scholarship concerned with the

151. I do not regard Shakespeare's Cleopatra as an exception to this observation. Arguably, *Antony and Cleopatra* moves beyond tragedy and into romance. Certainly Cleopatra's "infinite variety" is unique, not characteristic; rather than embodying the contradictions of Renaissance sexual ideology, which becomes the central focus of the play, she provides an alternative ethos that is opposed to the public/political world: i.e., the conflict is between love and duty. Finally, Cleopatra is not the sole hero of her play, as Lear, Hamlet, Macbeth, Othello, Coriolanus, and the Duchess of Malfi are of theirs.

relation of tragedy to history has emphasized the foundations of tragedy in the failures of the past.[152] With its relentless, subversive scrutiny of obsolete modes of heroism, tyrannical forms of government, unjust social systems, and inadequate sexual ideologies, tragedy is seen to play a radical role of negation, to clear the way for a new order by participating in the dissolution of archaic cultural formations. Not only has this scholarship rescued Renaissance drama from being assessed in terms of a nonreflective identification with the construct of unified hierarchy known as the "Elizabethan world picture"; it has also been invaluable in calling attention to tragic discourse as an historical process that plays a crucial role in the course of cultural change. But in correctly emphasizing the function of tragedy as a social critique, these analyses have tended to assume that the tragic exposé of social injustice is more real than the focus on loss and death, thus underestimating tragedy's considerable allegiance to the past. As Webster's elegiac conception of the Duchess's death makes clear, no matter how pronounced the criticism of the past and sympathy for the future may be in a play, the separation between past and future that is the defining purpose of radicalism never occurs within Jacobean tragedy. Instead, attention is focused on the radical act as one of sacrifice and extinction, and the future is diminished in deference to the past: "We that are young / Shall never see so much, nor live so long."[153] In this context Jacobean tragedy can be viewed not as

152. See especially Jonathan Dollimore, *Radical Tragedy: Religion, Ideology and Power in the Drama of Shakespeare and His Contemporaries* (Chicago: University of Chicago Press, 1984); Franco Moretti, " 'A Huge Eclipse': Tragic Form and the Deconsecration of Sovereignty," in *The Power of Forms in the English Renaissance*, ed. Stephen Greenblatt (Norman, Okla.: Pilgrim, 1982), pp. 7–40; Whigham, "Social and Sexual Mobility"; Cohen; and Heinemann. For other scholars who have addressed the issue of subversion and authority in Tudor-Stuart drama, see Greenblatt, *Renaissance Self-Fashioning*, esp. pp. 193–254, and "Invisible Bullets: Renaissance Authority and Its Subversion," in *Political Shakespeare: New Essays in Cultural Materialism*, ed. Jonathan Dollimore and Alan Sinfield (Manchester: Manchester University Press, 1985), pp. 18–47; and Montrose, " 'Shaping Fantasies.' "

153. I owe this point to Frye, who, quoting these lines, which are the last two lines of *King Lear*, comments (p. 6) that in Shakespeare the social contract that forms at the end of a tragedy is always a diminishment of the present and future: "the heroic and infinite have been; the human and finite are."

radical, but as conservative and nostalgic: a lament for a lost past from the point of view of the aristocracy. Seventeenth-century English tragedy tended increasingly to become a predominantly aristocratic form.

How can we reconcile the evident radicalism of Jacobean tragedy with its equally compelling nostalgia? As is well known, great tragedy, unlike comedy, has erupted in Western history in infrequent, irregular bursts, particularly in fifth-century Athens and sixteenth- and seventeenth-century Europe. Attempting to account for tragedy's simultaneous alliance with the past and future, Timothy J. Reiss has joined other scholars in pointing out that in each of its major appearances, tragedy has accompanied the rupture of a familiar order, in which "the essential relationships between physical, social, and religious life are now losing their reference to any 'experience of totality.'" At the same time, however, in both ancient Greece and Renaissance Europe, the major developments in tragedy coincide with the rise of science, the struggle to realize an emergent rationality for which analytic, referential knowledge, rather than mystery and mythical thinking, becomes "the true expression of reality." Reiss argues that during this process of change, "a sense of injustice appears, compounded of ignorance, fear, unfulfilled desire, and suffering, the mark of an 'absence' which of necessity escapes organization"—that is, meaninglessness. The function of tragedy is not simply to represent irreconcilable ambiguity, suffering, and injustice, but also to contain these ruptures precisely by defining them, giving them meaning and form. Tragedy's unique role in this process is to underline the moment at which the previously meaningless becomes legible and articulate, what Reiss describes as "*the moment of accession to referentiality*." Whereas other discourses (e.g., history) "take for granted the possibility of a discursive ordering of chaos, of the as-yet unknown . . . tragedy *performs* the overcoming of that 'absence,'" the enclosure of meaninglessness that "disappears as the very consequence of its naming." Reiss also emphasizes a dislocation between the protagonist and spectator of a tragedy. The protagonist is active but blind or, in the terms of this book, trapped in the past; the spectator, on the other hand, becomes conscious of a capacity to organize and to know, to create a future: "the discourse of tragedy may be ambiguous internally, but that is just the point: it is an ordered and enclosed ambiguity. . . . It presupposes a knowledge." By clearly defining and finally immobilizing the destructive ambiguities of suffering and injustice, then, tragedy provides an affirmation that a future imposition of order is possible.[154]

As Reiss makes clear, once tragedy has performed its function in the processes of cultural change, tragic plays may continue to be written, but no further development takes place within the genre. As he recognizes, these conceptions take different forms when embedded concretely in distinctive cultural situations. Reiss's formulations thus become particularly helpful for understanding the changing representation of love and sexuality in English Renaissance tragedy. As we have seen by examining *Tamburlaine*, in Elizabethan tragedy, created during a period of relative patriotism and optimism, the private life plays a marginal role in the representation of a heroism of action, to which it is at best subordinate, at worst destructive. In this context love and sexuality are constructed from a dualizing perspective that either idealizes or degrades women and eros, removing them from the significant center of action. Such a perspective of course lingers as a conceptual option in our culture, and as John Donne's marriage sermons, written between about 1620 and 1630, make clear, it remains prominent in Jacobean and Caroline England. Although this dualistic sensibility is never superseded, during the late sixteenth and early seventeenth centuries it gradually recedes before the Protestant idealization of marriage, a more multifaceted sexual discourse that elevates the private life and grants greater centrality to women as necessary protagonists in its enactment. Conjoined with a complex of sociocultural factors, including both the absolutism and pacifism of the king and the attempt to halt and consolidate the social mobility of the sixteenth century, the heroics of marriage becomes the primary subject of Jacobean tragedy. While *Othello* dramatizes the beginnings of this process by scrutinizing the de-

154. Timothy J. Reiss, *Tragedy and Truth: Studies in the Development of a Renaissance and Neoclassical Discourse* (New Haven, Conn.: Yale University Press, 1980), pp. 19, 36, 20, 21 (italics his), 24, 35 (see, in general, pp. 1–39). On p. 36 he remarks that "the reaction to tragedy . . . would be at once the fear of a lack of all order and the pleasure at seeing such lack overcome."

cline of the heroism of action, *The Duchess of Malfi* manifests its logic completely by granting full attention and distinction to the private life and making visible the pivotal role of the female hero in the process of cultural change. During the development of Jacobean tragedy, the dualizing sexual discourse becomes associated with the disappearing past, the heroics of marriage with the promise of the future. But, as we have seen, the heroics of marriage breaks down, both from external (and reactionary) opposition and from its own unresolved contradictions. As these ambiguities assume greater centrality in tragic representation, they are immobilized within a final, elegiac tribute to the lost past, a process of containment clarified in the deaths of Desdemona and the Duchess of Malfi. In this way tragedy serves its complex function of articulating the need for a future by destroying the past and then mourning its disappearance. Once again this point becomes clear from examining the tragic representation of sexuality, in which no further development takes place. Either the scrutiny of the private life becomes increasingly involuted, focusing on corruption and extremes, as in the depictions of female villainy and incest in *The Changeling* (1622) and *'Tis Pity She's a Whore* (1629); or the portrayal of endurance and suffering becomes increasingly static, as in *The Broken Heart* (1629). Fresh impulses in the development of the English drama are no longer articulated in tragedy, but in a less demanding and idealistic form, tragicomedy.

4

Transforming Sexuality:
Jacobean Tragicomedy and the
Reconfiguration of Private Life

i

Jacobean tragicomedy is the last original formal creation of English Renaissance drama meant for a public audience. Despite many illuminating studies, no explanation has ever accounted for all of the oddities of this hybrid genre, the most prominent of which remains the striking discrepancy between the aesthetic inferiority of many of the plays and their undoubted historical importance, including their contemporary popularity and the crucial role they played in the long-term development of seventeenth-century drama.[1] Explanations that center on Shakespeare's ro-

---

1. See, e.g., Arthur C. Kirsch, *Jacobean Dramatic Perspectives* (Charlottesville: University Press of Virginia, 1972), pp. 3–4: "Though Jonson's reputation may have been higher among the literati and Shakespeare's influence may have been more profound and enduring, it was [Beaumont and Fletcher] who clearly dominated the repertory of the English stage for the better part of the seventeenth century. . . . It was only in the 1670s . . . that the authority of their dramaturgy began to be questioned, and even then it continued to exercise a considerable influence, especially upon Restoration comedy. No English dramatists before or since have had so extraordinary an influence." In *Dramatic Character in the English Romantic Age* (Princeton, N.J.: Princeton University Press, 1970), Joseph W. Donohue, Jr., explores this long-ranging influence of Fletcherian characterization. For studies of the reputation of Beaumont and Fletcher, see Lawrence Wallis, *Fletcher, Beaumont and Company: Entertainers to the Jacobean Gentry* (New York: King's Crown, 1947); and William W. Appleton, *Beaumont and Fletcher: A Critical Study* (London: Allen & Unwin, 1956).

mances are clearly inadequate to any historical inquiry into the form. Not only did Shakespeare retire over a decade before the end of James's reign, when the majority of tragicomedies were produced; but analyses of his romances cannot fail to focus on the miraculous reconciliations, the overcoming of suffering and injustice, that illuminate his last plays but that pointedly contrast with the deflating, irreverent levity characterizing the bulk of late Jacobean tragicomedies. Known as "the Beaumont and Fletcher plays," that bulk is largely the product of John Fletcher, who (though he had collaborators, primarily Francis Beaumont and Philip Massinger) became the chief playwright of the King's Men and dominated the Jacobean stage from Shakespeare's retirement in 1613 to his own death in 1625.[2]

Dryden himself tells us that it was Beaumont and Fletcher who provided the primary imaginative link between Renaissance and Restoration drama: "Their plays are now the most pleasant and frequent entertainments of the stage; two of theirs being acted through the year for one of Shakespeare's or Johnson's. . . . Their plots were generally more regular than Shakespeare's, especially those which were made before Beaumont's death; and they understood and imitated the conversation of gentlemen much better; whose wild debaucheries, and quickness of wit in repartees, no

2. The designation "the Beaumont and Fletcher plays" generally refers to approximately fifty plays written by Beaumont, Fletcher, and a variety of other collaborators. Assessments of the precise number vary slightly. As reported by editors Arnold Glover and A. R. Waller in *The Works of Francis Beaumont and John Fletcher* (Cambridge: Cambridge University Press, 1905–12), vol. 1, p. v, the second Beaumont and Fletcher Folio (1679) contained fifty-two plays. Alfred Harbage, *Annals of English Drama: 975–1700*, rev. S. Schoenbaum (Philadelphia: University of Pennsylvania Press, 1964), assigns fifty-six plays to Beaumont and Fletcher. The authorship of the plays (particularly the possible collaborations between Shakespeare and Fletcher) has inspired a much wider debate. The most extensive and impressive work can be found in Cyrus Hoy, "The Shares of Fletcher and His Collaborators in the Beaumont and Fletcher Canon," *Studies in Bibliography*, 8 (1956), 129–46; 9 (1957), 143–62; 11 (1958), 85–106; 12 (1959), 91–116; 13 (1960), 77–108; 14 (1961), 45–67; 15 (1962), 71–90. For further information on authorship studies, see Denzell S. Smith, "Francis Beaumont and John Fletcher," in *The Later Jacobean and Caroline Dramatists: A Survey and Bibliography of Recent Studies in English Renaissance Drama*, ed. Terence P. Logan and Denzell S. Smith (Lincoln: University of Nebraska Press, 1978), pp. 52–53.

poet can ever paint as they have done. . . . I am apt to believe the English language in them arrived to its highest perfection: what words have since been taken in, are rather superfluous than ornamental." Dryden, of course, later recognizes the superiority of Shakespeare. But acknowledging Shakespeare's obvious greatness does not nullify the point that it is Fletcher, much more than Shakespeare, whose influence can be discerned in the most enduring and delightful of Restoration dramatic creations, the comedy of manners.[3]

Recognizing the extent of Fletcher's influence, studies of the large Beaumont and Fletcher corpus tend to fall into the now outmoded opposition of "critical" versus "historical" analyses generated by the dominance of the new criticism. Concentrating on what is defined as "the text itself," the former variety have helped greatly in underscoring thematic patterns and subtly unraveling the tone of the plays, but are ultimately defeated by the plays' artistic mediocrity.[4] The second version of this approach takes two forms. The first attempts to account for the blend of established conventions, novel techniques, and ingenious structural devices peculiar to tragicomedy by tracing their generic origins in classical and medieval drama, as well as in romantic story.[5] Such analyses tend to stress the importance of the sixteenth-century Italian poet-

3. John Dryden, "An Essay of Dramatic Poesy," in *Essays of John Dryden*, ed. W. P. Ker (Oxford: Clarendon, 1926), vol. 1, p. 81. Though Ben Jonson is another obvious influence on the comedy of manners, he did not focus on the battle of the sexes, as Fletcher and his collaborators did.

4. See, e.g., J. F. Danby, *Poets on Fortune's Hill: Studies in Sidney, Shakespeare, Beaumont and Fletcher* (London: Faber & Faber, 1952); Philip Edwards, "The Danger Not the Death: The Art of John Fletcher," in *Jacobean Theater*, Stratford-upon-Avon Studies, no. 1, ed. J. R. Brown and B. Harris (London: Edward Arnold, 1960), pp. 159–77; Philip J. Finkelpearl, "Beaumont, Fletcher, and 'Beaumont and Fletcher': Some Distinctions," *English Literary Renaissance*, 1 (1971), 144–64; Cyrus Hoy, "Renaissance and Restoration Dramatic Plotting," *Renaissance Drama*, 9 (1966), 247–64; Clifford Leech, *The John Fletcher Plays* (London: Chatto & Windus, 1962); Marco Mincoff, "Fletcher's Early Tragedies," *Renaissance Drama*, 7 (1964), 70–94; Michael Neill, "'The Simetry, Which Gives a Poem Grace': Masque, Imagery, and the Fancy of *The Maid's Tragedy*," *Renaissance Drama*, N.S. 3 (1970), 111–35; and Nancy Cotton Pearse, *John Fletcher's Chastity Plays: Mirrors of Modesty* (Lewisburg, Pa.: Bucknell University Press, 1973).

5. The most important of these studies is Eugene Waith, *The Pattern of Tragicomedy in Beaumont and Fletcher* (1952; rpt. Hamden, Conn.: Archon,

playwright Guarini, whose pastoral tragicomedy *Il Pastor Fido* (1589, translated in 1601) and whose critical pronouncements defining the form directly influenced Fletcher, particularly in writing his own definition of tragicomedy. These influence studies are weakened by the fact that Fletcher's generic definition, though unique, is nevertheless notoriously inadequate and fails to account for his work.[6] Indeed, Fletcher's pastoral tragicomedy *The Faithful Shepherdess* (1608), the only one of his plays directly influenced by Guarini, was a drastic failure. His later work reveals that he largely abandoned the premises that he had pedantically tried to impose on a reluctant readership when the play was published sometime before the end of 1610.

A second, historical approach attempts to place the Beaumont and Fletcher plays in the Tudor-Stuart dramatic tradition, which they are viewed as concluding. Because it endeavors to account for the contemporary popularity and influence of the plays, this approach is more effective.[7] Yet Fletcherian tragicomedy is too often dismissed as an inward-turning, decadent form, an exhausted re-

1969). See also Madeleine Doran, *Endeavors of Art: A Study of Form in Elizabethan Drama* (Madison: University of Wisconsin Press, 1954), pp. 186–215.

6. See John Fletcher, *The Faithful Shepherdess*, in *Stuart Plays*, ed. Arthur H. Nethercot, Charles R. Baskervill, and Virgil B. Heltzel; rev. Arthur H. Nethercot (New York: Holt, Rinehart & Winston, 1971), p. 559: "A tragicomedy is not so called in respect of mirth and killing, but in respect it wants deaths, which is enough to make it no tragedy, yet brings some near it, which is enough to make it no comedy, which must be a representation of familiar people, with such kind of trouble as no life be questioned, so that a god is as lawful in this as in a tragedy, and mean people as in a comedy." The tragicomedy *The Two Noble Kinsmen*, however, concludes with the death of one of the heroes. Cf. Giambattista Guarini, "The Compendium of Tragicomic Poetry," in *Literary Criticism: Plato to Dryden*, ed. Allan H. Gilbert (Detroit: Wayne State University Press, 1962), p. 511: "He who composes tragicomedy takes from tragedy its great persons but not its great action, its verisimilar plot but not its true one, its movement of the feelings but not its disturbance of them, its pleasure, but not its sadness, its danger but not its death; from comedy it takes laughter that is not excessive, modest amusement, feigned difficulty, happy reversal, and above all the comic order."

7. See, e.g., Kirsch; Wallis; T. S. Eliot, "Ben Jonson," in his *Elizabethan Dramatists* (London: Faber & Faber, 1962), p. 77; and Una Ellis-Fermor, *The Jacobean Drama: An Interpretation* (London: Methuen, 1936), pp. 201–26. Danby and Finkelpearl also attempt to place the Beaumont and Fletcher plays in the Tudor-Stuart dramatic tradition.

view of a disappearing past; consequently this perspective over-looks the fresh impulses in the plays and so misconstrues their content and diminishes the curious fact of their lasting influence. This view also assigns Beaumont and Fletcher a major role in creating and pandering to what is conceived as the jaded, aristocra-tic, courtly half of an increasingly polarized seventeenth-century theater audience, the "rival traditions" outlined by Alfred Har-bage. Recent scholarship has been refining Harbage's oppositions between Puritans and cavaliers, middle-class and courtly aristocra-cy, and public and private theaters, largely by demonstrating that the social and cultural environment in which the drama partici-pated was considerably more complex than he recognized.[8] To date these revisionary studies have focused primarily on Jacobean tragedy and satire and on Caroline drama; the odd phenomenon of Fletcherian tragicomedy has yet to be viewed as a development of late Jacobean culture with a relation to the future as well as the past.

In this chapter I suggest that Jacobean tragicomedy can best be understood as participating in an ongoing process of cultural trans-formation. Specifically it can be seen as facilitating processes of artistic change by mediating between future and past dramatic forms, an accomplishment most discernible in the tragicomic rep-resentation of love and sexuality. When tragicomedy is viewed in this way, as "a form moving in time" (the phrase is Fredric Jameson's),[9] the logic behind its fantastic structural devices, puz-zling levity, and discordant juxtaposition of conventions and val-ues often thought to be mutually exclusive begins to become more clear.

8. See, e.g., Margot Heinemann, *Puritanism and Theatre: Thomas Middleton and Opposition Drama under the Early Stuarts* (Cambridge: Cambridge Univer-sity Press, 1980); Walter Cohen, *Drama of a Nation: Public Theater in Renais-sance England and Spain* (Ithaca, N.Y.: Cornell University Press, 1985); Jonathan Dollimore, *Radical Tragedy: Religion, Ideology and Power in the Drama of Shakespeare and His Contemporaries* (Chicago: University of Chicago Press, 1984); A. J. Cook, *The Privileged Playgoers of Shakespeare's London* (Princeton, N.J.: Princeton University Press, 1981); and Martin Butler, *Theatre and Crisis, 1632–1642* (Cambridge: Cambridge University Press, 1984).

9. Fredric Jameson, *The Political Unconscious: Narrative as a Socially Sym-bolic Act* (Ithaca, N.Y.: Cornell University Press, 1981), p. 148.

Jameson's fully developed theory of the relation between ideology and genre defines literary form as "a socio-symbolic message . . . [that is] immanently and intrinsically an ideology in its own right." With its stress on perpetual struggle and conflict, Jameson's conception of genre as endeavoring to contain the contradictions generated by social transformation is valuable for understanding all dramatic forms. But his "notion of the text as a synchronic unity of structurally contradictory or heterogeneous elements, generic patterns and discourses" becomes especially useful for conceptualizing the hybrid tragicomedy, which, I argue, is a form whose constituent elements themselves embody and articulate the processes of cultural change. In elaborating his theory Jameson discusses romance (with a particular mention of Shakespeare's last plays) as a response to a critical moment of socioeconomic transition:

> As for romance, it would seem that its ultimate condition of figuration . . . is to be found in a transitional moment in which two distinct modes of production, or moments of socioeconomic development, coexist. Their antagonism is not yet articulated in terms of the struggle of social classes, so that its resolution can be projected in the form of a nostalgic (or less often, a Utopian) harmony. Our principal experience of such transitional moments is evidently that of an organic social order in the process of penetration and subversion, reorganization and rationalization, by nascent capitalism, yet still, for another long moment, coexisting with the latter. So Shakespearean romance . . . opposes the phantasmagoria of "imagination" to the bustling commercial activity at work all around it.[10]

Whether or not we accept Jameson's emphasis on the various phases of class struggle or the centrality of capitalism, the socioeconomic developments he describes are undeniably relevant to Jacobean England.[11] Fletcher's plays, participating in the same

10. Jameson, p. 148.
11. It should be acknowledged that Jameson's formulations are sometimes problematic for the Renaissance. Though Shakespeare's romances do not yet recognizably articulate conflict "in terms of the struggle of social classes," plays by many of Shakespeare's contemporaries (e.g., Marlowe, Middleton, and Webster) certainly do. As we will see, Shakespeare tends to be a conservative in the representation of class conflict.

conditions that Jameson argues constitute Shakespeare's romances, comprise a strikingly different response.

As I have tried to show throughout this book, various levels of cultural change combine and compete in the dramatic representation of sexuality and are particularly important to the shifting conception of the relation between public and private life. As is well known, English Renaissance drama is informed by an aristocratic vision of order that is conceived politically in terms of hierarchy and rank and rhetorically in terms of a system of analogies and correspondences that conjoin individual, society, and cosmos.[12] Thus the landscape of love and sexuality becomes an arena where spiritual, social, and psychic energies meet, conflict, and/or unite. Fully articulated in Protestant moral literature, one dominant sexual ideology, which I have called the heroics of marriage, attempts to unite public and private life and, contrasted with a dualizing sensibility that idealizes or degrades women and eros, is enacted in Elizabethan comedy, where sexual tensions are evoked but contained within a harmonious, stable social structure symbolized in marriage. Jacobean satire severely scrutinizes orthodox comic and social order by highlighting and exposing these tensions. And, in Jacobean tragedy, the contradictions and paradoxes inscribed in the two dominant modes of Renaissance sexual discourse explode into destruction and protest. Whether it is evoked to be affirmed, scrutinized, or subverted, though, the politically orthodox "Elizabethan world picture" always provides the informing principle of order in English Renaissance comedy and tragedy. With its pronounced emphasis on archaic, fairy-tale material and its abstract projection of a Utopian future, Shakespearean romance also remains well within orthodox discursive terrain. In Fletcherian tragicomedy however, this situation no longer prevails. In these plays

12. The classic statement of this world view is E. M. W. Tillyard's *The Elizabethan World Picture* (Harmondsworth: Penguin, 1963). Recent scholarship has rightly subjected Tillyard to a profound critique, not so much for being inaccurate as for being myopic and incomplete: i.e., Tillyard identified his "world picture" with Elizabethan orthodoxy and ignored the existence of multiple world views and the complexity of social life in Renaissance England. Cf. *Political Shakespeare: New Essays in Cultural Materialism*, ed. Jonathan Dollimore and Alan Sinfield (Manchester: Manchester University Press, 1985), pp. 5–6.

spiritual, sociopolitical, and psychological realities begin to be constructed by the dramatists without mourning or protest as separate
and distinct levels of being. The effort to unite them is represented
parodically as deluded, anachronistic, a little absurd: Fletcherian
tragicomedy displays a new willingness to dismiss the cultural
formations of the past.[13]

The resulting differences in the representation of sexual change
among the major dramatic genres can best be perceived in terms of
contrasting formal/ideological conceptions of the past and future.
The future is not problematic in either comedy or tragedy. In
comedy the future is assured and deflected by the focus on the
harmonious present and the symbolic affirmation of the status
quo. In tragedy a diminished future recedes in significance before
the overwhelming concern with the failures of the present and the
past. When the heroics of marriage breaks down, for example,
tragedy clarifies the need for constructing some new relation between private and public life, while only peripherally indicating its
form or conditions; instead of envisioning a specific future, tragedy destroys the past and then contains its own contradictions by
mourning the destruction. Like tragedy, tragicomedy depicts present conditions as inadequate and uncertain; however, a newly dismissive irreverence toward the past allows a workable, even a
desirable, future to be more fully imagined and affirmed.

These processes become most clearly discernible in a revised
conception of the relation between public and private life, the formation of which can be traced in the tragicomic representation of
love and sexuality. The new and distinctive way in which
Fletcherian tragicomedy treats these issues can best be viewed in
contrast to Shakespeare. What follows focuses on three plays:
Shakespeare's *Troilus and Cressida* (1602), *The Two Noble Kinsmen*
(1613, probably a collaboration between Fletcher and Shakespeare), and *The Knight of Malta* (1618, probably a joint effort by
Fletcher and Philip Massinger). These plays share a deflating, ironic view of human nature and destiny, conveyed through similar
clusters of themes and motifs that gain their significance from the

13. See Cohen, p. 391, for the idea that a Utopian view of the future as
expressed in Shakespeare's romances may actually prove the most historically
accurate.

ways they combine to illuminate the protagonists' encounters with erotic love. In each of the three plays, the figure of a bewildered knight pursues an idealized love in a courtly, chivalric setting, and in each instance the interplay of hero, quest, and setting dramatizes a destructive attachment to anachronistic sexual values. The analysis will demonstrate the ways in which these themes and motifs are differently arranged, weighted, and proportioned from play to play and from playwright to playwright. This kaleidoscopic view of matching and modulating motifs does not merely have the advantage of distinguishing Shakespeare's imagination from Fletcher's, but also of stressing the continuity that is present in the process of generic change. The move from Shakespeare's bitter pessimism to Fletcher's witty irreverence articulates the final relinquishing of a treasured Renaissance cultural vision of the past; and this shift in sensibility can best be viewed as a development that was gradual and continuous, rather than as a departure that was violent and abrupt.[14]

ii

Before going on to examine these plays about questing knights, it will be useful to review some points about the originating cultural conditions of chivalry and to recall some defining themes of the incorporation of chivalry in literature. What follows is an extremely selective and synthetic sketch, meant to highlight issues concerning chivalry that remain relevant to the development of English Renaissance drama.

One distinguished historian of the topic, Maurice Keen, has recently defined chivalry as "a word that came to denote the code and culture of a martial estate which regarded war as its hereditary profession." Flourishing between, roughly, 1100 and the begin-

14. Cf. Jameson, p. 97: "Just as overt revolution is no punctual event . . . but brings to the surface the innumerable daily struggles and forms of class polarization which are at work in the whole course of social life that precedes it, and which are therefore latent and implicit in 'prerevolutionary' social experience . . . so also the overtly 'transitional' moments of cultural revolution are themselves but the passage to the surface of a permanent process in human societies. . . ."

ning of the sixteenth century, this medieval phenomenon, though related at various points in its development to Christianity and the church, derived its Christian tone primarily from the fact that chivalric groups arose and operated within a Christian society. Originating with the warrior groups of the early Middle Ages, chivalry evolved essentially as a mode of secular power that provided an alternative to the church. Knighthood comprised an estate of aristocratic, elect warriors in search of personal glory, "with a general commission to uphold justice and protect the weak":

> From its beginning to its close, men going forward in the hope of magnifying their names and fortune in knighthood is the basic theme of . . . [chivalric] history. . . . Religious priorities were not the driving force behind its ethic, which . . . [was often seen as confounding] the pursuit of spiritual merit with the pursuit of worldly honour. Even where the crusade was concerned, it was not the new approbation and the indulgences that the Church reformers of the eleventh and twelfth centuries had extended to the warrior estate that moved nine knights out of ten, but the glamour of martial glory and social esteem. Chivalry essentially was the secular code of honour of a martially oriented aristocracy.[15]

Keen and other historians agree that the relative lack of concern with national boundaries in the medieval world allowed chivalry to become an international phenomenon. Consolidating and articulating its basic premises in twelfth-century France, the knightly ideal reached its height of influence and breadth of dissemination in the fourteenth and fifteenth centuries, when, Georges Duby argues, "the ruling class needed to grow more rigid in defence of its threatened privileges, and when the king's authority was struggling to base itself more firmly on intermediary bodies and made use of the categories of knightly morality to strengthen loyalties and foment military order. Chivalry . . . played a fundamental role in the great *mise-en-scène* of authority." During this period, chivalric and political history were intertwined, as politically motivated princes began forming their own orders of chivalry. No

15. Maurice Keen, *Chivalry* (New Haven, Conn.: Yale University Press, 1984), pp. 239, 252, 243.

matter how much the idealistic chivalric code was violated, Duby contends, it lay at the center of the system of education for the upper classes and became "the object of unanimous veneration."[16]

Recent historians, then, have stressed the crucial role chivalry played in the conduct of late medieval power relations. They have also agreed that no new developments in the formation of the chivalric code took place after the beginning of the sixteenth century. Keen attributes the decline of the military and political functions of chivalry in the Renaissance to the new and advanced military technology that enabled warfare to take place on a larger scale and brought about the appearance of permanent, national standing armies, which in turn required princes to evolve more efficient systems of taxation for their support. These alterations in the conduct of warfare caused the conception of the individual knight valiantly upholding justice and protecting the weak to attenuate to the concept of "the officer whose business it is to fight the King's enemies." Other Renaissance historians have stressed the humanist emphasis on classical education and distaste for the chivalric glorification of violence. Like Keen, they have described the increasing value placed on lawyers and administrators with professional, rather than military backgrounds in the formation of the secular nation state in the Renaissance.[17]

Keen contends that while the military and political functions of chivalry died in the sixteenth century, the enduring legacy of the chivalric ethic was located not in contemporary social and economic conditions, but in conceptions, such as ideals of honor and nobility, courtliness to women, and the emphasis placed on the individual quest for glory and adventure.[18] Many of these points

16. Georges Duby, "The Knightly Way," review of Keen in *Times Literary Supplement*, 29 June 1984, p. 720. See also Keen; and Arthur B. Ferguson, *The Indian Summer of English Chivalry: Studies in the Decline and Transformation of Chivalric Idealism* (Durham, N.C.: Duke University Press, 1960), pp. 4, 11–13, 76.

17. Keen, esp. pp. 247–53. See also Ferguson, pp. 169–220; Frank Whigham, *Ambition and Privilege: The Social Tropes of Elizabethan Courtesy Theory* (Berkeley: University of California Press, 1984), pp. 13–26; and Lawrence Stone, *The Crisis of the Aristocracy, 1558–1641* (Oxford: Clarendon, 1965).

18. Keen, pp. 249–53.

are arguable. Keen's separation of ideals and conceptions from socioeconomic conditions, an attempt to correct earlier historiography that emphasized the large quantity of fantasy material in the chivalric ethos, is based on a positivist distinction between fiction and fact that equates the former with illusion and the latter with reality. His arguments consequently do not account for certain complexities. For example, recent scholarship has demonstrated convincingly the very contemporary sociopolitical functions of the chivalric aesthetic in the late sixteenth-century cult of Queen Elizabeth, as well as the use of chivalric motifs as devices symbolic of monarchical power in the courts of the early Stuarts.[19] These are points to which I will return; here it suffices to note that it is impossible, even inaccurate, rigorously to separate "ideals" from socioeconomic conditions in the analysis of cultural phenomena like chivalry or the drama. As Pierre Francastel puts it, "Each society founding an economic and political order also creates a figurative order and simultaneously generates its own institutions, ideas, imagery, and displays."[20]

When combined with literary analysis of the characteristics of chivalric romance, Duby's account of the social conditions generating the formation of knighthood in twelfth-century France suggests intriguing connections among the institutions, ideas, and images that combined to construct the phenomenon of chivalry. In the area around Cluny that Duby has studied, the title "knight" emerged noticeably as a description of the topmost layer of the

19. See, e.g., Stephen Orgel and Roy Strong, *Inigo Jones: The Theatre of the Stuart Court* (London: Sotheby Park Bernet; Berkeley: University of California Press, 1973); Roy Strong, *The Cult of Elizabeth: Elizabethan Portraiture and Pageantry* (London: Thames & Hudson, 1977), *Splendor at Court: Renaissance Spectacle and Illusion* (London: Weidenfeld & Nicolson, 1973), and *Van Dyck: Charles I on Horseback* (New York: Viking, 1972); Frances A. Yates, *Astraea: The Imperial Theme in the Sixteenth Century* (London: Ark Paperbacks, 1985), esp. pp. 29–120; Stephen Orgel, *The Illusion of Power: Political Theater in the English Renaissance* (Berkeley: University of California Press, 1975); Louis Adrian Montrose, "Celebration and Insinuation: Sir Philip Sidney and the Motives of Elizabethan Courtship," *Renaissance Drama*, N.S. 8 (1977), 3–35; and Arthur Marotti, "'Love Is Not Love': Elizabethan Sonnet Sequences and the Social Order," *ELH*, 49 (1982), 396–428.

20. Quoted in Georges Duby, *The Chivalrous Society*, trans. Cynthia Postan (London: Edward Arnold, 1977), p. 3.

aristocracy around 1100. Approximately one hundred years earlier, however, the knighthood (*la chevalerie*), composed primarily of descendants of the great lords of the Carolingian period, had been subordinate to the small group that owned fortified castles and dominated the aristocracy. Around 1100, Duby argues, the title "knight" had become "a noun emphasizing the military function and service and was preferred to adjectives indicating the varying lustre of birth." Throughout the twelfth century the knights emulated the lives of socially superior castle owners, and gradually the lines segregating levels of the aristocracy began to blur. Duby cites several developments that occurred during this process of fusion and have interesting implications for the representation of chivalry in Renaissance drama. It was during this period, for example, that those who bore arms were separated from other men and became an exclusive, homogeneous group. The church hastened this process by spreading an ideology of peace (*la paix de Dieu*) that justified the knights' violence and held up the *miles Christi* for the approval of the entire lay aristocracy. As greater nobles began to behave like knights and to assume the title, the value attached to noble birth increased, fusing with the existing military ethic. The popularization of the idea of noble birth brought a change in the attitude toward kinship in aristocratic society, a shift that strengthened family solidarity within the framework of the lineage. As knights began to leave their masters' castles and settle their own estates, they adopted the idea of inheritance as a value, and the entire, newly unified aristocracy began to close itself off through the control of marriage.[21]

Thus, in tracing the origins of chivalry and attempting to account for its enduring prestige, Duby presents a picture of negotiation and reciprocity among levels of the upper classes. Upwardly mobile figures—the knights—provide the established elite—landowners—with a newly sanctioned conception and mode of power. The elite, in turn, expands to include and appropriate the knights, while preserving as well as transmitting its ideals of exclusivity and inherited privilege.

Duby amplifies this picture of an aristocracy redefining and consolidating itself with a more detailed analysis of the mobile mem-

---

21. Duby, *The Chivalrous Society*, p. 80: see in general pp. 79–87.

bers of the knightly class known as "youths." The term "youth," he contends, which is frequently found in narratives of the period, could apply to a churchman but was much more often used to designate a warrior at a well-defined stage in his career. No longer a child, the youth had passed through the educational process necessary for a military career and had been received into the company of warriors; specifically, he had taken up arms and been dubbed a knight. What the youth had not yet done was to form his own family and settle his own estate. "In the world of chivalry," that is, a warrior ceased to be called "youth" when he had established himself, founded a family, and become head of a house: "the stages of 'youth' can therefore be defined as the period in a man's life between his being dubbed knight and his becoming a father." (As we will see, the heroes of the three plays under consideration in this chapter are all quite pointedly represented as being in precisely this transitional condition.) Duby stresses that, owing to techniques of aristocratic estate management in twelfth-century France, this condition of apprenticeship could last unduly long. Sons of the nobility often became knights between the ages of sixteen and twenty-two, when their fathers commonly were about fifty and still firmly in control of their households and property. Regarded as potentially troublesome, sons were encouraged to leave home. Youth, consequently, became a time of impatience, turbulence, and instability. Without fixed positions knights became wanderers, joining together as roving bands of companions in quest of winning glory in tournaments and war.[22]

Duby and other historians have connected the shape of knightly activity with the fact of the distinct shortage of marriageable daughters. Although this condition can be attributed in part to the church's complex prohibitions against incest, it also resulted from fears that early marriage would fragment and dissipate a family's patrimony. Remarrying widowers were rewarded with the most acceptable brides. Sons, particularly younger sons, were often condemned to an indefinitely prolonged youth. Duby argues that knights' adventures in fact were often quests for wives: "the desire

---

22. Duby, *The Chivalrous Society*, p. 113. This discussion of youth is from pp. 112–22. On p. 117 Duby points out that in France, as in England, the rules of primogeniture often left younger sons at sea.

to be married seems to have dominated the behaviour of a 'youth,' encouraging him to shine in combat and to parade at sporting events."[23] This turbulent and unstable group, then, sustained the Crusades and was responsible for tournaments, as well as for some unruly behavior patterns of sexual luxury and concubinage. For the most part, however, the youths were kept in a suspended state of celibacy and danger.

The presence of this group at the heart of aristocratic society, Duby continues, helped to sustain certain chivalric ideas and myths. Youths, for example, constituted the main audience of chivalric epics and romances. Their special situation goes a long way toward explaining the complex of idealized emotions—a suitor seeking recognition and favor at the hands of a remote and (often socially) superior lady and usually meeting frustration—that constitutes courtly love.[24] The phenomenon of courtly love is of course much debated by literary historians. Did it actually exist? Did courtly lovers accept sublimation, rather than hoping to consummate their love? Or was this configuration of passions actually adulterous, as is often assumed? It is more important for this book that such a complex of emotions was projected in the first place and that, in combination with Neoplatonic and especially Petrarchan influences, it was eventually transmitted to Renaissance England. Whether courtly love affairs remained unconsummated, and therefore stressed idealization of women and transcendence of sexual passion, or were adulterous, and so allied with sin, the conception of courtly love dissociates eros from marriage and from the concrete enactment of social relationships as well. Furthermore, the English version is entirely masculine, focusing exclusively on male desire, removing woman from significant action, and limiting her to the static role of the inspirational object of that desire.

---

23. Duby, *The Chivalrous Society*, p. 118; see also pp. 119 and 113, where Duby explains that youth could last as long as twenty-five to thirty years.

24. See Duby, *The Chivalrous Society*, pp. 121–22. See also Herbert Moller, "The Social Causation of the Courtly Love Complex," *Comparative Studies in Society and History*, 1 (1958–59), 137–63. For a representative debate about courtly love, see *The Meaning of Courtly Love: Papers of the First Annual Conference of the Center for Medieval and Early Renaissance Studies*, ed. F. X. Newman (Albany: State University of New York Press, 1972).

In his analysis of the chivalric romance, Eric Auerbach stresses a turning away from the representation of historical and political actuality in the "refinement of the laws of combat, courteous social intercourse, [and] service of women" that comprise the content of the genre. By insisting that in the romance "the feudal ethos serves no political function," Auerbach does not mean that no symbolic relation exists between the political conditions of feudal life and the content of romance. Rather, he views the romance's glorification of knightly adventure as the determined effort of a single class to render itself exclusive and to idealize its activities.[25] That this imaginative endeavor should involve the extreme delicacy of the courtly romance and the pointed literary evasion of verisimilitude characterizing its construction of a mysterious world of adventure that seems to exist solely for the knight to prove himself worthy becomes more understandable when we recall Duby's picture of knights, particularly youths, as upwardly mobile, socially positionless, sexually frustrated, and perpetually imperiled: "Dedicated to violence, 'youth' was the instrument of aggression and tumult in knightly society, but in consequence it was always in danger: It was aggressive and brutal in habit and it was to have its ranks decimated."[26] In attempting to refine and "civilize" its conduct, the knightly class that created and responded to courtly romance developed a notion of itself as "a community of the elect, a circle of solidarity . . . set apart from the common herd," whose adventures were distinguished by having an absolute value enhanced precisely by their removal from quotidian social and political concerns.[27] The evolving notion of courtesy insisted that nobility of birth was not sufficient for the ideal knight, who must also possess valiance, sensitivity, and refined manners. As Auerbach contends, this emphasis on inner values expanded the potential of the ideal of nobility but did not render it less selective: "Courtly culture gives rise to the idea, which long remained a factor of considerable importance in Europe, that nobility, greatness, and intrinsic values have

---

25. Eric Auerbach, "The Knight Sets Forth," in his *Mimesis: The Representation of Reality in Western Literature*, trans. Willard R. Trask (Princeton, N.J.: Princeton University Press, 1974), p. 134; see generally pp. 123–42.

26. Duby, *The Chivalrous Society*, p. 115.

27. Auerbach, p. 137.

nothing in common with everyday reality."[28] Thus the chivalric ideal as developed in medieval France, with its stress on absolute merit, accommodated some social mobility while retaining an emphasis on aristocratic superiority, class solidarity, and exclusivity.

Along with other scholars, Auerbach points out that the role of sexual love and women in this process was that of inspiring males to valorous achievement, an idea that originated in the courtly romance. But Robert Hanning stresses the significance of the inclusion of love in the representation of chivalry as the beginning of a conception of struggle between public and private life. According to Hanning, twelfth-century narrative depended on the paradigm of love and prowess reinforcing each other; at the same time, plots were generated originally by construing this relationship as problematic. Defining the representation of chivalry in the romance as "the statement of idealized interaction between impulses toward love and aggression in courtly men and women," Hanning continues: "By investigating, and representing, the tensions between love and prowess, and by focusing on the manner in which knights and ladies become conscious of these tensions, the chivalric romance makes of its adventure plot the story, nay the celebration, of the necessity of men (and women) to face the fact of their private destiny, and to attempt to attain that vision which, born within the recesses of the self, makes of life a process of dynamic self-realization." According to Hanning, there was "an inherent conflict of aim" between the knight's quest for personal happiness and his role in "a historical or pseudo-historical narrative action that transcends personal careers." Hanning argues that this problem eventually disappeared as the chivalric plot attained full autonomy and became a metaphor for the protagonist's quest for individual fulfillment. In its fully developed, original literary form, then, the chivalric romance both introduced and resolved a view of the relation between public and private life as problematic.[29]

How do the literary and historical formations of chivalry in twelfth-century, feudal France relate to the representation of chivalry and its accompanying sexual ideologies in Renaissance En-

28. Auerbach, p. 139.

29. Robert W. Hanning, *The Individual in Twelfth-Century Romance* (New Haven, Conn.: Yale University Press, 1977), pp. 4, 11.

gland? The relationship proposed here is neither direct nor precise, but involves instead an interesting series of overtones and implications. In particular, understanding the originating conditions of the chivalric ethic in its combined sociopolitical and aesthetic manifestations can help to account for the enduring usefulness and prestige of chivalry in sixteenth- and seventeenth-century culture. Especially suggestive for Renaissance England is the coexistence of religious change and social mobility—an expanding and consolidating of the aristocracy—with a pronounced aesthetic effort at refinement and idealization accompanied by an evasion of verisimilitude, and with a significant attempt to resolve the relationship between public and private life that is perceived as problematic. All these are processes that chivalry was originally designed both to articulate and to conceal. This combination of conditions suggests that one of chivalry's primary ideological functions was to facilitate violent processes of change by idealizing and—potentially—denying them, thus mediating between the shifting cultural formations of the present and the past.

As is well known, the Tudor monarchs encouraged the chivalric style and ethic to maintain unity and order after the religious upheavals of the Reformation and the turbulence created by social mobility in the sixteenth century. Roy Strong has demonstrated in exhaustive and elegant detail the ways in which Elizabeth I in particular brilliantly manipulated chivalry to create an elaborate symbolic code that, by suggesting uninterrupted tradition and (however speciously) lack of self-interested political involvement, invested her monarchy with an aura of stability and legitimacy.[30] Splendid chivalric rituals, involving tournaments, tilts, and superb pageantry, were developed to celebrate the queen's Accession Day and the Order of the Garter, a deliberate revival of a medieval chivalric order that was originally formed to unify and bind an aristocracy to its prince. As Strong shows, the "image of the age" was primarily feudal and medieval. The Elizabethan obsession with heraldry, the "ostentatious displays of coats of arms" that Strong views as "the pedigree mania of the new families," has been well documented; in addition, major Elizabethan products in architecture and literature displayed a recognizably medieval aesthet-

30. Strong, *Cult of Elizabeth*, esp. pp. 16, 114, 161.

ic. Evoking the legends of King Arthur and the mythical origins of Britain in Troy, unprecedented public displays of the monarch employed chivalry as "a vehicle which enhanced the Crown with ancient feudal glory. It was the Queen as the fount of honour made visible to her people."[31]

Much as it had in twelfth-century France, the celebration of the warrior-knight as the ideal figure at the center of aristocratic society contained a considerable amount of evasion in its Elizabethan development. Not only did this idealization deny the burgeoning influence of middle-class values and the impact of commercial urban life; its pageants, tilts, and tournaments, nostalgically glorifying individual valor, ignored the changing nature of warfare and the increasing value being placed on administrative and professional rather than military skill. Yet as the unproblematic retention of a Catholic saint (Saint George) at the center of a post-Reformation public ritual indicates, Elizabethan chivalry functioned eclectically, keeping alive a number of possible applications of its imagery. Far from being merely nostalgic, the relative indeterminacy of this "deliberate cult and reinvigoration of archaisms" helped to subdue the trauma of religious and social change.[32] With its focus on the monarch as the "Lord's Annointed," for example, the celebration of Elizabeth as a "sacred Virgin whose reign was ushering in a new golden age of peace and plenty" provided a new and crucial focus for pre-Reformation religious loyalties.[33] The medieval configuration of courtly love, transmitted to England in its Renaissance, Petrarchan version, offered a familiar symbolic structure in which a powerful, remote, chaste, socially superior woman conferred favor on, and withdrew it from, knights who fought to serve her. Elizabeth's brilliant political manipulation of this aesthetic structure facilitated the peoples' acceptance of a female (and unmarried) monarch; further, the entire chivalric configuration of Gloriana and her knights also gave upwardly mobile young men a tactful role in which to seek a position and a usable form in which aggressive ambitions could be delicately pursued. As recent scholarship

31. Strong, *Cult of Elizabeth*, pp. 164–74, 116, 185. See also Stone, p. 352; and Yates, pp. 90, 108–9, 175.

32. Strong, *Cult of Elizabeth*, p. 185.

33. Strong, *Cult of Elizabeth*, p. 114. See also Yates, pp. 29–120.

has demonstrated, the learned symbolic pageants that adorned the chivalric state festivals functioned jointly as entertainments, policy statements, and allegories of personal striving.[34] Thus Elizabethan chivalry partly disguised and partly articulated the changing nature of courtiers, from feuding nobles seeking regional martial dominance to adept politicians functioning as cultural agents of the centralized nation-state.

Although this delicately balanced political aesthetic worked reasonably well until late in Elizabeth's reign, the alliance between art and power shifted noticeably after her death. It was not simply that the elaborate, eclectic, unifying mythology failed to survive the charismatic queen; James himself specifically rejected it. James regarded himself as (and was) a learned prince of peace, taking a dim view of military violence. "And although it be praise-worthy and necessarie in a Prince, to be *patiens algoris* and *aestus*, when he shall have adoe with warres upon the fieldes; yet I think it meeter that ye goe both clothed and armed then naked to the battell; except you would make you light for away-running," he advises Prince Henry in *Basilicon Doron*.[35] Throughout the sixteenth century the humanist distaste for chivalric violence that James shared had remained largely passive. Indeed, early English humanists managed to absorb and transform the military ideal of the warrior-knight to include the entire governing class; in this revised version, the knight became an educated, nonviolent figure who "should more effectively with his learning and wit assail vice and error."[36] In the

34. See Strong, *Cult of Elizabeth*; Orgel; Yates; Montrose; and Marotti. See also Leah Marcus, "Shakespeare's Comic Heroines, Elizabeth I, and the Political Uses of Androgyny," in *Women in the Middle Ages and the Renaissance: Literary and Historical Perspectives*, ed. Mary Beth Rose (Syracuse, N.Y.: Syracuse University Press, 1986), pp. 135–53.

35. *The Basilicon Doron of King James VI*, ed. James Craigie, Scottish Text Society (London: Blackwood, 1944), vol. 1, p. 175. See also Strong, *Cult of Elizabeth*, pp. 58, 187; and Orgel and Strong, p. 47.

36. Thomas Elyot, quoted in Ferguson, pp. 219–20. The entire quotation is as follows: "A knight hath received that honor not only to defend with the sword Christ's faith and his proper country, against them which impugneth the one or invadeth the other: but also, and that most chiefly, by the mean of his dignity (if that be employed where it should be and esteemed as it ought to be) he should more effectually with his learning and wit assail vice and error, most pernicious enemies to Christian men, having thereunto for his sword

early seventeenth century, however, historians such as Selden, Speed, and Camden began applying a less mythical, more scientific, approach to Tudor chivalric stories, maintaining in their accounts the chivalric ideal of an elect community of loyal nobles, but demythologizing the Tudor fabrications of its origins. Those who sought to revive the glories of Elizabethan chivalric symbolism and all it represented centered their hopes on Henry, Prince of Wales. Yet even in the celebrations created for and by this prince, the knightly ideal became increasingly revised and attenuated. The final blow to the attempted revival was delivered when Henry died in 1612. And James's notorious sale of knighthoods further damaged the prestige attached to that rank.[37]

Chivalric symbolism did not, of course, disappear from Jacobean aesthetics and politics. "Everyone in the early seventeenth century was busy calling in the past to redress the balance of the present," Lawrence Stone explains, in reference to the Renaissance affirmation of medieval ideals.[38] But the once inclusive and flexible Elizabethan chivalric mythology increasingly associated itself with political absolutism and became the property of an ever more rigid and exclusive class of aristocrats. In Elizabethan England, for example, the elaborate chivalric festivals displaying the monarch had been designed as spectacles for the public, a unifying political function that was dispersed and augmented by the queen's famous progresses around the country. In contrast, Jacobean chivalric imagery was increasingly absorbed and transformed by the masque, a creation designed solely for an exclusive courtly audience, seeking images of its own heroism that were more and more isolated from public values and sentiments. In tracing the transformation of Re-

---

and spear his tongue and pen." For the humanist attack on chivalry, see Ferguson, pp. 169–73; Strong, *Cult of Elizabeth*, p. 180; and Norman Council, "Ben Jonson, Inigo Jones, and the Transformation of Tudor Chivalry," *ELH*, 47 (1980), 259–75.

37. See Council; Strong, *Cult of Elizabeth*, pp. 180–87, and "Inigo Jones and the Revival of Chivalry," *Apollo*, 86 (1967), 102–7; and Mary C. Williams, "Merlin and the Prince: The Speeches at Prince Henry's Barriers," *Renaissance Drama*, N.S. 8 (1977), 221–30. For James's sale of knighthoods, see Stone, pp. 71–82.

38. Stone, p. 751.

naissance chivalric representation, Stephen Orgel has revealed a narrowing, rigidifying process that reached its peak in the inflexible, destructive illusions of Charles I.[39] Thus in Jacobean and Caroline England, the elements of evasion, fantasy, and nostalgia always latent in chivalric mythology became increasingly prominent and increasingly subject to articulate opposition.

These processes are represented in the drama as a transformation and critique of heroism. When the heroism of public action embodied in the figure of the warrior-knight and excluding women as active participants in public life begins to be severely scrutinized as corrupt, inadequate, and reactionary, the drama offers an alternative conception of a heroism that connects public and private life, is symbolized in marriage, and is associated with the future. In Elizabethan drama the heroics of marriage takes comic form as a collective affirmation that assures the future but also deflects it. In contrast, Jacobean drama grants to the heroics of marriage all the prestige of tragic expression by attempting to unite public and private life and to confer on them equal distinction; yet this effort breaks down, and the future recedes into collective mourning for the past, the consolation of tragedy. Although it does not represent a future, tragedy nevertheless demands one by destroying the past. What follows focuses on the ways in which the hybrid genre tragicomedy fulfills this demand; in redefining the relationship between chivalric heroism and sexuality, tragicomedy revises both comedy and tragedy and gives the future a form.

iii

Ever since the publication of the First Shakespeare Folio, determining the genre of *Troilus and Cressida* (1602) has remained notoriously problematic. As Kenneth Palmer puts it in his recent introduction to the Arden edition, "*Troilus* is essentially a schematic play, an exercise in dramatic paradigms; it takes any man, or any situation, and looks at either in a variety of ways, *each one valid for a specific kind of play*. It is this which accounts for much of the diffi-

39. Orgel, passim. See also Strong, *Cult of Elizabeth*, pp. 16, 114, 185, and *Van Dyck*, pp. 20, 43, 224, 246; and Orgel and Strong, p. 47.

culty which we find in characterizing the play: comedy, tragedy, satire, tragic farce and the rest have been propounded and justified; *and all are right.*"[40] It is the play's hybrid nature, particularly its unusual mixture of traditional elements, that gives it an interesting relationship to tragicomedy.

However *Troilus and Cressida* is classified, it comprises a piercing critique of the heroism of action and the chivalric ethos that defines and governs it. With its origins in one of the major myths of Western civilization, its population by the majority of the West's great epic heroes, and its inclusion of both ancient and medieval legends, the play manages to convey a wide-ranging indictment of the childish and willful falseness of human endeavor. It is well known that *Troilus and Cressida* can be viewed as Shakespeare's bleakest and most pessimistic play. In it he strips the ancient and medieval materials of their glamorous energy, exposing with unusual contempt the military and emotional conflicts involved in the Trojan War as petty, grandiose, and in every way needlessly destructive. The greater part of the play focuses on a hiatus in the fighting, a period of inaction when both the motives for battle and the preoccupations of the protagonists are examined and revealed as trivial, vicious, and deluded. The combined effect is frequently shocking or puzzling; often it is bitterly funny. Apt summary comments within the text range in tone from Agamemnon's pompous, wistful bewilderment—"The ample proposition that hope makes / In all designs begun on earth below / Fails in the promis'd largeness" (1.3.3–5)—to Thersites' caustic expression of the degraded extension of this logic of failure and disillusionment—"All the argument is a whore and a cuckold: a good quarrel to draw emulous factions, and bleed to death upon" (2.3.74–76). The plot is amorphous, varied, and diffuse; it is often difficult to remember precisely what happened and when.[41]

Shakespeare is clearly employing a variety of devices that purposely alienate the audience and prohibit sustained sympathy.[42]

40. Kenneth Palmer, ed., *Troilus and Cressida* (London: Methuen, 1982), p. 83, italics his. All quotations from the play, identified in the text by act, scene, and line numbers, are from this edition.

41. Cf. Barbara Everett, "The Inaction of *Troilus and Cressida*," *Essays in Criticism*, 32, no. 2 (1982), 119–39.

42. Cf. Palmer, pp. 53, 64, 69.

For example, no represented action or emotion escapes the bitter choric commentary either of Pandarus's debased voyeurism or of Thersites' devastating, scurrilous wit. One of the play's other distancing devices is Shakespeare's frequent insistence on the legendary nature of the characters and their story, a recurring motif that he uses to underscore the futility of their choices and actions, already predetermined and familiar to the audience. Although this self-conscious manipulation of legend adds to the play's irony, it also gives the action a timeless, inclusive quality that implies a scrutiny of all of Western civilization. Along with the play's inclusive and generalized preoccupation with the follies and emptiness of Western history, however, the significance of its action is augmented when it is considered as a peculiar product of English Renaissance culture. *Troilus and Cressida* is a very late (1602) Elizabethan play that—unusually, even exceptionally, for Shakespeare—centers entirely on the warrior aristocracy, a focus that is scrutinized from within the group, but is never varied by the representation of the activities or points of view of other classes. As we have seen, class exclusivity is one of the inherent features of the literary and historical formations of the knightly ideal. When we recall that the Elizabethan elite manipulated the aesthetics of chivalry as a means of defining and consolidating the upper (particularly the governing) classes, the attack on chivalric values in *Troilus and Cressida* comes into view as a biting critique of the aristocracy. Specifically, the play presents the Elizabethan aristocracy as a class without a future.

It is interesting, then, to consider *Troilus and Cressida* as a critique of chivalric heroism written at a belated stage in Elizabeth's reign, when the cult she had inspired was wearing thin. The chivalric myth that Britain was founded by the Trojans, so important to the Tudor political aesthetics of display, becomes the starting point for the play's attack, making the Trojans the more dedicated protagonists of chivalric values. During the scene (2.2) in which the Trojans debate the motives and purpose for their war against the Greeks, Troilus fully articulates the peculiar idealism of chivalry. In answer to Hector's protest against the futility of the war, he insists on the absolutism of nobility and honor, which, he declares, exist in spite of reason, possessing an innate value precisely because they are divorced from practical, everyday concerns:

"Reason and respect / Make livers pale, and lustihood deject / . . . .
What's aught but as 'tis valued?" (2.2.49–53). To Hector's argument for upholding the "moral laws / Of nature and of nations"
(2.2.185–86), which require the return of Helen to her husband,
Troilus opposes what he regards as the greater good of the valorous individual's quest for glory; his opposition articulates the
oddly self-absorbed conception of the world as designed especially
to provide adventures for knights seeking to prove their worth that
is characteristic of the chivalric romance:

> Were it not glory that we more affected
> Than the performance of our heaving spleens,
> I would not wish a drop of Trojan blood
> Spent more in her [i.e., Helen's] defence.
> But, worthy Hector,
> She is a theme of honour and renown,
> A spur to valiant and magnanimous deeds,
> Whose present courage may beat down our foes,
> And fame in time to come canonize us.
> [2.2.196–203]

Although Trojan idealism (and hence Trojan self-destructive-
ness) is greater than that of the Greeks, the actions of both sides are
defined and governed by the common language of chivalry.
Throughout the play Shakespeare equates the absolutism of chivalry, its idealized emphasis on innate nobility and the quest for
individual valor, with an evasion of brutal circumstance and a rigid
attempt to stop time and arrest the flow of history. As John Bayley
has demonstrated, in all of Shakespeare's other plays, time is at
most restorative, at least an agent of significance. But the action of
Troilus and Cressida, engulfed in an isolated present tense, renders
time meaningless: "In the formal impact of *Troilus* there is neither
past nor future: everything takes place in and ends in, the present
. . . the absence of value is contained and revealed in the absence of
time."[43] The play is full of images of inertia (embodied, for example, in the "sleeping giant" Achilles), frustrated actions, and
aborted growth. "Checks and disasters / Grow in the veins of

43. John Bayley, "Time and the Trojans," *Essays in Criticism*, 25 (1975), 55–
73.

actions highest rear'd / As knots, by the conflux of meeting sap, / Infects the sound pine and diverts his grain / Tortive and errant from his course of growth" (1.3.5–9), Agamemnon ponderously explains.

The connection of military prowess and abstract idealism with narcissistic self-absorption and the rigid resistance of history that defines chivalry in the play is, of course, most fully embodied in Troilus; specifically, it is symbolized by his youth. The play abounds with references to Troilus's youth, ranging from Pandarus's tedious description of his scanty beard ("you know he has not past three or four hairs on his chin . . . why, he is very young" [1.2.113–17]); to Hector's conception of the dangerous irrationality of his brother's youth ("Paris and Troilus, you have both said well, / And on the cause and question now in hand / Have gloz'd, but superficially—not much / Unlike young men, whom Aristotle thought / Unfit to hear moral philosophy" [2.2.164–68]), as well as its tender vulnerability ("No, faith, young Troilus; doff thy harness, youth / . . . . Let grow thy sinews till their knots be strong / And tempt not yet the brushes of the war" [5.3.31–34]); to Ulysses' perception of Troilus as "the youngest son of Priam, a true knight; / Not yet mature, yet matchless" (4.5.96–97); to Troilus's characteristically self-conscious eulogy to his own love ("Never did young man fancy / With so eternal and so fix'd a soul" [5.2.164–65]). Indeed, the combined references to this subject are so insistent, reiterated from so many different points of view, that it is possible to recognize in the combination of idealism, violence, abstraction, self-absorption, and rigidity that constitutes youth a developmental stage in life that has been frozen into a static condition, the defining condition of chivalry in the play. At this point it is helpful to recall Duby's description of the knightly class of youths as turbulent, transitional figures ("not yet mature yet matchless") who, looking forward to marriage and fatherhood, were nevertheless often younger sons forced to live in a state of prolonged suspension. While the future remained at best a remote possibility, the knights immersed themselves in the present tense, seeking glory in tournaments and sustaining violent military activity.

In *Troilus and Cressida* the chivalric suspension of the future is clarified in the representation of love and sexuality. For the purposes of this book, the most important characteristics of eros in the play are that it is private, abstract, destructive, static, and conceived entirely in terms of male desire. Secrecy, of course, was one of the main tenets of courtly love; it is a theme much emphasized in the play's main source, the *Troilus and Criseyde* of Chaucer (c. 1385), often considered the greatest story of courtly love to emerge from medieval Britain.[44] Whereas in Chaucer's version the love story is the central focus of the poem, though, in Shakespeare's play it comes relatively infrequently into view. As Kenneth Palmer demonstrates, the "love plot," although related analogously to the representation of the war, itself occupies only 33 percent of the play. Until Act 4 no one but Pandarus deals with the lovers as lovers; and only after he is betrayed in Act 5 does Troilus publicly acknowledge himself to be Cressida's lover.[45] As is often pointed out, though Troilus is willing to risk destruction to fight for the "theme of honour," he does nothing to save Cressida from the Greeks, immediately resigning himself to the "hateful truth" of her departure (4.4.29) and presenting "nightly visitations" (4.4.72) as the sole possible alternative for the lovers' future.[46]

The divorce of Troilus and Cressida's love from public knowledge and activity—its completely private nature—does not enhance a sense of idealized, rarefied intimacy, as it is meant to do in Chaucer; instead it serves to emphasize the irresolvable conflict that love and sexuality present to the heroism of action. As noted above, the introduction of women and sexual love into the medieval courtly romance provided a motif in which it was possible to reconcile potentially conflicting impulses of eros and aggression, the endeavors of private and public life, by assigning to eros the crucial (if static) role of inspiration. In Chaucer, Troilus's wooing of Criseyde does act as a spur to valorous deeds.[47] Similarly, in

44. See C. S. Lewis, *The Allegory of Love: A Study in Medieval Tradition* (London: Oxford University Press, 1977), pp. 176–97.

45. See Palmer, p. 39.

46. See, e.g., Robert Ornstein, "*Troilus and Cressida*," in *Modern Shakespearean Criticism: Essays on Style, Dramaturgy, and the Major Plays*, ed. Alvin B. Kernan (New York: Harcourt, Brace & World, 1970), pp. 311–19; and David Kaula, "Will and Reason in *Troilus and Cressida*," *Shakespeare Quarterly*, 12 (Summer 1961), 271–83.

47. Cf. M. C. Bradbrook, "What Shakespeare Did to Chaucer's *Troilus and Criseyde*," *Shakespeare Quarterly*, 19 (1958), 311–19.

Elizabethan drama we have seen the chivalric resolution of potentially conflicting public and private endeavors dramatized as successful in *Tamburlaine*. But in *Troilus and Cressida* sexual love is presented as purely destructive of military action and prowess. With the possible exception of Hector, the play's lovers are notoriously inert. The action begins with Troilus simultaneously unarming, expressing melancholy in love, and conceiving of himself in consequence as effeminate and weak (1.1.9–12). At one point Helen's role is defined as unarming Hector (3.2.145–50). Paris, "like one besotted on [his] sweet delights" (2.2.144), selfishly avoids going to the battle he created because "my Nell would not have it so" (3.2.133). And in one of the play's surprising twists, it is revealed that Achilles is refraining from battle less out of petty pride, as the text deceptively reiterates, than out of love for one of Priam's daughters. In the revelation of Achilles' love, Ulysses makes firm and explicit the irreconcilable opposition between eros and action, private and public concerns, along with the allegedly greater value of the latter terms:

Achill.   Of this my privacy
       I have strong reasons.
Ulyss.   But 'gainst your privacy
       The reasons are more potent and heroical.
                     [3.3.190–92]

That women and eros are depicted as subversive of public action does not score a point for misogyny in the play, nor does it demonstrate the superiority of military heroism. Instead, these representations serve to underscore the delusions of chivalry by emphasizing the evasive emptiness of its predominant sexual ideology, in which women, idealized as themes of honor and renown, in fact play at best a peripheral and at worst an antagonistic role in the chivalric conception of glorious male action. Along with Troilus, two warriors, Aeneas and Agamemnon, explicitly define woman's role as the inspiration and source of male action, but neither of them has anything to do with women in the play, and Agamemnon's pompous pieties about the causal relation of love and war are formulaic and absurd: "We are soldiers, / And may that soldier a mere recreant prove / That means not, hath not, or is not in love" (1.3.285–87).

What makes Agamemnon's remarks absurd is their lack of relation to circumstantial reality. But Troilus, who is in fact in love, displays the same quality of evasive abstraction in his response to Cressida. As is often observed, he is much more interested in the subtle movements of his own will and desire than he is in the actual Cressida, whom he regards as an empty vessel waiting to contain his love. "Sleep kill those pretty eyes, / And give as soft attachment to thy senses / As infants empty of all thought" (4.2.4–6), he begs. Troilus responds to Cressida's departure with entranced, self-pitying inertia, concentrating not on her welfare, but on the refinement of his own desire. "Cressid, I love thee in so strain'd a purity / That the blest gods, as angry with my fancy, / More bright in zeal than the devotion which / Cold lips blow to their deities, take thee from me" (4.423–26), he rhapsodizes, letting her go.

The brilliance of Shakespeare's conception of Cressida is that she is construed, and construes herself, entirely in terms of male desire. Gradually she relinquishes any grasp of an existence separate from men's need of her, which she correctly perceives to be hopeless. Her greatest bewilderment occurs when she attempts to declare the independence of her feelings for Troilus by separating them from his desire for her. As she recognizes in this scene of her confusion, she has at most "a kind of self," and Troilus is not much interested in her feelings apart from their response to his.[48] Accordingly, Cressida's alienation is clarified when, attempting to adjust her actions to the subtle momentum of male desire, she considers herself abstractly, as a "thing":

48. Cf. Ornstein; and Gayle Greene, "Shakespeare's Cressida: 'A Kind of Self,'" in *The Woman's Part*, ed. Carolyn Ruth Swift Lenz, Gayle Greene, and Carol Thomas Neely (Urbana: University of Illinois Press, 1980), pp. 133–49. The most subtle and perceptive study of Cressida's position in the play that I have come across is Janet Adelman, "'This Is and Is Not Cressid': The Characterization of Cressida," in *The (M)other Tongue: Essays in Feminist Psychoanalytic Interpretation*, ed. Shirley Nelson Garner, Claire Kahane, and Madelon Sprengnether (Ithaca, N.Y.: Cornell University Press, 1985), pp. 119–41. About Cressida's complete identification with male desire, Adelman comments (pp. 124, 136), "In the context created both by her own fears and by Troilus' expectations, there is no true choice. She reestablishes her dignity both for herself and for Troilus by retreating from self-revelation and from love. . . . For ultimately the necessities of Troilus' character, rather than of Cressida's, require her betrayal of him. Cressida's betrayal in effect allows

Yet hold I off. Women are angels, wooing:
Things won are done; joy's soul lies in the doing.
That she belov'd knows naught that knows not this:
Men prize the thing ungain'd more than it is. . . .
Therefore this maxim out of love I teach:
"Achievement is command; ungain'd, beseech."
[1.2.291–98]

Whose joy does Cressida refer to? Certainly not her own: her knowing maxims articulate a determination to conceal and nullify her own desires. The process is successful; her definition of herself as a male achievement at the end of this speech is echoed by Troilus's instantaneous response to the news that Cressida must leave Troy: "How my achievements mock me!" (4.2.71). The construction of Troilus and Cressida's attachment, then, depends entirely upon the fact that Cressida and her love exist only in the terms generated by male desire. Given these conditions, Cressida's surrender to another man's needs when she is separated from Troilus is inevitable, a necessary preservation of her identity. That Troilus dimly recognizes and partially accepts these conditions from the start is indicated by his dread of being overwhelmed by love ("I do fear besides / that I shall lose distinction in my joys" [3.2.24–25]), by his association of love with death (3.2.20), and by his overriding fear—indeed, it could be argued, his assumption—that Cressida will betray him (4.4.5–95). As we have seen throughout this book, in its origins in male subjectivity and its divorce from circumstantial reality, the abstract idealization of women coexists inevitably with the possibility of their degradation. What's aught but as 'tis valued? One man's object of strain'd purity will be another's daughter of the game. When Diomedes

---

Troilus to blench and still stand firm by honor; it serves to free him from a union ambivalently desired while allowing him to continue to think of himself as the embodiment of truth." As Adelman makes clear (pp. 137, 140), Shakespeare is far from "exposing" these emotions, which are presented as sympathetic, "part of the play's implicit identification with Troilus' fantasy. . . . For the effort to keep Troilus pure seems to me finally evidence of Shakespeare's failure to dissociate himself from the fantasies explored in the creation of Troilus; and insofar as the play consequently embodies Troilus' fantasies, Cressida as a whole character must be sacrificed."

speaks of prizing Cressida at her own worth, as though she were an independent entity, he is, of course, describing an impossibility (4.5.131–32). Troilus makes this fact clear when he is finally unable to assign to Cressida a comprehensible identity separate from his own desire: "This is, and is not, Cressid" (5.2.145).[49]

In terms of dramatic structure, neither Troilus's love nor Cressida's betrayal generates actions or consequences: each is devoid of suspense, predictable. In choosing to represent this aspect of the Trojan story, Shakespeare is interested in redefining the origins and nature of the chivalric legend, not in refashioning its well-known outcome. Another way to say the same thing is that chivalric idealism and sexuality are depicted as static and, perceived as such, preclude dramatic development. As is often argued, the lovers' interaction, epitomized in their oddly self-conscious vows (3.2), centers on an evasion of time and change. That Troilus does not die in the play denies the audience the unifying tragic consolation of witnessing a completed life cycle and underscores the state of suspension and inertia that characterizes the play and is symbolized in the hero's perpetual youth. Specifically, the destructive quality of chivalric idealism is perceived as a willful resistance to history, an inability to envision alternatives, to imagine and pursue the future.

What are the unwisely rejected alternatives to chivalry suggested in the play? Ulysses seems at first to be the one dynamic character, willing to move, plan, and engage actively with a possible future. Yet Ulysses also proves to have an insufficient grasp of the real. His witty and observant policies are as ineffectual as Troilus's love; and his eloquent remarks about time, despite their air of knowledge and experience, articulate not a committed acceptance of the processes of history, but a disillusioned exposé of human weakness, couched in a romantic and cynical portrayal of shallowness, fickleness, and disloyalty to the past.[50]

The only concept of a workable future in fact appears as a mere suggestion in the play's brief representation of women and mar-

49. For an interesting recent study of the mechanisms of desire in the play, see René Girard, "The Politics of Desire in *Troilus and Cressida*," in *Shakespeare and the Question of Theory*, ed. Patricia Parker and Geoffrey Hartman (New York: Methuen, 1985), pp. 188–209.

50. This tone characterizes both of Ulysses' famous speeches, particularly his speech on time (3.3.145–90).

riage. As we have seen, both Cressida and Helen are static, incapable of generating action; functioning solely as objects of the male quest for glory, they obediently fulfill the role predetermined for them by the dualistic, chivalric sexual system in which they are inscribed. In contrast, Cassandra, Andromache, and Hecuba do initiate independent action, pointedly opposing themselves to the chivalric ethic. Like Helen and Cressida, Andromache, Hecuba, and Cassandra are antagonistic to military action; they are clearly depicted not as depleting the men they love, however, but as trying to keep them alive. Though the prophet Cassandra's legendary doom is to be ignored, the Trojan queen Hecuba, who does not even appear in the play, manages to outwit Ulysses by keeping the greatest Greek hero, Achilles, from battle until chance (i.e., Patroclus's death) renders her scheme ineffectual.

Interestingly, whereas Helen is associated with rape and adultery and Cressida with extramarital liaison, both Hecuba and Andromache are loyal wives. Hector elaborates the association of marriage with the survival and perpetuation of society in the Trojan debate scene, when he opposes Troilus's chivalry as immoral and irrational:

> Nature craves
> All dues be render'd to their owners: now
> What nearer debt in all humanity
> Than wife is to the husband? If this law
> Of nature be corrupted through affection,
> And that great minds, of partial indulgence,
> To their benumbed wills, resist the same,
> There is a law in each well-order'd nation
> To curb those ranging appetites that are
> Most disobedient and refractory.
> If Helen then be wife to Sparta's king,
> As it is known she is, these moral laws
> Of nature and of nations speak aloud
> To have her back return'd: thus to persist
> In doing wrong extenuates not wrong,
> But makes it much more heavy.
>   [2.2.174–89]

Nevertheless, in the brief glimpses we are granted of Hector as a husband, his attitude toward marriage is dismissive and contemptuous. We learn at the beginning of the play that "he chid Andromache" (1.2.6), and although this action is clearly unusual, the one scene in which Hector appears with his wife shows him rudely rebuking her efforts to prevent his death (5.3). Furthermore, Hector almost instantaneously rejects the priority he himself places on marriage and survival in favor of the chivalric quest. His vision of marriage as the symbol of an ordered society is merely suggested, rather than developed: it is not the emotional focus of the play. The pervasive view of sexuality is instead articulated by Troilus in his argument to continue the war:

> I take today a wife, and my election
> Is led on in the conduct of my will:
> My will enkindled by mine eyes and ears,
> Two traded pilots 'twixt the dangerous shores
> Of will and judgement—how may I avoid,
> Although my will distaste what it elected,
> The wife I choose? . . .
> We turn not back the silks upon the merchant
> When we have soil'd them, nor the remainder viands
> We do not throw in unrespective sieve
> Because we now are full.
> [2.2.62–71]

As has been pointed out, Troilus's reasoning here is self-contradictory and muddled. More important for these purposes, though, Troilus equates sexuality with soilure, and his conception of a surviving marriage is one of inevitable corruption, regret, and ennui. Insofar as the future in *Troilus and Cressida* is suggested, then, it is associated with marriage; but that future is belittled, rejected, and, like Andromache, shunted aside. The degraded extension of this logic of intransigence is given its most vivid expression by Thersites, who, defining Menelaus as the central figure of Greek identity, speculates on the Greek inability not only to enact, but even to imagine alternatives to the dishonored condition of the humiliated cuckold: "To what form but that he is, should wit larded with malice and malice forced with wit turn him to? To an ass were nothing: he is both ass and ox; to an ox were nothing: he is both ox and ass. To be a dog, a mule, a cat, a fitchook, a toad, a lizard, an owl, a puttock, or a herring without a roe, I would not care; but to be Menelaus I would conspire against destiny. Ask me not what I would be, if I were not Thersites" (5.1.56–64).

The resolute denial of the possibilities of metamorphosis or transformation expressed in Thersites' speech makes explicit the play's direct refutation of the Utopian values of romance. That chivalric ideals—Helen's inspiration, Cressida's fidelity, Troilus's Hector's, and Achilles' honor—should be revealed as their opposites implies the lost value of those ideals and gives the play its special bitterness. Mark Rose has argued that "Shakespeare, who came to maturity in the 1580s at the height of the Elizabethan revival of chivalry, was not ready to write anti-romances like *Don Quixote* or *The Knight of the Burning Pestle*. He was . . . too deeply possessed by the absolute world of fidelity. He could write about the death of chivalry or the corruption of chivalry but he could not distance himself sufficiently from its imaginative claims to burlesque it."[51] As we have seen, the fundamental characteristic of the pessimism of *Troilus and Cressida* is depicted as the lack of a future. The legacy of the Trojans to their British descendants is disease: as Troilus puts it, "there is no more to say" (5.10.22). The implicit critique of Elizabethan society suggests that the existing aristocratic conceptions of heroism are bankrupt, leaving the elite without adequate models of behavior. Chivalry has lost its ability to mediate and to facilitate cultural change.

iv

Jacobean tragicomedy significantly revises these materials. In his discussion of the relation among ideology, genre, and cultural change, Jameson points out that "traditional generic systems—tragedy and comedy, for instance, or lyric/epic/drama—which in earlier social formations have their own objectivity and constitute something like a formal environment or historical situation into which the individual work must emerge and against which it must define itself, are for the contemporary critic the occasion for the

51. Mark Rose, "Othello's Occupation: Shakespeare and the Romance of Chivalry," *English Literary Renaissance*, 15 (1985), 293–311. Cf. G. K. Hunter, quoted in Palmer, p. 87: "The regular collapse of the grand gesture into incompetency and frustration does not mean, however, that the gesture was never grand anyway."

stimulation of essentially differential perceptions. On such occasions, even if the critic 'classes' the text as a whole in this or that traditional genus . . . the thrust of such a decision is to define the specificity of this text and mode *against* the other genre, now grasped in dialectical opposition to it." Thus even a text as difficult to classify as *Troilus and Cressida* can be grasped in terms of its direct and explicit rejection of the traditional materials of romance. But in tragicomedy the focus shifts, and the dialectical process Jameson describes occurs not only with the hindsight of critical analysis, but also, to a certain extent, within the play itself. Relying entirely on traditional materials, tragicomedy consciously revises their emphases so as to demystify, without necessarily rejecting, the terms of legitimate authority and recognized, shared cultural values that make these materials legible and articulate. Jameson describes the relationship between genre and what he calls the "historical moment" of a literary text as being "understood to block off or shut down a certain number of formal possibilities available before, and to open up determinate new ones, which may or may not ever be realized in artistic practice."[52] In this regard the unconventionality of *Troilus and Cressida* can be discerned as the play's decisive shutting off of new possibilities, specifically, its insistence on portraying chivalry as an inescapable cultural dead end. Tragicomedy, which also deflates chivalry, represents it in contrast as decidedly less powerful; further, in attempting to negotiate the present and the past by focusing on the chivalric ethos, tragicomedy manages to suggest alternative modes of conduct and conceptualization for the future.

The Two Noble Kinsmen (1613) presents a particularly interesting example of this process. Like *Troilus and Cressida*, *The Two Noble Kinsmen* is taken from Chaucer; it is a dramatization of *The Knight's Tale*. Something of the play's peculiar combination of deference and irreverence toward its medieval and classical materials is immediately evident in the Prologue's impertinent tribute to Chaucer:

> Chaucer, of all admired, the story gives:
> There constant to eternity it lives.
> If we let fall the nobleness of this,

52. Jameson, pp. 141–42 (italics his), 148.

And the first sound this child hear be a hiss,
How will it shake the bones of that good man,
And make him cry from under ground, "O fan
From me the witless chaff of such a writer
That blasts my bays, and my famed work makes lighter
Than Robin Hood!"

[Prologue, ll. 13–21][53]

The mixture of tones in the Prologue, with its barely concealed intent to deflate the past, could, of course, be attributed to the joint authorship of Shakespeare and Fletcher. Though evidence about the authorship of *The Two Noble Kinsmen* remains conflicting and inconclusive, scholars are nearly unanimous in discerning two distinct styles in the play, generally granting Fletcher the lion's share and attributing the first act and large parts of the last, with a few scenes in the middle, to Shakespeare.[54] Clifford Leech argues, for example, that the project was initiated by Shakespeare and brought to completion by Fletcher. Detecting the predominant presence of "Fletcher's deflating hand," Leech sees the younger playwright's attitude toward the elder as one of distinct irreverence.[55] Leech's case is extremely convincing, yet the mixed, uncertain evidence about the play's authorship renders relatively useless any effort to understand it in terms of authorial intent. If we view tragicomedy instead as both product and agent of an ongoing process of cultural transformation, we can better understand the odd juxtaposition of

53. William Shakespeare and John Fletcher, *The Two Noble Kinsmen*, ed. Clifford Leech, in *The Two Noble Kinsmen, Titus Andronicus, and Pericles*, ed. Sylvan Barnet (New York: New American Library, 1966), pp. 44–176. All quotations from the play, identified in the text by act, scene, and line numbers, are from this edition.

54. For an excellent summary bibliography for the play, including authorship debates, see G. R. Proudfoot, "*Henry VIII, The Two Noble Kinsmen*, and the Apocryphal Plays," in *Shakespeare: Select Bibliographical Guides*, ed. Stanley Wells (London: Oxford University Press, 1973). Other informative studies of the play's authorship include Paul Bertram, *Shakespeare and "The Two Noble Kinsmen"* (New Brunswick, N.J.: Rutgers University Press, 1965); A. Hart, "Shakespeare and the Vocabulary of *The Two Noble Kinsmen*," *Review of English Studies*, 10 (1934), 274–87; Marco Mincoff, "The Authorship of *The Two Noble Kinsmen*," *English Studies*, 33 (1952), 97–115; and Kenneth Muir, *Shakespeare as Collaborator* (London: Methuen, 1960), pp. 98–147.

55. Leech, pp. xxiv, xxxii of his edition of the play.

generic discourses, mixture of tones, and unresolved sexual and moral issues that characterize *The Two Noble Kinsmen*, not only as a representation of the inadequacy of the past, but also as an attempt to find accurate terms in which the future can be defined and appropriated.

Once again this process is discernible in the play's representation of love and sexuality. Like that of *Troilus and Cressida*, the action of *The Two Noble Kinsmen* is constructed in the specifically chivalric terms of the heroism of action. The major authority figure, the Athenian duke Theseus, and the heroes of the play, the Theban cousins Palamon and Arcite, are presented as warrior-knights; and the trappings of chivalry—the duels, armor, courtesy, and tournaments, along with the absolutist code of honor—constitute the bulk of the play's material and dominate its tone.

As I have tried to show, in the dramatization of chivalric stories, women and eros, though often symbolically important, play peripheral and static roles. In *Troilus and Cressida*, for example, although the love story is analogous to the war plot, it occupies the stage for only about one-third of the time. In *The Two Noble Kinsmen*, however, love and sexuality become not simply the predominant, but the exclusive focus of the play. The story centers on the rivalry between Palamon and Arcite, who, having been captured and jailed by Theseus after his triumph over the Theban ruler, Creon, fall in love simultaneously with Theseus's sister-in-law, Emilia, whom they spot from the window of their prison cell. This event marks the beginning of the rivalry that divides the previously inseparable pair of loving cousins into jealous and hostile competitors, whose newly, and sexually, inspired hatred becomes the major issue needing resolution in the play.

When sexual love becomes the central subject of an English Renaissance comedy or tragedy, it is conceived in the complex terms of the heroics of marriage and is usually opposed to a dualistic mentality that either idealizes or degrades women and eros and, in chivalric stories, is often associated with some version of courtly (or Petrarchan) love. In the first act of *The Two Noble Kinsmen*, these traditional oppositions immediately take shape. The play begins with an elaborate ceremonial, the wedding of Theseus and Hippolyta, which is quickly interrupted by three queens, begging Theseus temporarily to abandon his wedding and to wage a sur-

prise attack against the evil Theban ruler, Creon, who refuses to
bury their husbands, his defeated enemies. In protesting the urgency of their suit, the queens are particularly insistent that Theseus
undertake his quest in their behalf before consummating his marriage. Why? Eros, they claim, will utterly overwhelm his capacity
to reason and subvert his ability to act:

> When her arms,
> Able to lock Jove from a synod, shall
> By warranting moonlight corslet thee, O when
> Her twining cherries shall their sweetness fall
> Upon thy tasteful lips, what wilt thou think
> Of rotten kings or blubbered queens, what care
> For what thou feels't not, what thou feel'st being able
> To make Mars spurn his drum? O if thou couch
> But one night with her, every hour in't will
> Take hostage of thee for a hundred, and
> Thou shalt remember nothing more than what
> That banquet bids thee to.
>   [1.1.174–85]

The queens equate marriage with sex and assume that consummated sexual love inevitably will subvert heroism. Theseus refuses
to delay his wedding, couching his opposition to the queens' reasoning specifically in the epic, adventurous terms of the heroics of
marriage. His wedding becomes "this grand act of our life, this
daring deed / Of fate in wedlock"; marriage is "a service whereto I
am going / Greater than any was; it more imports me / than all the
actions that I have foregone / Or futurely can cope" (1.1.163–64,
170–73).

These traditionally competing views of sexuality dominate the
first scene of the play and seem to indicate familiar terms in which
the dramatic conflict will be constructed. As a pointed deviation
from *The Knight's Tale*, in which a bevy of queens confronts
Theseus after his marriage to Hippolyta has taken place, the interrupted wedding underscores the motif of sexual debate. Yet
despite the explicitness, immediacy, and care with which the terms
of erotic conflict are established, they are quickly and surprisingly
dismantled. Having elegantly elaborated the heroics of marriage,
Theseus promptly abandons it, suddenly agreeing after all to

postpone his wedding and rushing off to defend the queens by subduing the evil Creon. As a result, the heroics of marriage is reduced with startling immediacy to a tenuous suggestion that never recurs in the play. Still more surprisingly, the rationale for Theseus's sudden change of heart proves elusive: the play provides no evidence to support the queens' fears that eros will deplete the male potential for heroic action.[56] Instead the queens' insistence on an inevitable conflict between public and private life rapidly proves as irrelevant and unreal as the heroics of marriage. The queens disappear from the play at the end of the first act, when the central conflict is revealed as constructed instead between erotic love and friendship. As it turns out, then, the play will not center on an antagonism between public and private life or on an attempt to link the two; it will focus exclusively on the conflicts of private life, conceived as a separate domain.

Thus neither the heroics of marriage nor the dualistic sexual sensibility appropriately defines the situation of the leading protagonists of *The Two Noble Kinsmen*. Nonetheless, that situation is constructed entirely in the terms of these customary Renaissance sexual sensibilities; no new, more relevant terms are introduced. The effect is one of odd and pointed dislocation. Defined, on the one hand, in the chivalric terms of the heroism of action, the plot concentrates exclusively on private life, which usually receives at best peripheral attention in the representations of this mode; on the other hand, though a serious focus on private life is characteristic of the heroics of marriage, the attempt to construct marriage as an epic adventure and to confer on it equal distinction with public service, so crucial to that ideology, is reduced to virtual insignificance, adding little to the tone of the play.

56. If anything, the play proves the queens' fears false. The only sexual relationship actually consummated in the main plot is that of Theseus and Hippolyta, and their marriage and love are shown to be happy (e.g., 3.6.200–201). Hippolyta's response to the queens' reasoning about her sexual powers is to tell Theseus she is "much unlike / You should be so transported" (1.1.185–86). If, however, the audience can be assumed to be aware of Theseus's legendary sexual history, then an ironic light is cast on the "happiness" of the pair. For a fascinating discussion of Renaissance versions of Theseus's many exploits, see D'Orsay W. Pearson, "'Unkinde' Theseus: A Study in Renaissance Mythography," *English Literary Renaissance*, 4 (1974), 276–98.

These conceptual dislocations take a variety of concrete forms. Particularly striking are the truncated or deflected ceremonies in the play. Eugene Waith has argued that although the depiction of spectacular ceremony, usually demonstrating "the awesome difference between human and divine intrigue," characterizes the early staging of chivalric romance in Renaissance England, by the first decade of the seventeenth century "the material and techniques of the early dramatized romances had become old-fashioned if not downright ludicrous."[57] Shakespeare's deliberate introduction of archaic ceremonies into his final romances constitutes a boldly self-conscious manipulation of anachronistic material designed to enhance the effects of wonder and miraculous restoration. *The Two Noble Kinsmen* similarly abounds with romantic and chivalric ceremonies: Theseus's wedding, the pleading queens, the burial of the queens' husbands, May Day games, a stylized duel between Palamon and Arcite, a series of three spectacular theophanies in Act 5, a climactic tournament. Yet the majority of these displays either are disrupted or their focus is deflected. Theseus and Hippolyta's wedding, which begins the play with such splendor, is interrupted and, receiving no further attention, eventually takes place without comment offstage. While a series of May Day games and a banquet occur, once again, offstage, the attention of the audience is riveted instead on what is being defined by representation as the far more urgent private quarrel between the two kinsmen, who meet in the woods and resolve to determine their destinies once and for all in a duel. But the fatal duel is interrupted by Theseus, who, discovering that the banished Arcite has violated his decree by remaining in Athens and that Palamon has escaped jail, rashly orders that they shall both die. Theseus eventually gives way to the persuasion of his royal entourage and alters his decree to demand instead a decisive, climactic tournament: the winner will marry Emilia; the loser will be executed. In one of the play's most pronounced dislocations, the tournament takes place offstage while the action focuses instead on the lonely figure of Emilia, who cannot bring herself to witness the determination of her fate. After

57. Eugene Waith, "Shakespeare and the Ceremonies of Romance," in *Shakespeare's Craft: Eight Lectures*, ed. Philip H. Highfill, Jr. (Carbondale: Southern Illinois University Press, 1982), pp. 113–37.

Arcite wins the tournament, Palamon and his brave company are taken, onstage, to their execution. But this solemn moment is interrupted when Arcite falls from a horse and dies, and Palamon is summoned to marry Emilia after all.

Far from creating a sense of wonder, the revelation of the capricious power or benevolence of the gods, these anachronistically represented, truncated ceremonies and deflected foci emphasize instead a confusion about the actual sources of conflict in the play, as well as the lack of appropriate terms to define what those conflicts might be. Very few of the characters can decide what is important to them. As we have seen, Theseus is immediately persuaded to alter his insistence that his wedding will go forward despite the pleading queens. While Theseus's sudden abandonment of the heroics of marriage seems to reinforce the queens' conception of an inevitable antagonism between public and private life, this conception, like Creon's evil, is shortly revealed to have very little to do with the major conflicts in the play. A similar movement occurs when we first meet Palamon and Arcite in Thebes, agonizing over Creon's evil and determining to escape its consequences ("How dangerous if we will keep our honors / It is for our residing, where every evil / Hath a good color, where every seeming good's / A certain evil" [1.2.37–40]). Yet the kinsmens' potential participation in public corruption also turns out to have no importance. This pattern of red herrings is reiterated when, jailed in Athens, the kinsmen staunchly espouse stoicism, only to be immediately drawn to the world outside their cell in the figure of Emilia picking flowers below them. These representations demonstrate not the arbitrariness of the gods, but the characters' unwillingness or inability to commit themselves, the lack of firm ground on which decisions can be made and a future formulated. The emphasis is striking when perceived in contrast to *Troilus and Cressida*, where action is erroneously but firmly grounded, characterized by its rigid wrongness: Troilus and Hector adhere disastrously to past vows. In contrast, Palamon and Arcite, swearing to leave Thebes, in the next moment respond instantly, mechanically, to the battlecall to defend her. Later, swearing eternal friendship, they spot Emilia in mid oath and become enemies immediately. These ironies are too deliberately placed to allow any respect for their dignities. The authority of

Theseus is similarly undercut. Often his orders are simply ig-nored.[58] He usually changes his mind anyway, and when he does make it up, his decisions appear pointlessly cruel. His command that one of the kinsmen must die in their struggle for Emilia, for example, is an invention of the playwrights'; the pointed deviation from Chaucer merely emphasizes the harsh, arbitrary, human irra-tionality of the monarch's decree.

The anachronistic representation of spectacular ceremonies that, failing to create or reveal wonder, are interrupted by more urgent actions; the juxtaposition of conflicting sexual ideologies that are introduced and then discarded; the depiction of antagonisms and resolutions that are defined and then dismissed as irrelevant—the play's restless, groping disruption of traditional associations is epitomized in its treatment of sexual love. As we have seen, the detailed concentration on sexual love in a dramatized chivalric sto-ry, where eros is usually assigned the symbolic, static, and largely invisible role of inspiration for heroic action, is itself a dislocation. Although subjecting it to irony, *The Two Noble Kinsmen* retains the courtly love configuration of the remote, superior lady and her frustrated suitors, along with the polarizing combination of sexual sublimation and sexual disgust that traditionally accompanies that syndrome. When Palamon first spots Emilia he declares, "Behold, and wonder. / By heaven, she is a goddess," adding, "Do rever-ence / She is a goddess, Arcite" (2.1.192–95); Arcite immediately points out an alternative approach: "I will not [love her] as you do, to worship her, / As she is heavenly and a blessèd goddess: / I love her as a woman, to enjoy her" (2.1.222–24). Yet for Palamon the

---

58. The exchange between Theseus and Emilia in 5.3.28–34, when he commands her to view the tournament and she refuses to go, is typical:

Hipp.	You must go.
Emil.	In faith, I will not.
Thes.	Why, the knights must kindle
	Their valor at your eye. Know of this war
	You are the treasure, and must needs be by
	To give the service pay.
Emil.	Sir, pardon me,
	The title of a kingdom may be tried
	Out of itself.
Thes.	Well, well, then, at your pleasure.

only alternative to the idealization (i.e., sublimation) of sexual love is loathing and disgust. Recognizing himself as a soldier of Venus, he offers an invocation to the goddess that articulates a terrible tribute to the destructive power of eros, echoing that of the queens. But where the queens' distrust of consummated sexual love involves a fear of its subversion of public action, Palamon's erotic nausea is pristine, rooted in a straightforward aversion to what he perceives as the humiliating, persistent, anarchic power of the sexual act. Addressing Venus before his final combat with Arcite, he overlooks the great lovers of history and myth, dwelling instead on adulterers, boasters ("large confessors"), a "cripple [flourishing] with his crutch," the "pollèd bachelor," and

> a man
> Of eighty winters . . . who
> A lass of fourteen brided. 'Twas thy power
> To put life into dust: the aged cramp
> Had screwed his square foot round,
> The gout had knit his fingers into knots,
> Torturing convulsions from his globy eyes
> Had almost drawn their spheres, that what was life
> In him seemed torture.
> [5.1.107–15]

The intensity of Palamon's aversion to eros would be extraordinary in any case, but its context makes it astonishing. Palamon is on the verge of risking his own life and the lives of his fellow knights in order to win the woman he loves. Interestingly, marrying Emilia is never an explicit concern of the kinsmen, who quarrel only over the right to love her.[59] This situation results partially from the kinsmens' imprisonment and consequent lack of options; more to the point, however, is the irrelevance of marriage to courtly love. That marriage is never an issue in *Troilus and Cressida* has nothing to do with the desire or personality of either Troilus or Cressida; instead it is a condition of the chivalric sexual system in which they are inscribed.[60] In *The Two Noble Kinsmen* Theseus

59. See, e.g., 2.1.215–79.
60. Cf. Lewis, 13, 14. Henry Ansgar Kelly's case in *Love and Marriage in the Age of Chaucer* (Ithaca, N.Y.: Cornell University Press, 1975), pp. 229–42,

forces marriage on the cousins, who, entirely preoccupied with their own desires, clearly consider Emilia's feelings irrelevant. After defeating Palamon in the competition for Emilia's hand, Arcite shows little eagerness for victory, remarking bitterly, "Emily, / To buy you I have lost what's dearest to me / Save what is bought" (5.3.111–13). When Arcite falls off a horse and dies, Palamon wins Emilia after all, but he takes small joy in his triumph. "That we should things desire which do cost us / The loss of our desire! That nought could buy / Dear love but loss of dear love!" (5.4.109–11), he exclaims.

That the kinsmen should risk their lives for Emilia while taking no notice whatsoever of her feelings, or, indeed, of her, recalls the fact that chivalric love is construed exclusively in the terms of male desire. Yet once again the play presents a dislocation, a disruption of traditional sexual logic. The chivalric ethos that inscribes the protagonists demands that the lady be superior, remote, and static, a treasured object of desire. Thus, on one level, Emilia occupies the same structural position as Cressida; she is passively swept up into the conflict engendered by male desire and forced to occupy a place within it. Indeed, she frequently underscores her own helplessness, which she tends to equate with innocence. "I am guiltless of election" (5.1.154), she assures herself, insisting, in one of the play's finest lines, "I am bride-habited, / But maiden-hearted" (5.1.150–51). On the other hand, the play reveals that the state of Emilia's mind and heart is considerably more complex than this elegant duality will allow. It is another false formulation. Emilia plays a frequent and decisive role in swaying Theseus; and, like the kinsmen, she expresses a sense of conflict between heterosexual love and same-sex friendship (see 1.3.55–66).

Emilia is also given several soliloquies, in which she reveals her struggle to define her own role in the kinsmens' lethal courtship. While the climactic tournament between the cousins takes place offstage, audience attention is riveted on Emilia's conflict between physical desire for either or both of the kinsmen and terror that she will be responsible for one of their deaths: "Arcite may win me /

---

where he argues that Chaucer's Troilus and Criseyde actually undergo a clandestine marriage, is unconvincing, ignoring both Chaucer's irony and the ambivalence with which such marriages were regarded by the church.

And yet Palamon wound Arcite to / The spoiling of his figure. O what pity / Enough for such a chance? If I were by, / I might do hurt" (5.3.57–61). Unlike Cressida, then, Emilia plays a prominent role as an independent actor in the play and is more often the subject of representation. Is she merely a passive victim in regard to choosing a mate, or is she unwilling to assert her prerogative as a subject and make a choice? The play cannot decide; nor can it come up with satisfactorily flexible terms that would define Emilia as both subject and object. Most important for these purposes is the fact that the play inscribes her in a chivalric sexual system that denies her status as an independent actor and then subverts that system by insistently scrutinizing her choices and desires. The resulting effect is again one of *The Two Noble Kinsmen* groping for new terms in which to define conflicts—trying, in effect, to change the subject.

The dislocations of the traditional emphases of chivalric sexuality transform idealistic lovers and their treasured object of desire and source of inspiration into three ambivalent narcissists, for whom love becomes an isolated, compulsive experience. "I must love and will," insists Palamon (3.6.262); Arcite remarks sadly, "And I could wish I had not said I loved her, / Though I had died. But loving such a lady / And justifying my love, I must not fly from't" (3.6.40–42); and Emilia hopes at one point that "If well inspired, this battle shall confound / Both these brave knights, and I a virgin flow'r / Must grow alone, unplucked" (5.1.166–68). The play's deflected focus on Emilia's struggles, along with the representation of the kinsmens' self-absorption, suggests that a newly conceived subject would center not on a conflict between public and private life, between society and the individual, or between marriage and virginity, but on desire in conflict with itself. Such a conception is, of course, individualistic and can be elaborated in psychological terms. Indeed, the best studies of the play have relied on the psychoanalytic conception of individual development to argue, as Philip Edwards does, that *The Two Noble Kinsmen* concerns the "movement from one state to the next, the unavoidable process of [i.e., individual] growth," a process that the characters view with melancholy and alarm.[61] Clifford Leech adds that "the

---

61. Philip Edwards, "On the Design of *The Two Noble Kinsmen*," in Leech's edition of the play, pp. 243–61.

Fletcherian drama is a drama about men's refusal to live as individuals."[62]

There is much in the play to sustain these readings. In contrast to *Troilus and Cressida*, in which the attack on chivalry articulates a critique of an entire civilization, *The Two Noble Kinsmen* tests chivalric idealism against private (primarily sexual) experience alone. In *Troilus* the suspended condition of the hero's youth comes to symbolize a society without a future, but in the later play the heroes' insistence on their youth can be perceived in psychological terms as individuals' unnatural recoil from experience and, specifically, from sexual love. "Dear Palamon, dearer in love than blood / And our prime cousin, yet unhardened in / The crimes of nature, let us leave the city / Thebes, and the temptings in't, before we further / Sully our gloss of youth," urges Arcite (1.2.1–5); when imprisoned later, he again expresses the desire to escape the corruption of adult life, this time explicitly associating his notion of inevitable contamination with sex: "Let's think this prison holy sanctuary, / To keep us from corruption of worse men. / We are young and yet desire the ways of honor / That liberty and conversation, / The poison of pure spirits, might like women / Woo us to wander from" (2.1.130–35). When Emilia expresses a nostalgia for her childhood, whose innocence she sees as embodied in a girlhood friendship that she insists "may be / More than in sex dividual" (1.3.81–82), Hippolyta points explicitly to an element of perversity in her sister's response: "Now alack, weak sister, / I must no more believe thee in this point, / . . . than I will trust a sickly appetite / That loathes even as it longs" (1.3.86–90). As Hippolyta's remark implies, Emilia's negative view of heterosexuality tends to be dissociated, like Palamon's, from any motivation or context but itself; what Theodore Spencer observes of the kinsmens' attitude toward Thebes applies equally to all three of the protagonists' attitudes toward eros: "Palamon and Arcite look back in disgust at Thebes before we have been given any satisfactory reason for their disgust."[63] Thus dissociated, their troubled equation of their youth with a sexual innocence they are reluctant to relinquish begins to seem less like the pathetic or awesome

62. Leech, p. xxxviii of his edition of the play.
63. Theodore Spencer, "*The Two Noble Kinsmen*," in Leech's edition of the play, p. 232.

suffering of the victims of Fate and more like anxiety, the claustrophobic suffering of neurosis. A feeling of confinement results from the refusal to grow.

There is, then, powerful evidence to support a view of the play and its protagonists as conceived in individualistic and psychological terms; to see the play, that is, as a representation of neurotic suffering. As we have seen, Palamon summarizes his experience with an eloquent emphasis on the mixed nature of desire: "That we should things desire which do cost us / The loss of our desire! / That nought could buy / Dear love but loss of dear love!" This conception of the play can be developed further by looking at the subplot of the Jailer's Daughter. "Subplot" is actually a misleading term, for although this story serves the traditional function of commenting on, mocking, and amplifying the main plot, it also steals the show. As the production history of *The Two Noble Kinsmen* makes clear, the Jailer's Daughter is the most compelling part in the play.[64] Funny, affectionate, and courageous, this young woman, although already engaged to be married, falls in love with Palamon while he is in jail and, out of both pity and a desire to win his love, takes the huge risk of releasing him from prison. Following him into the woods and losing her way at night, she goes mad with a combination of frustrated desire and fear that her father will be punished for Palamon's escape. Like the major protagonists, then, the Jailer's Daughter is caught in an unresolved dilemma of desire ("Why should I love this gentleman? 'Tis odds / He never will affect me; I am base, / My father the mean keeper of his prison, / And he a prince; to marry him is hopeless, / To be his whore witless" [2.3.1–5]); and she attempts to abandon this dilemma by discounting rationality ("I love him, beyond love and beyond reason, / Or wit, or safety: I have made him know it. / I care not, I am desperate" [2.5.11–13]).[65]

---

64. This fact was especially prominent in the summer 1986 RSC production in Stratford-upon-Avon at the Swan Theater.

65. Cf. the scene (1.2) in which Palamon and Arcite, despite their reiterated repugnance for their homeland, fight for Thebes in instantaneous violation of their principles. "Leave that unreasoned," Palamon states in reference to the blatant moral contradiction, and Arcite expresses the same unwillingness rationally to attempt to determine the course of his own life: "Let th'event / That never erring arbitrator, tell us / When we know all ourselves, and let us follow / The becking of our chance" (1.2.113–16).

Thus the Jailer's Daughter shares with the major protagonists an unbalancing anxiety and ambivalence about sexual love, and her story elaborates the play's exclusive and intensive emphasis on the individual's problems of private life. Her madness is treated by a doctor, who explicitly defines her problems as psychosexual in origin ("for this her mind beats upon" [4.3.79–80]), and who prescribes sexual intercourse with her (now reinstated) fiancé, pretending he is Palamon, as the solution. That the Jailer's Daughter is subjected to a bedtrick recalls the play's emphasis on the mechanical impersonality of sex; but rather than inspiring repugnance, as they do in the main plot, the mechanisms of desire are analyzed with apparently benevolent scientific detachment from traditional moral codes:

Doct. [to Wooer]. If she entreat again, do anything:
                Lie with her if she ask you.
Jail. Ho there, doctor!
Doct. Yes, in the way of cure.
Jail. But first, by your leave, I' th' way of honesty.
Doct. That's but a niceness:
        Ne'er cast your child away for honesty;
        Cure her first this way, then if she will be honest,
        She has the path before her.
Jail. Thank ye, doctor.
Doct. Pray bring her in and let's see how she is.
Jail. I will, and tell her her Palamon stays for her.
        But, doctor, methinks you are i' th' wrong still.
                    [5.2.17–26]

The Doctor, however, is not wrong; the bedtrick works. The Jailer's Daughter moves happily, if obliviously, into a future of marriage to a man who loves her. So what if she imagines he is someone else? Her madness and cure are wholly encompassed in the comic mode, as becomes apparent earlier in the play when she joins a group of weavers rehearsing a morris dance for May Day celebrations. Like the androgynous hero, the Jailer's Daughter follows eros into an uncharted terrain. As in Emilia's case, in the story of the Jailer's Daughter female desire is both granted centrality and presented as a problem to be managed and resolved by powerful men. But the transformation of the authority figure from reigning monarch to doctor changes both the meaning and the tone of the episode. While the Duke commands Emilia's marriage by a harsh and arbitrary decree, the Doctor is presented instead as discovering what the Jailer's Daughter "really" wants by releasing repression, ferreting out her desire. What do women want? asked Freud, and proceeded to reply. The answer provided in the Jailer's Daughter plot of *The Two Noble Kinsmen* is that what women want is the illusion of marrying a prince.

Thus several important points emerge from the episode of the Jailer's Daughter. First, it presents a strikingly self-conscious early example of what Jameson describes as the constitution of the psychological subject, in which reality is construed individualistically, in and through the terms of an autonomous psyche.[66] Second, the Doctor's power to resolve the situation by defining its terms ("I will . . . / But doctor, methinks you are i' th' wrong still") recalls Michel Foucault's argument that precisely by granting the medical and helping professions the powers of definition, modern sexuality has subjected itself to their regulatory rhetorical control.[67] In *The Two Noble Kinsmen* the Doctor is much more successful at regulating sexuality in the Jailer's world than Theseus is in his court, a fact that distinguishes the conceptualization of the Jailer's Daughter's story as distinctively modern and associates it with the future.

Although the Jailer's Daughter plot is the most appealing aspect of *The Two Noble Kinsmen*, its terms and conceptions cannot be said to encompass the entire action. The future that is suggested and affirmed in the play's subplot is in fact not available to the major protagonists. Like the Jailer's Daughter, Emilia and Palamon move into a nonchivalric future symbolized in marriage, but unlike her, they move with no illusions and great reluctance: Arcite is left behind. The most telling contrasts between the stories are clearly discernible in the ideological terms that link gender, genre and class. The dilemma of the Jailer's Daughter centers on her lower-class status and is constituted entirely in the comic mode. "I am base," she announces the moment she comes onto the stage and, contrasting her wooer with Palamon, exclaims, "Lord,

66. Jameson, p. 124.
67. Michel Foucault, *The History of Sexuality*, vol. 1: *An Introduction* (New York: Pantheon, 1978).

the / diff'rence of men!" (2.1.58–59). But the sweet levity that sets the tone of her episode is strikingly absent from the combination of piquancy, bitterness, brutality, and absurdity that characterizes the interactions among the aristocrats, whose dilemmas are by no means entirely comic. In contrast, for example, to the Doctor's cavalier dismissal of virginity, traditional sexual and moral configurations (in their chivalric form) receive greater deference in the main plot. Thus the scene in which Palamon and Arcite arm each other and discuss their former, heroic comradeship is one of the nicest in the play. The theophanies in Act 5 are neither mocking nor interrupted, but perform without parody their traditional romantic function of simultaneously suggesting and concealing the outcome of the action.

Although chivalry and its romance are continually deflated as inadequate, then, their devices still play a defining structural role. As we have seen, the continuing false conflicts and disruption of traditional associations oscillate between defining the world in human and/or divine terms. When Palamon declares, "I must love and will," is he referring to the divine commands of Fate, the social demands of chivalric honor ("I saw her first"), or the private compulsions of the individual psyche? The play is unclear and, ending with the death of one kinsman and the marriage of another, settles for the characteristically tragicomic note of compromise. "Let us be thankful / For that which is, and with you leave dispute / That are above our question" (5.4.133–35), says Theseus, addressing the gods; but his final vision of inscrutability emphasizes the perversity of the human mind, unaccountably, irrationally, bringing unnecessary suffering upon itself:

> For what we lack,
> We laugh, for what we have, are sorry; still
> Are children in some kind.[68]
> [5.4.130–33]

The focus on love and sexuality in the plots of *The Two Noble Kinsmen* both links and distinguishes social classes in the play's

---

68. Interestingly, Freud describes anxiety as a "riddle" in *Introductory Lectures on Psychoanalysis*, trans. James Strachey (New York: Norton, 1966), p.

projected conception of the future. In both cases the future is attached to creating a realm of private experience that begins to be construed in individualistic terms and is increasingly divorced from public life or, in the vocabulary of dramatic representation, from traditional heroism. Yet there are crucial differences in tone. Although the Jailer's Daughter is treated with poignant and affectionate condescension, the irony that encompasses the aristocrats is often bitter and demanding. The parody that highlights their indecisiveness is accompanied by a residual, elegiac lament that mourns their attenuated heroism and compromised authority. As the Doctor's comic triumph in the subplot makes clear, the elegant, inadequate conception of chivalry has a future, but that future depends on the ease with which the fantasy component of the aristocratic ethos can be knowingly manipulated for the power of its illusion by an increasingly confident professional class.

Though *The Two Noble Kinsmen* does not abandon chivalry, then, it sets up the conditions in which chivalry can be abandoned. The restless realignment of discourses in the play renders it what one critic describes as an open-ended text, or a text devised to "unsettle the reader [or viewer] into becoming a critic of, rather than a complicit participant in," its conventions: "refusing to lay issues to rest because irresolution is part of the meaning, the open-ended text passes its tension on to the reader, who must actively struggle with the unsettling questions raised but left unresolved by the prior narrative."[69] In Fletcher and Massinger's *The Knight of Malta*, chivalric heroism and sexual love are again brought into conflict and realigned according to a newly established centrality of private experience; but when the constituent elements of these issues are distinguished and revised in the later play, a clearer resolution emerges, taking the shape of a distinctive split between public and private life.

393: "The problem of anxiety is a nodal point at which the most various and important questions converge, a riddle whose solution would be bound to throw a flood of light on our whole mental existence."

69. Joseph A. Boone, "Modernist Maneuverings in the Marriage Plot: Breaking Ideologies of Gender and Genre in James's *The Golden Bowl*," *PMLA* 101 (May 1986), 377.

The Knights of Malta are a chivalrous order of Christian soldiers, zealously defending their faith, militantly chaste. In spite of the intimate association of celibacy and idealism required by their order, three of them—one an initiated knight, Mountferrat, and two, Gomera and Miranda, about to be invested into the order—are in love. This situation, already dramatic, is complicated by the fact that they all love the same woman, Oriana, sister of Valetta, the Grand Master of the Knights of Malta. As in the former two plays, then, the conflict appears to be constructed between chivalric (public) heroism and private (sexual) life. *Troilus and Cressida*, however speciously, subordinates erotic experience to the more prestigious and exacting demands of public life; in contrast, *The Two Noble Kinsmen*, however inadequately and reluctantly, begins to acknowledge the pressing importance of the private sphere. But *The Knight of Malta* represents the conflict between the two domains as impossible to reconcile; and in the polarization between the two, the weight of sympathy and value—and the opportunity for heroism—has switched decisively to favor the private life.

Far from exploring chivalry as an idealized mode of being flexible enough to command the emulation of an entire society, Fletcher and Massinger focus on the most extreme and remote manifestations of the chivalric code. As noted earlier, the associations of chivalry with religion were peripheral and accidental rather than central to its development; indeed, these were precisely the associations that dropped away in the Renaissance, while more powerful aspects of chivalric idealism, such as the glorification of individual valor and emphasis on an exclusively meritorious class of men, remained part of chivalry's enduring appeal. Similarly, far from being central to chivalric idealizations, knightly chastity was an enforced condition of youth, often considered temporary and represented in literary expression with an accompanying yearning to escape. By defining the knight's major function in *The Knight of Malta* as killing infidels, Fletcher and Massinger subtly recall the Catholic Crusades. Further, by conjoining military heroism with religion and permanent celibacy, they succeed not only in rendering the elitist appeal of chivalry remote and specialized, but also in surrounding it with an aura of anachronism and irrelevance. Thus *The Knight of Malta* augments the critique of chivalry by depriving it of centrality. In *Troilus and Cressida* Shakespeare bitterly identifies chivalric idealism as the dominant form taken by the willful, evasive destructiveness of an entire civilization. In *The Two Noble Kinsmen* chivalry proves poignantly and reluctantly inadequate to what are depicted as the more urgent, if decidedly less glamorous, concerns of private life. But in *The Knight of Malta* chivalry loses its power to threaten, inspire, and destroy, and this attenuation is never associated with loss. Instead, the play consigns chivalry to the margins, deftly exposing it not only as irrelevant but also as absurd.

The reduction of the chivalric code to unmitigated parody is clarified in the portrayal of Miranda, the title's "Knight of Malta" and the only one of the three protagonists destined to pursue the chivalric/religious ideals of the order. In considering the depiction of Miranda's quest, which involves overcoming sexual desire in order to qualify for knighthood, it is helpful to recall Eric Auerbach's argument that the medieval romance presented a world apparently designed for the sole purpose of providing the knight with a series of adventures in which he could demonstrate his valor; as a result, chivalric idealism tended to glamorize heroic endeavor precisely by dissociating it from the events of everyday life. But in *The Knight of Malta* the playwrights, like Cervantes, mock the unreal quality of the chivalric quest as a fantasy in the mind of the hero.

Miranda is among the most posturing of tragicomic heroes. More than Oriana, more than God, he loves the last-minute revelation, the dramatic rescue. How marvelous to appear—miraculously—at the very moment of disaster and deter its course through sheer force of personality and advantage of superior knowledge! Given the opportunity to save by the bell, Miranda rises to the height of his glory; lacking the opportunity, he quite literally *makes* a scene. When Oriana responds negatively to the clandestine sexual overtures of Mountferrat, that villain avenges himself by slandering her maliciously, accusing her of treason and endangering her life. The older and less agile Gomera challenges Mountferrat to a duel, which will determine Oriana's fate. When Miranda, far away on a military adventure, hears of this potential catastrophe, he does not, like Gomera, come forward publicly as Oriana's champion. Instead he persuades Mountferrat by subterfuge to let him (Miranda) take Mountferrat's place in the duel, disguised. Miranda then allows Gomera to win, after which he dazzles everyone, first by revealing himself, then by stepping forward to claim Oriana as his own.

Mir.	None has deserv'd her
	If worth must carry it, and service seek her,
	But he that saved her honor.
Gom.	That's I *Miranda*.
Mir.	No, no, that's I *Gomera*, be not so forward,
	In bargain for my love, ye cannot cozen me.
Gom.	I fought it.
Mir.	And I gave it: which is nobler? . . .
Gom.	I undertook first, to preserve from hazard.
Mir.	And I made sure no hazard should come near her.

[2.5][70]

Addressing Oriana, whose life has been hanging in the balance, Miranda continues:

> Such another fright
> I would not put ye in, to owne the Island,
> Yet pardon me, 'twas but to shew a Soldier.

[2.5]

Miranda, though, does cause "such another fright," not only to Oriana, but to all the other characters, and this time he scares them even more. Oriana eventually marries Gomera and, when pregnant, is alienated from him by the machinations of the persistently evil Mountferrat. Through a triumph of miscommunication, Gomera thinks Oriana dead; meanwhile, she is not only alive, but she has given birth to his child. Miranda, unraveling these mishaps, prolongs everyone's misery for the sole purpose of dramatically restoring all the good to happiness and punishing the wicked with an amazing display of ingenuity. He even teases Oriana by posing as her enemy, pretending to threaten her with slander and her husband's death. He cannot resist. Wait until she realizes how

---

70. All quotations from *The Knight of Malta*, identified in the text by act and scene numbers, are from the Glover and Waller edition of the *Works of Beaumont and Fletcher*, vol. 7, pp. 78–163.

he, busily working behind the scenes, has actually engineered for her perfect happiness!

Fletcher and Massinger have clearly deflated chivalric endeavor to the level of ridiculous egotism. Once again, Miranda's bravado is associated with youth, a fact clarified by the contrast between his behavior and that of Gomera, the man who wins Oriana. Like Othello, Gomera is an older soldier who has fallen in love for the first time; unlike Othello, however, he recognizes marriage as his destiny, which he embraces with no trace of self-hatred or fear of the contradictory or psychologically subversive in his values or feelings:

> I am in love; laugh not: though time hath set
> Some wrinkles in this face, and these curl'd locks
> Will shortly dye into an other hew
> Yet, yet I am in love.
> [1.3]

The striking contrast between Othello, unwilling and ashamed to acknowledge the importance of his marriage or to admit its power over him, and Gomera, equally heroic but willingly surrendering his military career in order to marry, can be seen as a register of sexual change. It is a direct acknowledgment of Gomera's frankness and dignity that although Oriana's brother has selected Gomera as her mate, she herself affirms the choice.

Like Cressida and Emilia, Oriana functions for much of the play as a victim and object of male desire. When she is neither silent nor in a stupor, she spends a considerable amount of time wavering in her affections between Gomera and Miranda. Like the Jailer's Daughter, she needs male authority figures to regulate her sexuality by making up her mind. But at the end of the play she wakes up, asserts herself, and makes a choice of her own: "Thy eye was ever chaste, thy countenance too honest," she tells Miranda, rejecting him, "And all thy wooings was like Maidens talk" (5.1). In the exchange in which she and Miranda agree to part, we can recognize the two predominant forms of English Renaissance sexual discourse asserting and distinguishing themselves:

> *Mir.* Husband, Wife,
> There is some holy mystery in those names
> That sure the unmarried cannot understand.

Ori.   Now thou are strait, and dost enamour me,
So far beyond a carnal earthly love;
My very soul doats on thee, and my spirits
Do embrace thine, my mind doth thy mind kiss,
And in this pure conjunction we enjoy
A heavenlier pleasure than if bodies met;
This, this is perfect love.

[5.2]

Perfect love! For all her saying so, Oriana does not choose celibate, Neoplatonic contemplation for her future course. Instead she returns to her husband and newly born child. The play ends with Miranda's investiture as a Knight of Malta, happily pledging himself to a career of celibate heroism. Thus *The Knight of Malta* represents public and private life as irreconcilably separate, but newly equivalent, spheres: Gomera gives up his vocation as a knight, but heroically embraces a private destiny instead. The wish-fulfillment resolution of tragicomedy can be seen in the parting exchange just quoted between Miranda and Oriana. Here Oriana insists that the two sexual ideologies that we have seen to be conflicting—a dualistic system that either idealizes and sublimates or rejects and degrades women and eros ("perfect love") and the heroics of marriage (the "holy mystery . . . / That sure the unmarried cannot understand")—will coexist peacefully in her mind. Furthermore, this resolution is achieved exclusively in the private sphere and defined in the terms of the individual psyche: specifically, it is located in female desire. Regarded once again as separate from public life, both women and eros nevertheless retain the discursive centrality granted them by the heroics of marriage. The fact that women are being conceived and represented by men locates the tragicomic wish-fulfillment in the nexus of potential contradictions that are left unexplored in the play.

The wished-for resolution of traditionally conflicting sexual sensibilities articulated in *The Knight of Malta* can be recognized as the same resolution pursued by Charles I and Henrietta Maria, the first English royal couple to idealize themselves domestically, as husband and wife. At the same time the queen was the center of a Neoplatonic cult that glorified chastity, and Charles represented himself as the solitary heroic knight of the Van Dyck portraits. As in the case of Queen Elizabeth, scholars have analyzed the self-presentations of these Stuarts in terms of political power.[71] From the perspective of this book, the attempt of king and queen to idealize themselves in conflicting sexual representations becomes yet another sign of their political fragility and illusions. But the fact that these monarchs felt the need to idealize their marriage, along with their chastity and military heroism, also indicates the way in which private life had gained a new stature and prestige.

Throughout this book the changing stature of the private life in Renaissance England has been suggested by a conjoined examination of moral, religious, and dramatic texts. I have tried to show how moral and dramatic languages combine to create and transform dominant sexual sensibilities: that is, to underscore the ways in which traditionally literary and nonliterary discourses function similarly as well as reciprocally in the production and transmission of sexual values. Thus the increasing prestige of marriage helps to account for the development of comedy and tragedy, which in turn augment and perpetuate the enhanced dignity of private life through their representations.

In arguing that dramatic and moral texts function jointly to produce and transform dominant sexual sensibilities, I have attempted to show the ways in which focusing on aesthetic issues (e.g., dramatic structure and form) can illuminate the workings of cultural change in the English Renaissance. Thus the specific deployment of wish-fulfillment patterns in romantic comedy, including the containment of potential sexual conflict in the final marriage scenes, clarifies the new effort to idealize marriage in Elizabethan society; and the lineaments of the unresolved struggle for sexual equality can be traced as a disjunction between content and form in Jacobean satire.

These modes of analysis suggest that traditionally literary (in this case dramatic) texts can best be related to the rest of social history neither by comparing the arrangement of plots and the depiction of characters to actual human behavior, nor by relegating literature to the realm of escapism. Rather it is suggested that the

71. See, e.g., Jonathan Goldberg, *James I and the Politics of Literature* (Baltimore, Md.: Johns Hopkins University Press, 1983), pp. 94–95; and Butler, p. 55.

characteristic cultural logic of dramatic texts can be discerned by tracing the changing location of conflict and the shifting nature of subject matter, aesthetic processes that can serve as registers of social and sexual transformation. Recognizing that aesthetic categories as such have a sociohistorical logic also allows us to apply them fruitfully to texts that are usually considered "nonliterary." Thus focusing on the construction of marriage as a heroic endeavor, the repeated, traditionally "literary" rhetoric that suffuses the Protestant tracts, helps to explain the emergence of the private life as a tragic subject in Jacobean England, while it also delineates a new ideology in the process of formation.

The increasing prestige of private life is defined and represented in Renaissance dramatic, moral, and religious writing in the heroics of marriage, a discourse that unites public and private life and attempts to confer on them equal distinction. When this discourse breaks down in tragedy, tragicomedy endeavors to change the terms of dramatic conflict, moving toward redefining the relation between public and private life as separate but equal spheres. That such a division would generate its own set of contradictions takes us out of the Renaissance and into the domain of modern discourses and problems. Born of the same inconsistencies that eventually undermine its coherence, the heroics of marriage articulates the sexual conflicts to which future generations will be heir.

Index

Library of Congress Cataloging-in-Publication Data

Rose, Mary Beth.
  The expense of spirit.

  Includes index.
  1. English drama—Early modern and Elizabethan, 1500–
1600—History and criticism. 2. English drama—17th century—
History and criticism. 3. Love in literature. 4. Sex in literature.
5. Women and literature—England—History. 6. Women—
England—History. 7. Literary form. I. Title.
PR658.L63R6 1988   822'.3'09354   88-47742
ISBN 0-8014-2189-6